CLARA'S
HEART

CLARA'S HEART

Joseph Olshan

JONATHAN CAPE
THIRTY-TWO BEDFORD SQUARE LONDON

First published in Great Britain 1986
Copyright © 1985 by Joseph Olshan

Jonathan Cape Ltd, 32 Bedford Square, London WC1B 3EL

British Library Cataloguing in Publication Data

Olshan, Joseph
Clara's heart.
I. Title
813′.54[F]   PS3565.L82/

ISBN 0-224-02359-4

Portions of this novel appeared in *The Times* and in *Pig Iron* magazine.

For Patrick Omweg

... And every love is a screen for sadness.

SALVATORE QUASIMODO

1973

"Go wid ya muddar," she told him. "Go and grow to a man. And when you a man, you'll get a sign to come and hear de most hurtful part."

With that she had sent him away from her apartment in Brooklyn. He had taken the train back to Rye, where he packed up the rest of his things and prepared to move. David tried to believe in Clara's promise. He knew the ability to relay such a mysterious sign would certainly be within her command. But then he considered how many years it might take until she beckoned him back to hear what truly plagued her, this "hurtful part." Then he grew afraid that after he left for California, Clara would slip away to Jamaica and disappear forever into the dark folds of her country.

That night as he tried to sleep, David was beset by longing. He cast his mind back over the summer, the loneliest of his life. He kept thinking of Clara's bedroom down the hallway, abandoned and empty these past few months. It was still impossible to accept the house was sold and that tomorrow the moving vans would arrive.

He got up after a while, went to his window, and peered out over the lawns and woods of the property toward the Sound. A chorus of crickets was keeping up an endless shrill. He thought of all the nights this summer when he dived off the dock and swam hundreds of yards out into the gurgling black water. He smelled salty sediments of low tide and watched the silvery currents shifting beneath the moon. He wondered how he could possibly leave New York in such a state of confusion.

1

After an hour David realized sleep would never come. He walked to the hallway phone and called Rye Taxi. He dressed quickly in a sweat shirt and a pair of khaki pants that had been snug at the beginning of the summer but now were so loose they hung from his hips. He stopped in front of the mirror and ran a comb through his sandy hair. He had eaten little for the past two months and his soft, teenage face had melted away to sunken planes of cheeks. He grabbed a light jacket in case it got cool. As he crept toward the staircase, he noticed the light was still on in his mother's room. He left the house and hid among the rhododendrons while waiting for his ride to the train station.

He arrived in Manhattan well after midnight and from there hailed a taxi to Brooklyn. Traffic was light and in no time he was gliding down the familiar boulevard with tall elm trees where he and Clara used to stroll. Before the taxi reached the cemetery, he could make out the silhouetted shape of her solitary building. Moonlight foamed over the streets like a celestial breaker, and as the car drew nearer, the tombs began to gleam. When he arrived at the apartment house, David looked up to her eleventh-floor window and saw lights burning.

With trembling fingers, he handed the taxi driver $15 and did not ask for the change. He stood outside for a moment, certain he could feel the seasons faintly shifting. The humid air had acquired a cool edge and was sweet with a dried thistly fragrance. He walked into the building and buzzed Clara's apartment.

Through the tinny-sounding intercom came the voice that had echoed for the past five years through the cavernous house in Rye. Suddenly David felt eight years old again. "Who is it?" the voice challenged.

He caught his breath. "It's me, David."

There was a pause. "Child, what you come here fa now?" she demanded.

"I had to."

"Don't I said you must go wid ya muddar, go to de avocados?"

"I have to talk to you, Clara," he insisted.

"No more talking," she said, her voice softening yet emphatic. "Ya curiosity gwan kill us both out tonight," she muttered, and buzzed David through.

The old lumbering elevator took a while to descend from the upper floors. Once David stepped inside, he smelled fried plantain and cooking lard, noticing lovers' messages carved in knifepoint on the painted metal doors. He finally reached the eleventh floor and slowly made his way down the hall to 11 H. ("Remember *H* for Hart," Clara used to say.) He rapped loudly and listened to the slow shuffle of footsteps answering.

Clara opened the door only partway, wedging her strong body into the narrow space. "Ya not gwan beg me no more," she warned David. He cast his eyes down. "Ya understand?" He nodded. "Come in den." She opened the door and squeezed him into a hug. "Me old Hart child," she cooed, surprising him with her warmth. She drew away from him and he looked into her black face, drawn of late, still lineless, her small dark eyes twinkling and mischievous. Her arms were plump and her graying hair was swept beneath a paisley scarf that was wound into a turban. David smelled Touch of Fire.

He stepped through the doorway into the living room. Against a wall was the RCA console television Clara had inherited from his mother a few years back in Rye. It had recently broken down and, without enough money to have it fixed, she had removed the knobs and dials, leaving the instrument panel a series of holes. The set now reminded him of an ancient automobile retired to cinder blocks. They walked into her small kitchen where yellowed shades were drawn, the night throbbing beyond them. Her portable fan was on, panning back and forth like a searchlight. On the wall David noticed a drawing he had once given Clara for a birthday gift: the view of the Sound from her old bedroom, tangles of rose brambles, the slate pathway that wound back toward the water. There was a large pot slow-boiling on the stove.

"Cooking rice and peas," Clara said.

"So late?" David asked.

She turned away so that he would not see the wounded light in her eyes. "Can't sleep again, so me cook. Make plenty if you want to eat some." Then Clara grew suspicious. "Ya too quiet," she said. "Must be ya lie to me out dere into de hallway," she accused him. "You *did* come here to insist." Sighing, she cast her eyes up to the peeling plaster ceiling. "Somehow me was afraid you'd come like dis."

He took her chafed brown hands in his, looking at the scars she had gotten from working at the Copra factory in Port Antonio. "You must've known I'd come sooner than you expected."

She pulled away from him. "No, man. Ya too craven for ya own good!" she cried. "You'll soon learn life not so easy."

In Clara's tiny bedroom off the kitchen, a black-and-white television was blaring the voice of a boxing announcer. From where they were standing, she began to watch the fight, then advanced slowly toward the set and sat down on the bed. In the way she was suddenly lost to the program, David could tell Clara spent many insomniac nights in the sweet vacancy of late television. He went and sat next to her, waiting.

Eventually she turned to him and ruffled his hair. "You really looking fine, child since you lost dat weight. Eyes always were lovely. Eyes like ya muddar's eyes." Clara faced her television again. "So you and she pack and ready, prepared to gone away . . . to bliss?"

David nodded although Clara could not see, her own eyes mirroring skepticism.

"But don't ya muddar know war is on?"

"What war?"

"War everywhere. Out dere. As well as right here." Clara pointed to her heart. Suddenly fidgety, she motioned to the television. "Don't I tell you—war? Me love fe watch de fights. Go hit him, broke his ass!" she screamed burlesquely to the prancing figures on the screen. "Don't step back, pump dat boy so him won't be able to recite A,B,C."

David felt Clara finally understood that here so late in the loneliness of a sleepless night she would no longer be able to keep his wonder at bay. He shut his eyes, suddenly feeling weary. It seemed to him that her power pulsed through the room. He took a deep breath and touched her shoulder. Clara stiffened and glared back at him. "I told you once you'd get the sign when to come and hear everything," she whispered. "Why you don't wait till den?"

"Because I can't—I just can't leave until you tell me. Clara," he insisted, "I'm ready to know."

She gripped his arm. "But it ugly, man!" she cried. "A wretched thing."

"I understand that."

Groaning, Clara began to rock in place. "David Hart," she said. "Den let us go sit down in me kitchen and we'll talk it once more through. I will make us some coffee. And we'll talk it like old crones who don't have so much more time."

ONE

1969

His younger sister seldom cried those two months she was alive. He remembered her dark shiny ringlets of hair, her red sweating face, the sturdy body of his mother bathing her, wrapping her in white flannel, and the shrieking and howling that filled the house one morning when she would not wake up. His mother's eyes were a Slavic-looking green. He had never seen her weep before.

David was eight years old, confused by this twist of fate, unable to understand the depression his mother fell into over someone who had lived only a small part of his own lifetime. She refused to go out, drawing the curtains in their rambling colonial house, lowering a pall on their lives. Clutching his father by the shrouded windows, she wept for days. At first he was brought to a neighbor's to be kept away from his parents' grief, but he wailed until his mother came to bring him home. He refused to walk, so that she was forced to carry him. He knew he was too old, but he wanted to be younger, to hide himself in the protection of her strong arms. While she was carrying him, he imagined the ground to be hundreds of feet below them, the sky a glittering membrane just beyond his fingertips, beyond which little Edith was floating. He tried to press his lips to his mother's cheeks, but she twisted her head away. It was as if he were responsible for his sister's death.

It wasn't until late one evening when his mother's voice pierced through the depths of his sleep that he began to understand that she, too, felt responsible for Edith's death. Her conversation with his

9

father had been loud enough to travel along the upstairs corridors, through the empty bedrooms where she told David all his brothers and sisters would live.

"Why didn't I check her room? Why didn't I do something?" his mother cried.

"Lee, stop blaming yourself," his father told her.

"But, if I'd just rocked the crib, or maybe even touched her. Anything!" Her voice cracked as she spoke.

"I'm not going to discuss this anymore. You're driving both of us nuts," Bill said.

"You blame me," she said, her voice going low. "I don't care what you say. I know you do."

"How could I possibly blame you?"

David would hear these discussions in the morning before his father left for work and on the weekend when his father left for golfing. His father would look at him and say, "Mother is still unhappy today. Try to play quietly. Try to help her if she cries."

"But what do I do?"

"Put your arms around her and say you love her and that you'll be patient and wait for her to bring you another brother or sister. Now come here and let me rub your head so I'll be lucky playing golf."

"If you're lucky, will you give me some of the money you win?" David asked.

"You little operator," Bill said, mussing David's hair with his knuckles.

Inside the house, where David learned about death, a dusty silence had bloomed. His mother had forbidden the cleaning ladies to come, and the rooms had quickly grown dingy. Dishes speckled with bits of rotting food remained in the kitchen sink for days. She refused to cancel the diaper service, and sometimes he had to answer the door to receive the packages of clean nappies. David brought them to the nursery, which was still unchanged, drawers filled with pink rompers, tall shelves lined with bottles of alcohol and Baby Magic and mineral oil. He would tiptoe inside, still able to smell Edith, who had smelled of Desitin ointment and Ammens powder. He remembered her bottom pink with diaper rash, how she was allowed to suck on his mother and he wasn't. He wondered if at some point she might crawl back from the dimension where she was hiding: back through a crevice in the closet that had given her away to the dark and beyond, something like the world locked inside the emerald band of crystal that rimmed the glass coffee table.

To escape the somber feeling in the house, David would stay in his room. He loved his carpeting. It was shaggy and bright blue like the painted blazer of a toy soldier. He had chosen it himself when the carpet man came. Now it looked ugly. There were bits of notepaper and lint wound in its long threads. He had dripped glue on it when he was pasting cutouts and could no longer comb his fingers through the way he combed them through the hair of their dog, Nipper, who sometimes snapped at him. He loved to turn on his air conditioning and feel cold air blowing in. That winter he put on sweaters and made the room as cool as the refrigerator. He drew pictures: of himself and his parents standing together in the garden, Edith lying near them on a bed of flowers; of the empty crib and basinet and Edith floating above them with an angel's halo. He took his butterfly collection, opened the glass frames, and fingered the tiger-swallowtails and the mourning cloaks and thought of his sister under glass. The powder of butterfly wings smudged on his fingers and he smelled its sweet must and wondered about death.

He'd wait entire mornings for his mother to leave her room. She'd wear her bathrobe and bedroom slippers all day long. He comforted her just as his father requested, but she said little to him in return and would spend the rest of the day walking around the house, raking her fingers through her ratty hair. She'd call her friends from the kitchen phone, wrapping herself in the white cord that stretched all the way to the pantry. While she talked, she took cans of beans and soup and oysters and lined them up on the kitchen table. David thought she was playing dominoes.

To her friends his mother talked about a disaster. Until then, "disaster" had been when cars flew off the highway or planes plunged from the sky or, when David was small, his mother talked in hushes to his father about "missiles" and then rushed to Shopwell to fill grocery baskets with these very cans of beans and soup.

Two weeks after Edith's death, his mother appeared at his bedroom early one morning and ordered him to get up. She told him he could dress himself, which made him feel important. They drove to B. Altman's in nearby White Plains. Going up the escalator, he watched how the ground floor with its six-foot mannequins and scented cosmetic counters fell away in favor of the toddler's department that fit magically into its place. His mother went through the racks and picked out pinafores, tiny Dr. Denton pajamas, and white baby shoes. She asked his opinion about a snowsuit and a jumper. David figured his mother was playing a game until she took out money and paid for the clothing. Then he hoped she had the power to bring Edith back.

His father got home from work late that evening and came through the kitchen door just as David was helping himself to a snack. David was forbidden to eat after dinner and froze in the act of stealing food, his body bathed in the refrigerator light. But as his father lumbered into the kitchen, he didn't seem to care at all that David was eating. It was drizzling and he wore a trench coat belted at the waist, which made his massive athletic shoulders look even wider. "Come here, pal," he said, grabbing David's hands and twirling him around like a top. "What did you do today?"

David shrugged. "Mom took me shopping."

"What you get?"

David peered at his father. A spotlight invaded the room from the garden and made his father loom like a giant. "Didn't get anything."

"Mommy buy herself anything?"

"She bought stuff for Edith."

David heard a pounding in the kitchen and didn't know what it was. Then he realized his father had banged the side of the refrigerator. A moment later his father had opened the metal door he struck, muttering to himself as he removed packages of cold cuts and a block of cheese. He made a quick sandwich without bothering to get a plate —which his mother always insisted upon—and told David to go play in the library before going upstairs to the bedroom.

But David knew something was about to happen. He waited a few moments before sneaking after his father, tiptoeing down the hallway and slipping inside the dark, abandoned nursery, which was right next to his parents' bedroom. "Are you out of your mind?" he heard. "Indulging yourself like that. And taking David with you!"

His mother said something David couldn't make out and then his father replied, "Bullshit! Of course you remember buying it. You're not suffering any lapse. You're just morbid. Morbid!" he yelled.

To David, the word conjured up a woman in a black dress with a bitter taste in her mouth. "Morbid," he would repeat to himself. "You're morbid, you know," he told his mother the next morning when he found her walking aimlessly around the house. She'd been crying; her face was bloated, her cheeks wrinkled as though she had been sleeping on frozen waffles. She had swallowed a yellow pill the neighbor who had looked after him had been urging her to take. The neighbor was one of the people who said, "You've got David now. You've got to be careful how this is going to affect him." His mother locked her room, ran a hot bath, and soaked in billows of suds. Later on, she dried herself off and took a nap. She wore a satin eyeshade to pretend it was night.

After that, his parents seemed to say less and less to each other. His father began to stay longer in Manhattan. David's bedtime would arrive and though he tried to stay awake, he fell asleep waiting for his father to get home. One night his father came home early, but instead of going upstairs to see his mother, he took the cold cuts from the refrigerator, dropping them into his mouth strip by strip as he made his way to the library. David followed him and sat by his legs while he made phone calls to California and to the Orient. His father let him say hello to someone in Australia and David told the person he spoke to that he should visit New York. David asked how long it took this invitation to travel across the world, and the person laughed and said in the voice of a fairy-tale prince, "About the same time it takes for you to blink your eyes."

His father took the phone back, David listening to him talk business language. *Maritime* was the only word he understood; his father was a maritime lawyer.

Suddenly, his mother was standing in her bathrobe at the doorway. Her face was paler than David had ever seen, her lips trembling, her eyes as troubled as Long Island Sound on those gloomy days when

14   Joseph Olshan

boats were warned. She had seen the light glowing on the telephone
up in the bedroom. She motioned for his father to get off the phone,
but he shook his head and kept discussing business.

The next morning David's father announced that he and David's
mother were going away somewhere. David asked why, and the answer was that his mother needed to rest away from Rye. His parents
couldn't take him along; they were going far, to a place where children
could not go, because there were no baby-sitters. They arranged for
a colored woman to stay with him while they were away. He cried and
cried the day they left, pinned behind the dark arms of this strange
woman, watching his mother, pale and woozy, hanging on to his
father, who was wearing a silly-looking straw hat. A limousine arrived
and whisked them away to the airport. Then came five endless weeks
during which David was afraid his mother would never get well.

"Her baby dead into the crib."

"You mean to say that happen up United States, too?"

"What you talking? If dem don't cure it, it must happen."

The supervisors were handing out piles of freshly laundered sheets to the chambermaids. The linen room was cramped with women and smelled of perspiration and starch. Clara felt weary as she received her stack of whites with their blue border. She hated this job.

"She trouble to look after," another supervisor went on. "Lock up in dat room all day, don't let you come and tidy."

"Which woman you talking?" Clara asked, taking a bottle of spray disinfectant from a shelf.

Ignoring her, the supervisors continued their discussion. "Too pretty a woman, she, to let go her life so."

"Where she locate?" Clara insisted.

"What you mean?" someone asked crossly. "Don't she in *your* wing?"

"I don't see her."

"What interest you so much?" another woman asked Clara. "Dis one not looking for wisdom."

"Cha, man, don't be nasty," a young maid piped up. "Miss Clara, de lady is in eight-thirty-five."

Clara quickly left the supervisors' quarters. "Go fly to find the white one, fallen angel," one of them muttered after her.

The maids at the Frenchman's Cove no longer approached Clara

15

with their troubles. Her advice had once been sought by everyone, but now the burden fell upon another woman, who was older than she, but not nearly so wise. Everyone in Port Antonio knew what had happened to the lady who used to give advice at the laundry gorge behind the town, her bright voice rising above the sibilance of muslin and colored cloth rubbing on the flat stones. Some said Clara had the strength of the beyond and could fight like a man. Some said she was secretly a Gypsy. The young, who didn't quite understand what had occurred, still revered her. "Dere she go, Miss Clara Mayfield," they would remark whenever they caught sight of her purple turban.

Later on when she put her ear to the door of 835, Clara could distinctly hear water running. " 'Ello, clack clack," she called, imitating the door knocker. "Step about, maid is here."

No one answered. She decided to ignore the Do Not Disturb sign and use her passkey.

The voile curtains were pulled shut, billowing softly with the trade winds. Beyond them Clara made out the quivering shadows of palmetto fronds and magnolia leaves. Although there had not yet been maid service, the room was tidied, the bed freshly made. Pastel-colored golf shirts were stacked on the antique dresser, bottles of perfumes and cosmetics arranged in a perfect semicircle on a vanity table. Next to them stood two brass-framed pictures of a little boy and a baby. "Lovely child," Clara muttered aloud as she looked closely at the boy, tsking under her breath when she noticed the baby. She heard dull splashing sounds of someone soaking in a tub.

"Maid is here," she said softly, knocking on the bathroom door.

"Come back later," spoke a hoarse voice from inside. "There's nothing for you to do right now."

"But you have your Do Not Disturb out dere from morning till night."

The woman did not answer.

"And ya not even enjoying the view. At least let me part the curtains."

"Please, no. Just leave them."

"You don't like our island?"

"I haven't seen it."

"For shame," whispered Clara. "These rich ladies have everything dem could ever want and still come to get so glum. She should only bear my life. When this island so lovely she stay inside soaking like a sow."

Defiant, Clara drew back the curtains and flung open the shutters. She walked out on the balcony. A shower had passed overhead only a few minutes before and she could see the dark stain of rain clouds trailing across the green wings of the hotel's far lawns and onto the fairway of the rolling golf course. A procession of plumeria blossoms scattered along the walkways and the air smelled like sour sap. She looked toward the half-moon-shaped bamboo bar near the swimming pool where her husband's old friend Alberga tended drinks. "Alberga certainly do get bald so till," she remarked out loud.

Something disturbed her idleness and she realized it was the lady in the bathroom calling for her. "You still here? You still here?"

"Hold on, coming," Clara called, and then, "you ras," she swore under her breath.

"I have a shaver in that gold lamé toilet case on the vanity table. Could you bring it to me?"

"Yes, ma'am," Clara said.

The bathroom was hot and a head of steam clung to the ceiling. An auburn-haired woman, surrounded by islands of fine suds, was soaking in the tub. She glanced bleakly at Clara, who noticed what looked like bruises below her eyes. Not sleeping well, she thought to herself. The woman had a wide, sensual face and looked vaguely Oriental. Her green eyes were flecked with yellow.

"Thank you," she said, reaching for the razor. Clara watched her lift a leg from the tub and hook it over the porcelain lip. It was a sturdy, muscular leg.

"How come you're inside on such a fine day?" she asked. "You should be playing tennis or golf."

"I hate golf," the woman said. "And there's nobody to play tennis with."

"What you saying? Lots of people leave their name down at the tennis pavilion."

"None of them are any good. It's not worth my while."

"Oh, so you must be champion."

"I used to be ranked. Back in the U.S."

"You lucky," Clara said. "But enough of this bathing now. You must get outside and enjoy yourself. Soaking is for where you come from."

The woman stared into the swirls of bath suds. "But I didn't want to come here."

Me can see this one hard to please and probably craven as well, thought Clara. "But you are here, so . . . let me tell you this. If you take ya worries with you, dem will dig their roots into new soil. You must bust up the gloomy. Play tennis. Exertion always good. Run the beach. There's a lovely path runners take down by the shanties. Or walk the river. Go to port where big ships come in from everywhere announcing themselves with they loud horn. I myself used to go and amuse with those ships when something pained me. Coming and going with cargoes of bananas and leather and silver. Quite busy."

The woman managed to make her eyes crinkle with a smile that was unable to grace her lips. "My name is Leona Hart," she said.

Clara nodded. "Clara Mayfield is mine."

When Leona made a move to get out of the tub, Clara reached for the robe, provided by the hotel, that lay folded on the toilet. She helped Leona put it on, and Leona wrapped the terry-cloth flaps tightly around herself and walked out into the bedroom. She smiled when she saw that Clara had ignored her wishes and opened the curtains. She looked out across the patio to the Mediterranean buildings that contained the dining room and ballroom. "It *is* lovely here, isn't it?" she said.

"One of God's chosen places," Clara said proudly.

"I'm hungry," Leona said unexpectedly. "I haven't eaten a thing all day."

"Let me call the room service for you. I will order something special. I have old faithfuls in the kitchen who will send me up something you never tasted before. We call it ackee."

"What is it made from? Maybe you should tell me first. I'm sort of picky."

"Don't worry. If you don't like it, we'll pitch it away. You're on

vacation. You must try something different. You're allowed caprice,"
Clara said as she went to the telephone table at the side of the
king-size bed. She dialed the kitchen. "Hello, where super dere?" she
said. "Tell him is Clara Mayfield calling from eight-thirty-five. Tell
him send me up a traditional. Yes, man, ackee and rice with a side
order of chocho. Wait, you have toto down dere?" She frowned.
"Don't you tell me it's not for guests. I have someone who grow up
in Jamaica longing fe eat it." She winked at Leona. "She want to taste
her childhood again."

Soon after Clara got off the phone, the ackee arrived: creamy yellow
vegetable mixed with an equal part of codfish and bits of bacon, onion,
and lots of black pepper. Leona looked at it. "This is like scrambled
eggs," she said, disappointed.

"No, sir. Favor scrambled eggs, but no eggs in dere. Just taste it."

Leona took the tray over to the bed and set it down on the table
next to the phone. She took a small forkful and tasted butteriness and
a slightly stringy texture of fresh fish that did not overpower the
flavor.

"This is wonderful. What spices are in it besides pepper?"

Clara smiled. "Secret spices, she said. "Tastes of another life."

Leona took big bites of the Jamaican dish. The rice was tender and
perfectly cooked. Once she had finished it, she suddenly felt tired and
lay back against the pillows. Ackee was the first full meal she had
eaten in days. The muffins and scones she had tried to eat in the
mornings made her stomach gurgle and feel bloated. She had been
getting nourishment from Swiss chocolate she bought at the magazine
boutique. "Ackee looks a lot heavier than it actually is," she told
Clara.

"Must be eaten by laborers at midday," Clara explained. "Can't be
too heavy. Would taste even better if you could get in downtown Port
Antonio. Ingredients fresher and they specialize."

"Maybe one day I'll hire a driver and go see the town."

"There's a bus runs by the hotel every hour. Goes to and from."

Clara began gathering up the plates. As she was taking them to her
portable cleaning station out in the corridor, Leona said, "You've
been very kind to me."

Smiling, Clara said goodbye and closed the door behind her. Down the long carpeted hallway, staring suspiciously, stood one of her underlings. "To ras wid you," Clara muttered under her breath. Then she remembered her friend Pella the Gypsy had prophesied that a white woman would change her life. Could this be she?

Bill had packed all of her clothing for the trip. Leona felt strange whenever she looked in the drawers and saw which of her things he had selected to bring. She had worn little of it since they had arrived ten days before. What could he have been thinking when he packed all her designer dresses and silk blouses to go to a resort? It was though in choosing impractical things for her to wear, Bill was dooming her to remain in bed. Still, it was her own fault, because she had been too numb to choose for herself.

It was remarkable how much energy she felt with something solid in her system. She decided to get dressed, and combed through drawers of glittery tops; linen skirts; and frilly, long-sleeved shirts. Finally she found a peasant blouse she had bought in Acapulco the previous year and a pair of knock-around cotton slacks. Putting them on, she waited for Bill to get back from having lunch with a client who had flown down to Jamaica.

At last he lumbered into the room, golf clubs on his right shoulder. He seemed surprised to find her sitting up so sprightly in bed. A smile ripened on his bold, angular face. His lanky, steel-colored hair, normally combed and plastered down carefully with men's hairspray, had gone awry on account of the humidity and was hanging over his eyes. His gray eyes were made even paler-looking by the presence of a suntan. "How you feeling?" he asked.

"I'm better," she said. "I'm feeling pretty good."

He grinned. "Getting a little of your vigor back?" he asked hopefully, putting his clubs behind the door. He sat down at the foot of the bed, grabbed one of her feet, and began massaging it.

"I don't know," she said. "I managed to eat all my lunch."

"Well, that's something," Bill said hopefully. "By the way, Joe asked if we would have dinner with him tonight. I said I didn't know because you'd been . . . well, I said you're still a little under the weather."

Under the weather, she echoed to herself. Why was it so difficult for him to admit what she was going through? He almost seemed ashamed. Maybe he felt he had to play down the misfortune in order to help her deal with the misery. "Did your client mention anything at all about what happened?" she tested him.

Bill's sun-weary expression sank even lower. "We got a condolence card from him, remember?"

"I was just wondering if he actually said anything to you."

Bill shook his head. "I met him at the course this morning. We played eighteen. And discussed the Saudi contracts. Then we had drinks and went over the papers."

Leona looked disgusted. "I can't believe he didn't say anything. He knows we're not down here on a vacation."

"Honey, it's difficult for people. They don't know what to say."

"If that's the case, having dinner with him would make *me* feel too awkward. You'd better just do it alone."

He looked at her forlornly.

"The answer is no."

Bill shrugged as he took *Time* magazine and went into the bathroom.

The momentary ease Leona had felt before dissolved, now replaced by the sadness she had been struggling with all along. Perhaps it would have been better if they had taken separate vacations; she would not be feeling so hemmed in. With Bill there, it often felt as though they were both trapped together in an elevator; the sensation hovered over everything they did.

She often wished he had been the one to walk into the nursery that morning. Leona remembered how the pale sunlight had curled the edges of the frilly shades she had had made to order. She'd felt so peaceful that morning as she pattered softly through the lightening shadows in her red bathrobe. For a moment she hovered above the crib, noticing how Edith had the longest lashes, the most delicate hands. Slowly she began to realize that something more than slumber kept her daughter so still. She reached down into the crib. Edith's limbs gave no warmth. Her eyes rolled up into their sockets. It was as though she had become a doll, her skin turned to plastic. Leona reeled back. Then she ventured forward again, winding her fingers around Edith's wrist. She felt its rasp and chill. She glanced back at the fringe of sunlight, which suddenly looked as menacing as flames. There was a shaft of pain at the front of her forehead and her breath couldn't come. Her own shrieks surprised her. Part of her was convinced that someone had played an evil joke and exchanged her warm, wriggling child for this motionless dummy lying in the crib.

The memories of what happened next were both jagged and blurred. Weeping in Bill's arms, the frightening call of an ambulance rupturing the quiet of that winter morning. Leona remembered its screeching arrival, the flashing orange lights blinding her eyes up at the nursery window. She remembered smelling exhaust and watching clear smoke rising and thinking that these white men getting out of their white vehicles were messengers sent from heaven to survey for the dead. Without an invitation, they scrambled up the stairs. Against her protest, they took a metal machine to Edith's frail body and clamped it to her like an octopus. Later Bill told Leona she had rushed at them in an attempt to claw them away from her daughter. She did vaguely remember struggling against Bill and the agony ripping her heart when she saw these strangers lifting Edith, whose body had grown as stiff as a board. Now, whenever Bill got undressed, Leona saw her bite marks on his shoulder. They had turned into scars.

And then came a terrible gap: caressing a child in your arms one day and without warning having it gone forever the next. Sometimes Leona wondered if because Edith was so much quieter and more contained than David had been, the characteristic had allowed her to slip soundlessly into death. In the days and weeks following the event, Leona would repeatedly check the crib, tracing the outline Edith's body had made on its tiny mattress during her two months of life. Perhaps if she combed through Edith's clothing and toys, she would be able to make sense of this abrupt change, this trick. Bill disagreed with this, pushing her to dismantle the nursery. She refused. The other day he had suggested she should not still be bedridden with depression. What was the use of trying to set up such a time limit? It reminded her of the way he'd carefully count up the time zones before calling Singapore or New Zealand on his Maritime accounts.

Who was to say that in exactly four weeks she would be beyond the worst of the pain? Who was to say it would not last two months or two years?

The irony of it all was that for the longest time she had never wanted to have children. But the year Leona turned thirty she felt fairly certain that Bill was fooling around with a blond English translator he had met on business in Saint Kitts. Instead of confronting him, Leona decided to get pregnant, thinking his real priorities would create too much of a conflict for him to continue the affair. She was right. Several years later, by the time Leona was pregnant with Edith, her marriage felt secure enough to raise a family. And she had been looking forward to raising a daughter.

The toilet flushed and Bill emerged from the bathroom in his boxers. His legs were too thin for his massive torso. The sight of him made her shudder inwardly. He came over and slipped his arm around her shoulders. "Sweet," he said, "you know I'd love to have dinner with you alone."

"But that's impossible, isn't it?"

"I can't do that to Joe."

She shook her head resolutely, thinking how she had wanted to wear the morning-glory-blue dress with the low-cut back he had brought her from Europe. She had even been thinking of putting a flower in her hair.

"Look," she said, "I really am feeling a lot better today. But I just don't feel up to having dinner with anyone else. You go and I'll order in if I get hungry."

Bill sighed. "All right."

He went to put on the television set. Leona watched the Jamaican version of "World News," the voices of the commentators soothing her nerves. The Caribbean lilt was even nicer to listen to than a British accent. Much more cheery and musical. She thought of the lovely maid who so effortlessly had been able to improve her spirits.

Later in the afternoon, she watched her husband put on his dinner clothes. Although he was handsome and well proportioned, there was nothing elegant about him. His everyday movements were jerky and unfinished, a sort of physical inarticulateness. He struck her as unsophisticated as he dressed in his beige cotton suit, toyed with his brittle hair, and sprayed it. When he finally left the room, she was relieved to be alone.

He had hidden the Valium. The doctor had told him to dole them out to her so that she wouldn't take too many and become dependent. The first place she looked she found them: in a side pocket of the golf bag, the bottle stuffed into the thumb of a golf glove. There was something sweet about his careful yet abortive deception. It made her feel weepy. She popped one, knowing he'd eventually find out—he kept track of how many he gave her—but she'd worry about that later.

Aquamarine shadows thickening around her, Leona tried closing her eyes. Her limbs were addled from nerves. She had a sense of her body hovering above the bed, turning sideways so that her head was facing the windows. Slowly, she slipped into cold sleep.

Edith and she were in a flimsy sailboat out on the Sound. They were on a broad reach, the mainsheet held snugly in her hand, wind rushing at their back as it forced the sail farther out. She was holding Edith on her lap, and as the boat heeled, she hunched forward, gripping the child between her upper body and legs. Soon there was nothing left to unfurl and they were traveling at great speed through a threatening chop. She looked back toward shore. In the distance, like a mirage, her house rose through stormy mist across a field of dark molten swells. She could see someone waving from the shore. She strained her eyes and then realized it was Clara, who seemed to be beckoning. The next thing Leona knew, the wind had overpowered the boat, which suddenly capsized, and Edith slipped from her arms. She got tangled up in line, thrashing frantically through the murky water to find her daughter. But Edith had already sunk into the turbulence of the Sound.

She woke up in choking screams, feeling strangled by the humid dark. The balcony was open and the moist sea air overwhelmed the air conditioning. Her hands were trembling. Her blouse was dripping. She glanced at her wristwatch: It was 7:30. Bill would be in the dining room. Leona wondered if she should call for him. She picked up the telephone, holding it uncertainly for a moment a few inches above the night table. It slipped from her fingers, making a frantic clatter, and tumbled to the floor. She sat there looking down at the dislocated receiver, listening to the buzzing tone. Eventually she could hear the hotel operator coming on: "May I help you? May I help you?" Leona slowly stood up, wobbled across the room to her husband's golf bag, and stuck her hand in the pocket.

When Leona opened her eyes the next morning, Bill had already left for the golf course. For the first time in the ten days they had been in Jamaica, she woke up ravenous. She ordered eggs, bacon, and almond croissants, and then called the magazine boutique for a copy of the *New York Times*.

By 10:30, the heat of the day was starting up like a powerful engine. Leona got out of bed and poked her head into the hall, where she saw an unfamiliar elderly woman in hotel uniform pushing a cart of linens. "Is Clara Mayfield working on another floor today?" Leona asked.

The woman looked up, a false smile curling her lips. "That is no business of yours. We have rules in this hotel about fraternizing with maids."

Leona was startled by her insolence. "I was just curious to know if she was here."

Silent, the maid stared down at the carpeting's gold and blue pattern of swashbucklers.

"Well, are you going to tell me?"

The woman looked up at her with challenge in her eyes. "Even fallen angels have days off."

"What?"

"I said, Clara Mayfield's day off."

Leona retreated into her room and closed the door. Fallen angel—what could that mean?

For once, Leona was anxious to get out and do something. She took her tennis racket out of the closet and practiced her ground strokes, but she quickly lost interest. Tossing the racket on the unmade bed, she sat down next to it, resting her elbows on her knees. Should she put on a bikini and go to the beach? Then she realized that it was a perfect opportunity to visit the town of Port Antonio. She quickly got dressed in a white blouse and a pale blue linen skirt. Leaving Bill a note, she walked through the main building of the hotel and asked directions to the Port Antonio bus. She went through the outer gates and stood alone on the roadway.

She waited for a half-hour before catching sight of a red double-decker diesel bus. She flagged it down and climbed aboard. As soon as she got on, Leona realized she was the only white passenger. The sleepy-looking black Jamaicans ogled her with a mixture of curiosity and scorn as the bus crawled along narrow roads toward the center of town. By turns she was able to peer deep into copses of jungle land and then out toward the sea, where English villas with their gardens had been built upon steep limestone cliffs. On the translucent water beyond, she could spy a white mass of coral beds and dark wands of seaweed.

Once she reached Port Antonio, Leona wandered aimlessly through the marketplaces. Drawn by the shrill cries of merchants, she inspected bolts of brightly colored cloth, straw dolls and hats and calypso figures. She sauntered through the stalls of outdoor butchers, looking at meat carcasses offered on hooks. Mongers held up wicker baskets full of glistening fish. Leona asked an elderly man if there was something authentically Jamaican to taste besides ackee, and was directed to a buxom woman with hoop earrings vending jerked pork from a barrel. Helping the woman was a bony twelve-year-old girl with large, fervent eyes. Her red pinafore was torn. Staring at Leona suspiciously, they sold her a strip of dried pork that was too peppery for her taste.

Several cruise ships had docked in Port Antonio for the day. Periodically, Leona found herself overrun by swarms of camera-toting tourists. She tried to see Americans from a Jamaican point of view. They were too demanding, overly curious. She pictured Bill out on the golf course with his client. He probably thought she was spending another day moping in the hotel room. As she made her way toward the harbor, Leona thought about David living alone with the woman from North Carolina. She didn't miss him. But was the woman making sure he ate properly and kept busy? She made a mental list of the things she'd do when she got back to America. Maybe she'd accept an offer to chair that committee to protect hundred-year-old oak trees in the town commons. Or lead a Girl Scout troop.

At the harbor, Leona skirted the berths of the cruise ships and went to look at all the merchant vessels. Some had black prows with gold Slavic lettering. If only she could sneak aboard and stow herself away, crossing the Atlantic to Romania to trace her ancestry. Boxloads of bananas were being loaded up a conveyor belt onto a Libyan tanker. Muscled dockworkers with bandannas wound about their closely cropped heads turned to leer at her. As she walked away from them, someone called out something about white pussy. She looked up at the flawless sky, watching a gyre of gulls lunging into the Caribbean after refuse. The air smelled like diesel oil and fish.

In the midst of her stroll, Leona stopped, realizing that all along she had been looking for a clue, almost expecting something to happen. It occurred to her that she was hoping to run into Clara on her day off. Perhaps that was why, when she got back into the center of town, she had little desire to return to the hotel. She was just passing the woman and child who had sold her the jerked pork when an idea struck her. She paused for a moment. It was worth a chance. "I was wondering if you might know of someone in Port Antonio?" she asked them.

"Can try me." The woman's toothless mouth stretched into a feigned obsequious smile.

"I was wondering if you knew a Clara Mayfield."

The monger glanced away nervously.

"Hi!" the little girl said in a squeaky voice. "She looking Clara Mayfield." Her face looked hollow and malnourished, and she fidgeted compulsively as she stood next to her mother.

"Shut up ya mouth," the woman said, and then turned to Leona. "If you seeking advice, she no longer advise."

"What?"

"There are Gypsies if you looking fortune."

Leona felt her stomach knotting. The jerked pork was beginning to repeat on her. "I'm sorry. I'm confused. I don't know what you're talking about."

"How you get her name?" asked the vendor.

"I met her at my hotel."

"Momma, don't you hear de song?" the little girl piped up. "To de hotel angel fall, to de hotel angel fall," she chanted.

There it was again, that expression. Shade was coming over the market, like a stain upon the merchant stalls. Leona felt it passing over her heart.

"Philippa, me ask you once already, don't be rude," the woman scolded.

But the little girl kept humming the melody, though she didn't repeat the words.

Leona peered down at the girl. "What are you talking about?"

"She don't mean a thing," the vendor said. "She just a child."

"High as Babylon, but she do fall," Philippa sang, dancing in a circle.

"If you continue like dat, you will see what happen," the woman upbraided her. She turned to Leona, annoyed now. "Please don't quiz us no more. Leave us. If you must, ask elsewhere."

The harried monger was now trying to grab hold of her mischievous daughter, but the girl wrenched away, in the process knocking over a metal cashbox that sent coins scattering on the ground. As Leona turned to leave, she heard them arguing.

The sun beat a path down the middle of the dirt road, and on either side of it bloomed a shadow that deepened below the rickety verandas where old ones sat with young toddlers. The heat had grown oppressive and Leona's blouse was drenched with sweat. She was growing tired. She wondered if all this business about "fallen angel" was just part of island strangeness. Her lips parted with thirst and she wanted to knock on one of the closely knit shanties and ask for a glass of water—until she remembered what she'd read about drinking water in the tropics. Each time Leona passed a group of

Jamaicans, all chatter ceased. Hawking vendors stifled their cries.

Suddenly, someone was tugging on the pocket of her skirt. Leona looked down and saw the pork vendor's little girl, whose eyes were wild. She glanced back into the marketplace; her mother was nowhere to be seen. "Clara Mayfield was de muddar of a cliff boy," Philippa panted. "Him jumped right off into hell, his heart left to de sea. But before him jump, him do shame."

"What shame?" Leona whispered "What shame?"

But her only answer came in the form of a piercing cry—"Come back here, you devil's child!"—and the little girl scampered off.

Clara was pulling the coverlet tightly over the hotel bed, her strong hands smoothing wrinkles out to the corners, where they disappeared. She was wearing a lovely strand of red coral. On one of her wrists, Leona noticed a long, zigzagging scar.

Clara caught her staring. "What fancy you?"

"Your necklace. I didn't see anything like it yesterday."

"Probably you don't go to the right part." Clara frowned. "I certainly wish I could have known you'd be in town. I would have arranged to meet you."

"On your day off?" Leona asked.

"Wouldn't be so much trouble. Although dem have a rule here— no fraternizing wid guests. I could be pitched out."

"I heard about that rule."

"Who tell you?" Clara said.

"I asked one of the maids about you."

Clara looked away. "I see," she muttered. Leona felt Clara was on the verge of saying something else, but then her head jerked slightly and she was silent. Her fingers meshed and unmeshed.

There was a loud rapping at the door; room service had arrived with the pot of tea Leona ordered. Clara seemed grateful to have another activity. Muttering something unintelligible to the waiter, she took the tray and set it on a bureau. Into a blue china pot, she began measuring several spoonfuls of dark, pungent tea.

"Did you stay at home yesterday?" Leona asked.

Clara nodded. "Just quiet. Writing letters to friends in Brooklyn."

"Brooklyn?"

"Can't you tell by me accent me come from Brooklyn? she said, stirring the water.

Leona laughed.

"One friend of mine has hairdressing parlor in Flatbush. I know some others."

Clara left the room for a moment and went outside to her linen station. She returned with a brown paper parcel. "I brought some bakery bun you should try. Sort of like fruitcake. How about we have our tea on the terrace?"

Leona got up. "You don't care if they see you having tea with me?"

Clara looked at her skeptically. "Do you?"

"Not in the least."

"Let them discharge me," Clara shrilled as she walked out into the sunlight. "I lived through worse than that."

As she followed, Leona shuddered inwardly, remembering, "angel fall" and the talk of shame. If Clara's son took his life, why should *she* be held responsible—unless Jamaican custom put the blame on a suicide's family? Was she the mother of a devil's child?

Clara, meanwhile, was pouring tea as daintily as a woman of refinement. She cut the bun into slices and put them on a plate. She waited while Leona took a taste; it was very much like dense raisin bread you could buy in the United States.

"You're married, aren't you, Clara?" Leona carefully phrased her question.

"Yes."

"Your husband works in town?"

Clara gazed blankly at her.

"I'm being too inquisitive?"

Clara shook her head. "No. My husband is working out the country just now. In Cuba."

Strange, Leona thought to herself. What could he be doing in Cuba? Maybe Clara and her husband were separated and she was loathe to admit it.

"So, you're alone right now."

"By circumstance," Clara said. "Though I can't say I regret. Despite anything, I don't allow myself to be regretful. Just can't live so."

Suddenly, beyond them, hotel sprinklers went on. The sun shone through the fine net of water and Leona could see a faint rainbow. A group of dark birds landed in the midst of the spray.

"Those are cling-clings," Clara said.

The birds got busy flipping their wings. A droplet of water hit Leona below the eye.

A long silence unwound. Clara was looking off into the depths of the hotel gardens. Leona crossed her legs tightly, looking at Clara's dark, thoughtful face, full-cut lips that had a slight natural pout, the native woman musing. Far away from the familiarity of her own country, Leona felt strangely clearheaded, more comfortable than she had felt in a long time.

Then Clara let go a throbbing sigh. "It's quite peaceful here in Jamaica, don't you feel?" she asked, though her sigh conveyed anything but calm.

"Soothing," Leona appended, taking a sip of tea.

Clara smiled. "It's a funny thing to be alone. You talk to yourself, but then you get to a point where you stop from listening your own voice, forget you're there. Sometimes I come home nights, take me dinner, and read. But I don't think at all. I get into such a dullness. But if someone should call over phone, I can say such marvels that they seem to draw from another place." She fanned her arms toward the sea. "Like from the coconut's head or the guango's heart, and pass out my lips perfect as fruit. I even joke about it to meself, calling it 'banana bright.' "

Clara stared into the empty pot of tea, her eyes shimmering with distance. Leona felt she suffered inwardly, but knew this perception was charged by things she had heard. She took another bite of bun. "You ever think going somewhere where nobody knows you?" she asked.

Clara looked fixedly at her. "What would be the purpose?"

"I feel that way a lot, just wanting to go someplace new and be someone else."

Clara shrugged. "Me, I just favor quiet and to manage me own concern. Hotel work involve you too much into a throng."

"Maybe *I* should get a job when I go back," Leona said.

Both women fell silent and continued to sip their tea. The sky filled up with gnarled clouds, and sprinklers pattered the guango leaves. A scent of dampened fronds suddenly filled the air.

Thunderstorms were for summertime, and yet here they were in the middle of March. David pressed his flushed face to the cold window of his bedroom and watched the hail. It was as though God had stolen his father's shagbag of golf balls and overturned them upon the world. He listened to the pelting noises and to wind tearing at the naked copper-beech trees. The Sound had turned the color of ashes. Waves became monsters and gnashed at the boathouse until they swallowed one side of it.

For a while David loved the storms and would pretend his lonely house was a great ship threading its way between the continents on a trip around the world. He took the windjammer his father had bought for him in Singapore and held it up to the window, superimposing it over distant whitecaps that could barely be seen through the sheets of rain. He undulated the sailboat, wondering what his father would do when he found out about the boathouse. Then he sat on his bed and reread his book about a sea otter who gets separated from his beloved mate and swims through lakes and streams to find her. Otters can swim faster than any man, and David would imagine himself a champion swimmer who turned into an otter on the last lap of a race and won the Olympics.

Glynnis, the lady who looked after him, was a nervous, rangy, middle-aged woman who smoked cigarette after cigarette. She sat in his father's library, blowing out foul plumes that gathered at the top of the bookshelves. She left a dirty smell in the kitchen. Bits of tobacco stained with lipstick clung to her teeth. The thunder, unseasonably strange in early spring, meant something evil where she came from. She would often hide in her closet, quivering and weeping. David kept asking her what was wrong, but her answers were always garbled and unclear.

One particularly severe night, Nipper, the wirehaired terrier, managed to get loose outside. Bounding across the half-frozen lawns and garden, he leaped into the street. David heard the sound of a car skidding and then the dog yelped. He hurried to the window. Glynnis was already outside, her scarecrow figure sprinting toward the road through a corridor of rain. When she reached Nipper, she knelt down and seemed to huddle into herself. She put her hands over her face. She then rushed over to the neighbors, and brought back a man with her to the street. By then, the car had driven away and the two of them bent over the dog.

David flew down the staircase and ran outside. As soon as Glynnis and the neighbor saw him coming, they held Nipper way above his head. The dog was struggling to get down, and David could see a gash bleeding from the side of his neck. Glynnis kept promising David that Nipper would be okay, but she had to leave him alone while the man rushed her and the dog to the animal hospital.

As soon as they were gone, the storm grew worse. The world seemed to be going crazy. For a while David paced the empty house, afraid of the bursts of thunder and of the Sound that continued to crash upon the dock. He gathered up his butterfly collection and his windjammer and went to hide under the bed. He pressed his hands over his ears and curled up into a ball.

He woke up with dust in his mouth and a stiff feeling in his neck. A pair of cold, scruffy hands were grabbing his ankles, pulling him out from under the bed. Glynnis had returned from the dog hospital but hadn't been able to find him. By now she was frantic. She didn't realize David had somehow slept through her calling and scolded him because she thought he was hiding. "Where's Nipper?" he said, looking around for his dog. She pulled him to her, trying to kiss him as the truth spilled from her tobacco-stained lips.

David broke away and ran out into the freezing rain. He ran down the stone pathway to the water. The wet slate was stained the color of charcoal and he smelled soggy ground and thought of earthworms in their burrows. He looked in awe at the damaged boathouse. Poking his head inside, he discovered the Sunfish was covered with huge splinters. He was desperate to tell his parents about Nipper and the boathouse. Glynnis had the telephone number of the hotel in Jamaica. David raced along the wet tide line, skirting dull, silvery bodies of dead fish, his sandy footprints erased almost immediately by the rain.

When he arrived back home, dripping wet, he demanded that Glynnis call his father. But she was reluctant. "I have to talk to him," David insisted.

"I'm not supposed to call unless unless an emergency," she drawled.

"But the dog!" David began to scream. "The dog!"

For a moment Glynnis stared at him as though he were crazy. "Okay, all right, chile, I'll call your daddy."

But first she made David get out of his wet clothing and swathed him in a large blue towel. She untacked a piece of paper from his mother's bulletin board in the kitchen and then picked up the phone. David listened to involved arrangements Glynnis made with various operators to place a call to Jamaica. The idea of speaking to his parents, who seemed to be on the opposite side of the world, made him feel somehow older. As soon as his father was on the line, David was handed the phone. He heard his father's voice amid the sounds of rushing steam. And as he broke the news about Nipper and the boathouse, he pictured a metal corridor of wires beneath the ocean that changed his voice into electricity and hurried it to Jamaica.

"Davey." His father's voice was echoing. "I'm sorry about Nip. Don't worry, we'll get you a new dog when we get home."

"Are you going to come home now?" David asked.

"I can't, pal. Your mom still needs to get rest."

"Nipper's dead," David said solemnly, realizing for the first time that Nipper and Edith were in the same place. Had they already found each other?

"I wish I could be there to make it easier." Something in his father's voice made it sound as though he were gulping his breath. "But we have to stay down here a little while longer."

For a moment David wondered if his father was crying. It was unthinkable. "Is mom still sick?" he asked.

"She's feeling better. Isn't that good?"

"Can she speak to me now?"

"She's not here. She went into town for a while. She needs to get out and have some air," his father explained. "Now, I want you to go and have some supper, and mom will call you later."

"Dad, can't you come home sooner?" David pleaded.

"Why? Is anything else wrong? Is Glynnis treating you okay?"

By now Glynnis had walked over to the stove. "I hate her." David spoke as softly as he could. "She isn't going to keep staying here, is she?"

"No, she's not," his father reassured him. "Don't worry about that. Just hang tight for a few more days."

But David was not reassured, and after he said goodbye to his father, he considered running away. He was all set to sneak upstairs and pack a bag when he noticed Glynnis had begun to roll hamburgers. She mixed a Duncan Hines cake and put it in the oven. That was too much temptation.

Before David called, Bill had been lying on the bed, staring out over the balcony, hypnotized by the weightless curtains swelling with warm air. He had been thinking of summers back home, when after finishing a round of golf or sailing halfway across the Sound, this would be his favorite time of day. He would be relaxing with a lager beer, convinced finally that there was nothing more he could do to push himself: that he couldn't try for a better golfing score; that there were no more barnacles to scrape from the boat; no more clients to call on the other side of the world.

But after he finished consoling David, Bill put down the phone and cursed life. He stormed around the room, swearing against God and the house. Just when he'd felt things might be getting better, there was more death, more damage to contend with. Then he noticed the limp cluster of hibiscus lying on the night table. He had stolen them from the ninth hole and wrapped them in a wet hand towel. Holding them before him like posies, he had come into the room hoping to delight her. However, when he discovered her gone for the second day in a row, he was glad rather than disappointed; it was the first positive step she had taken in weeks. He just worried how this sudden news would affect her.

Later on in the dining room, it was the old Leona who responded. "We'll get another dog," she said, playing the role of comforter. "We'll get a golden or a Labrador who can swim. I'll have the boat-house reinforced. We'll be able to collect insurance, right?" An architecture major in college, Leona had designed the boathouse herself. "This will give me a chance to fix the mistakes I made," she said, glancing around the room, where, among enormous potted palms, black waiters in white jackets hurriedly crisscrossed with crocks of oysters and stands filled with crushed ice and bottles of champagne. Light glinted off silver chafing dishes and womens' jewels. Leona looked radiant. Her shiny auburn hair feathered back with perfect symmetry. Her wide, handsome face was tawny from wandering among the open marketplaces. Her green eyes—remarkable how David's were replicas down to the amber flecks—were moist with this strange purpose she had suddenly found.

Bill distrusted her mood. It came from this Jamaican woman, who-ever she was, and Leona's sudden fondness for her seemed almost flirtatious. "Clara is a marvel," Leona had said. "The things she understands, and what she's endured. Her outlook is so positive." Leona was so absorbed with her day that she almost seemed dulled to what had happened at home.

The beautiful plates of their table setting were whisked away. Bill had wanted them to stay. He had loved looking at the glazed depic-tions of English hunting scenes. Crab-meat cocktail now enticed him, but he had no appetite. Leona devoured hers. Between bites, she began pressuring him to telephone his friend at the Bureau of Immi-gration in New York and arrange a visa for this woman he had never seen nor heard of—Clara Mayfield—who suddenly wanted to leave her homeland and come back to Rye with them. Leona often latched on to farfetched ideas, refusing to give up on them or compromise. He suggested perhaps she should correspond with Clara for a few months before having her emigrate; then they would see if it would really work. But Leona wouldn't hear of this.

Leona spoke up again. "It's good for me to be exposed to someone like Clara. When you broke the news to me about Nipper and the boathouse, I thought of how *she* would react, so I didn't let myself be shattered."

"In two days this Clara taught you how to be strong, is that what you're telling me?" Bill asked quietly.

Leona shrugged. "A lot of people in Port Antonio know who she is, Bill. She used to give advice."

"A prophet, no less."

The crabmeat cocktail was taken away and the main dish, Pompano, put in its place. Bill took a few bites and then sent it away as well. Leona began polishing off her shrimp scampi. At one point she looked up at him, her face purposeful, and explained, "I've got to try and gain back some of the weight I've lost."

"I like you thin," he managed to say. "It looks good on you."

She grinned at him sheepishly and he remembered one of their earliest conversations. They had just met at a winter party out on Long Island in the town where she had grown up. He had been shocked when in passing conversation she referred to herself as "fat." He had then looked at her more closely; she was more solid and muscular than he had realized, her face soft and dimpled. Later on she would grow lean.

"Lee Lee," her friends used to call her. She was wearing a white fur hat and a long black woolen dress. The house where the party was held, ironically, was near the Sound; in later years Bill would often hark back to a moment when a group of the guests had stood on the lip of a frozen marsh, looking across the water, and be amazed that one of the tiny lights they had seen on the distant shore had been the house he and Leona bought years later. As they talked that first evening, he was impressed to learn she had won large tennis tournaments without practicing very much, had master-planned a house with a contemporary design for friends of her parents.

After that they didn't see each other for a year and a half. Then one wintry night in law school, huddled over his studies, Bill suddenly remembered the magic of that party. He called Leona out of the blue and made a lunch date. By now she had finished college and had lost some weight. She acted cooler and more sophisticated. She was working as a buyer at Macy's.

A short time after they became involved, Leona began insisting they get engaged. Bill was afraid to commit himself to anything until he passed the bar, which was two years away. She refused to understand this and they were forced to break it off. After a month, Bill discovered he was too preoccupied with her to study. He finally called Leona and made a vow.

"Honey, what are you thinking?" he now asked her.

"Nothing, really."

"You're thinking how you really want to bring this woman home with us?"

She raised her eyebrows. "Yes," she said. "I am."

"Look, I realize we need a live-in. But there are agencies in New York."

Leona shook her head. "But there's only one Clara Mayfield. And she's made me feel better. I'm even looking forward to going home again."

"And if it doesn't work out?"

Leona shrugged and sat there gazing at him. "I feel like going for a walk," she said, suddenly rising from the table.

"But you haven't finished eating."

"I just want to be alone for a while. I'll see you back at the room."

He watched her weaving uncertainly through the formation of tables. She glanced back at him before stepping outside into the balmy night.

One morning David woke up with a strange feeling in his stomach. The house was quiet. Rubbing his eyes, he trudged downstairs to the kitchen, where he found the housekeeper sitting at the table surrounded by her suitcases. She was using one cigarette to light another. Between clenched teeth she said, "Your parents are coming home today." She looked sad to be leaving and David felt bad, though secretly he was glad she'd be gone, with her strange fears and her smoking. A neighbor came over to stay with him for a few hours after the housekeeper left.

A limousine pulled up and two people in white linen got out. They were so suntanned, David hardly recognized his parents. He saw someone with them in the back seat of the car. At first he thought they had offered her a ride, but then saw how dark she was, even darker than the woman from North Carolina. He was afraid she would get out of the limousine, too, and it would begin all over again: more cigarettes and strange moods. He forgot how happy he felt that his parents had come home when he saw the driver lifting an unfamiliar red carrying case and a large doubled-over valise out of the trunk.

As soon as they walked in the door, his parents encircled him with hugs. He peeked through the tangle of their arms and saw a red knitted coat. She had followed them through the door without an invitation, as though the house now belonged to her. They finally stepped apart and let him see.

"David, I want you to meet Clara," his mother said. "She's going to be living with us from now on."

41

Clara, in turn, touched his shoulder. She had a knot of silver bangles on her wrist, and her fingers were filled with gold rings. "What gwan, boy?" she asked him in a funny voice, the movements of her purple lips confounding him. "Ya muddar tells me you misbehave. Is dat true?"

"No, it's not true," David stammered, staring at her in disbelief. He turned to his father. "Why is she going to live with us?"

"Because we need her help around here. This house has always been too big for your mother to manage for herself."

David suddenly smelled a sugary cologne that seemed to be coming from within the folds of the woman's coat, from the pleats of her dress that was printed with blue moons. He studied the rest of her face, noting her smooth skin, the way her cheeks had small pouches that looked as though they could hold tiny prizes or force out a deafening whistle. She looked much stronger than the woman from North Carolina.

"Don't be 'fraid of me," Clara said. "Me not gwan gnam a bite o' you. Unless you don't behave, since me na take no trouble from children."

David's parents smiled at what Clara said, and then his father took her bulging luggage up the wooden staircase that led from the kitchen to a large bedroom, where Glynnis had slept. David ran after his father, his face burning.

"I don't want her here!" he cried.

Clara and his mother laughed.

He whirled around. "Get her out of here!"

Clara was amused. "Where you get such nasty talking?"

"David, shut up!" His mother turned to Clara. "I'm sorry."

"You mustn't act so dreadful wid a stranger," Clara scolded gently. "And you have an oddar guess coming if you act so 'round Clara."

Leona took her on a tour of the house. They first strolled through the living room and into the library, where Clara was impressed by all the floor-to-ceiling bookshelves filled with volumes of Bill's law. Then they went upstairs and Clara was shown a series of never-used bedrooms as well as Edith's nursery. David stood outside Clara's door until they arrived. "Yes, Miss Hart, yes, ma'am," Clara was saying as his mother showed her which sheets and towels to use before going off to unpack.

He stood aside, allowing them to enter a bedroom that once had been two smaller rooms. David remembered how in a mood of boredom the previous summer his mother had had the walls between them broken down. He watched Clara's eyes as they took in the empty walls, the twin beds, the mahogany dresser, and the Formica night table with its brass lamp. She went to the window and peered out over the weeping willows, the shriveled back garden, and the cold lip of the Sound. She sighed jaggedly and slowly began to unpack. From her larger suitcase she removed exotic-looking dresses—bold paisley prints, gold and aquamarine cottons, purple sarongs—and hung them in the closet. She took crimson and peach-colored turbans and put them on one of the closet shelves above her dresses. She put soft, roomy nightgowns in the dresser drawers as well as stacks of bleached white work uniforms that each had a small patch with palm trees sewn over the right breast pocket. David looked hard at her, figuring she was somewhere past what seemed like the distant age of forty. And yet she hadn't a wrinkle on her face, her arms were soft and plump. When Clara stopped to smile at him, he noticed her teeth were perfectly straight and white like rows of identical sea shells.

"But come in if you must come in. Don't maraud by de door."

"I don't want to come in."

"Suit yourself."

"I want you to leave," David told her.

Clara dropped the nightgown she was holding. "You want I to go back to where I come?"

"Yes."

"All right." Clara went to a bureau drawer and removed a pile of work uniforms. She brought them back to the double suitcase, carefully fitting them inside a pocket, and zipped it up. "Satisfy now?"

"They won't let you leave," David said.

Clara smiled wearily. "Honey, listen to me. No one control this one. If I wan go, I go. If I wan stay, I stay. You hear what I talking?"

"Why do you talk so funny?"

"What you mean funny? Everybody in Jamaica talks so. And you don't hear me talking yet. I can talk so you can't understand. I can talk deep bad."

"I don't believe you."

"Come in here and smell this." Clara tempted David with a pint-size bottle.

"What is it?" he asked, squirming away with embarrassment.

"Bay rum. When you sick, is good for fever."

David stepped inside the room and took a whiff of the clear fluid. He smelled berries and rubbing alcohol. "Yuuuuh," he said.

"You can stay," he told Clara finally. He didn't want her to stay, but he felt guilty about perhaps hurting her feelings and also didn't want to be the one responsible for her leaving so suddenly. He remained where he was standing, continuing to watch Clara remove toiletries from the clear plastic pouches of the Val-Pac. She took out a red porcelain bottle shaped like the figure of a woman and quickly misted herself behind the ears. "You like smell my Touch of Fire as well?" she asked.

David smelled the overly sweet scent that came from her knitted coat. Suddenly, he noticed a dark, hairy object in one of the pouches and reeled back, frightened.

At first, Clara couldn't figure out what scared him. "Cha, man, don't be a bebe. What you see is only one of my wigs."

"Why did you come here?" David asked, his eyes still trained on the hairpiece.

"Don't your muddar tell you I was working at the hotel where they staying? It was she who asked me to come."

David looked hard at her. "Are you scared of thunder?"

Clara glanced out her new window, as though a sign of a storm might be visible somewhere in the backyard. Then she sighed. "Look 'pon me, darling," she said. "Me na frighten of anything. I seen too much already. And certainly thunder don't trouble me."

David returned to his room and drew pictures of his family. He gave his parents dark skins because they had just returned from Jamaica. He drew Edith in a coffin deep in a swell of summer flowers. He couldn't decide whether or not to draw in Clara as well, then added her as an afterthought.

His father came in after a while and sat with him on his bed. "You look like you've been eating okay since we've been gone." He reached for David's stomach and pinched him, and David knew his father was teasing him about being overweight. "Who bought all those cookies in the pantry?"

"Glynnis. I didn't eat any of them," David insisted.

"Likely story," his father said jovially. "What you really need is exercise. We're going to have to get you into a little league or something when it gets a little warmer. I don't want you to sit around like you did last summer. Maybe you can try out for the swim team at the club. I think you might make it this year."

"I could have made it last year."

"Then why didn't you?"

"Because I was too nervous when I had to race all those other kids."

"But that's what it's all about."

David said nothing. Then he turned to his father.

"You said that Glynnis wouldn't stay and then you bring back this other lady with you."

"When I said that, I had no idea this was going to happen."

"You mean it was mom's idea?"

His father shrugged. "What do *you* think? Of course it was. Anyway, how do you like her so far?"

"I think I like her better than Glynnis."

"Well, that's not a bad start."

"Glynnis was deep bad," David said, remembering one of Clara's expressions.

His father looked at David curiously, then went back to his bedroom. David sharpened a few crayons in the hole at the side of his crayon box, then got up and turned on his air-conditioner. A moment later his mother was standing at his door. He was glad to see she was wearing normal clothing—not a bathrobe—and that she seemed to have energy again. "It's April," she complained. "Turn that thing off."

David got up and went to switch off the air-conditioner. She waited for the sound of the fan blades to die before she went on. "Did you run that while we were gone?"

David looked away. "No."

"I'll know when the electric bill comes in."

"I didn't." David insisted.

Suddenly, he smelled a wonderful odor. Sniffing, he asked his mother what it was.

Leona was amused. "Clara's downstairs cooking ackee," she explained. "We brought it all the way from Jamaica. Wait till you taste it. Got a great flavor."

They both went to stand at the top of the stairs. David heard clattering of pots downstairs, a song being sung, something like "Chi chi buddo." His mother went back to finish her unpacking.

The house swelled with shadows as he tiptoed down the carpeted staircase and sneaked through the long, creaky hallways. He caught a glimpse of himself in the gilded mirror of the entrance hall. His face suddenly *did* look rounder; he hoped he was imagining it—why did his father have to tell him he had gotten fatter? He slid in his socks over the black and white diamonds of marble tile in the front foyer and stopped at the outskirts of the kitchen. Across the room he spied a large Revere pot simmering on the stove, steaming up a strong foreign scent. The room appeared empty. Clara must have gone back upstairs. Hypnotized by the bright blue gas flames, he crept slowly forward, past a flank of glossy white cupboards with brass knobs and the butcher block where a small onion had been minced. He had just cracked the lid on the pot when a voice rang out! "Get ya duhty hands out dere!" He jumped a foot in the air, looking around wildly for the intruder. Clara had been sitting a gloomy sentinel on the wooden steps that led up to her bedroom, keeping an eye on dinner.

David beat a retreat to his bedroom, thinking that Clara was as scary as her wig. A while later, his mother passed by his room on her way downstairs. He followed her at a comfortable distance. When Leona got to the kitchen, she hovered over Clara, who was stirring something yellow and pulpy into a skillet where there was already something gray. "Let's have the breadfruit tomorrow," Leona said. "I hope they like this ackee as much as I do."

"Some toto is in the oven," Clara told her confidentially. "I make it for the little boy."

I am not a little boy, David almost shouted.

"Fabulous," Leona said.

He wondered how his mother and Clara had gotten to know each other so well.

This concern only deepened when Clara actually sat down to dinner with them at the kitchen table. Leona had told Bill she didn't want to make Clara eat alone the first night in America.

"This is Jamaican?" David asked, looking down at his plate. "It looks like eggs."

"That's what I thought when I first saw it," his mother said. "Try it."

"You go first," David told his father.

His father took a large forkful and chewed it matter-of-factly. "Pretty bland," he said, "but it's okay."

"Bland?" Leona glanced helplessly at Clara. "Don't you taste all the wonderful spices?"

Bill shrugged. "I'm not sure."

"It's taste you learn," Clara said loftily.

David dug in. "Tastes fishy to me," he said.

"There's very little fish in it," Leona told him.

"What kind of fish?" Bill asked.

"Cod."

"Ugh, no wonder," David said.

"Child, it's mostly vegetable," Clara explained.

Cod made David think of cod-liver oil, and he found it impossible to eat any more of the ackee. He asked if he could get some cold cuts and have a sandwich, and his father glanced at him jealously, although he kept eating the ackee. David went to the refrigerator, searching for the makings of a sandwich.

"That's the last time Clara is going to knock herself out," Leona told Bill once they had finished eating.

"I didn't ask for the island special," he replied.

"Don't be sarcastic," she warned him.

"Don't trouble it," Clara interrupted, getting up from the table and going to the oven. She took out a cookie pan filled with huge brown clusters.

"What are those?" David asked gleefully.

"Totos," Clara said. Her eyes were smiling at him. "Coconut-and-raisin cookies. I made them just for you."

Bill shut his eyes and then shook his head. "Look, I have to explain something to you." He addressed Clara in a pleasant tone of voice. "David shouldn't have sweets. He needs to lose weight. He has to wear huskies as it is."

"I do not!" David cried. He was shamed that his father had told Clara this secret.

Clara was looking wistfully at the pan of cookie clumps. She put them back in the oven.

"It's okay," Leona told her. "You and I will eat them. They're delicious." She glared at Bill. "And David will have one."

A brief silence followed.

"The first day home," Leona told Clara sadly.

"You both tired. And feel tension from your return," Clara advised her.

David stared at his mother, surprised and jealous that she was accepting Clara's opinion.

"You're the one who should be tired and tense," Leona said to Clara. "You've never even been here before."

Clara shook her head. "I feel lovely. This place suits me just fine."

Leona was suddenly peering at David, her eyes full of questioning. He knew their eyes were similar, except hers slanted slightly at the corners and crinkled when she laughed or cried. Kids at school teasingly asked if she was part Chinese—she looked different from other mothers. She reached for his plate, scraped his uneaten ackee onto hers, and divided it with Clara.

David watched as Clara learned the responsibilities of running the house, remembering her "nobody control me." His mother gave her the telephone numbers of the cleaning ladies and the gardener and left it for her to manage them and make sure they received their paychecks from the accountant in his father's law office. Clara could easily have assigned all the washing and ironing to the cleaning ladies, but after she inspected their work, she decided to do that part of the housekeeping herself. Food shopping she and Leona did together.

His mother treated Clara as though she were somebody special, and his father as he would an employee. He asked her to mail letters at the mailbox down the street, to polish his golf shoes—chores Clara seemed happy to accomplish. Shortly after her arrival, however, Clara actually argued with his father about the proper way to iron his shirts. He favored heavy starching. She tried to explain that careful ironing could give him the same effect and that starching would eventually ruin all his handmade shirts, which she claimed would last years longer if he would trust her. But his father stubbornly insisted the shirts be done his way. Clara held out that she should at least be given a chance to show him what she meant. To David's surprise, his father finally gave in. Later on, Bill was impressed with the job she did. He called her a wizard with the iron and she continued to press his shirts without starch. David soon realized he'd have to let go of any secret wish that Clara would displease his parents enough to be sent back to Jamaica.

Clara wanted certain changes in her bedroom. She already had been given the black-and-white television that used to belong in the sunroom. She asked Leona if her off-white walls could be painted pale yellow and was told the request had to be put before David's father. With the excuse of buying the evening's dinner, Clara ordered a taxi to the butcher shop in Rye, where she selected shell steaks, Bill's favorite. David came home from school to find her in the kitchen hovering over the wooden cutting board, shredding potatoes into thin shoestrings, which she later fried to a crisp in olive oil. Leona joined them in the kitchen and both she and David watched Clara's dinner preparations. She teased Clara about "the way to a man's heart," saying she never thought she would see the day when Clara relied on "womanly wiles" to get what she wanted.

The dinner that evening was a smashing success and several times Bill told Clara she had outdone herself. She took his compliments graciously, pursing her lips. Leona smirked.

The next morning, at the kitchen table, David was eating his Captain Crunch and Clara was reading the *National Enquirer* when his father came downstairs. She matter-of-factly put in her request to have her bedroom and bathroom painted. David's father glanced at him, sighed wearily, and then solemnly gave Clara the go-ahead. He made her promise, however, not to leave it up to Leona, but to get estimates because, he claimed, Leona would end up hiring someone expensive. Clara took this request to heart and spent the next week interviewing prospective painters. David got home from school one afternoon to find her arguing politely over an estimate with a stout, whiskered Italian man. The discussion got more and more heated until she was screeching in patois and he was fuming at her in Sicilian. Somewhere in the midst of their squabbling they struck a deal, and he was the one who ended up painting her room the beautiful pale yellow Clara dreamed of.

After the new color had dried, Clara made several attempts at rearranging her bedroom furniture, finally deciding the problem was she needed a double bed instead of twins. She didn't bother cooking up a special main course this time around, just focused on the shoestring potatoes. Her wish for the double bed was granted, and she managed to find it on sale somewhere in Portchester. It was only after the new bed had been delivered that the room began to take on the complexion of Clara's life.

The first thing she did was tack up drawings and watercolors, the artwork of her grandson, Derek, who was two years older than David. Derek already was able to accurately depict the contours of the human body, the curve of palm trees, the pastel bands of the Caribbean. She also hung up scripture quotations—penned parchments that were shellacked and mounted on scalloped wood. One of these was "The Lord is my Shepherd," which David felt was important to learn and recite before he went to bed, just as he had seen Clara murmuring her own prayers before she retired.

She put all her immigration papers and letters in her small red suitcase, which she kept in the closet behind her hanging dresses. She went to the five-and-ten and bought Styrofoam busts for her wigs and wiglets and lined the top shelf of the closet with the collection of hairpieces. When David saw the assortment, he imagined they were the shrunken heads of her enemies in Jamaica or perhaps even her ancestors. The styles of her wigs varied from soft bouncing scrolls to a dense-looking beehive. Only one of these hairpieces, a grapefruit-shaped bun, did Clara wear around the house. The others were saved for weekends or special occasions. She told David she saved the beehive for going to church.

Clara spread a piece of white lace over the mahogany bureau, where she began to collect tall amber drugstore bottles full of hand lotions; hydrogen peroxide, which she used for mouthwash; blue bottles of Milk of Magnesia for her stubborn constipation; and Doan's Pills for occasional backache. In the middle of this assortment of bottles she put an ivory cameo picture of her husband and a brass-framed photograph of her daughter in a white gown, taken the day of her first Communion.

Curious from the beginning about Clara's family, David sensed that it would be best not to ask her immediately about them. This was partly because he didn't understand how she could leave them and come to America. His mother told him that Clara had to live in America because in Jamaica she couldn't earn enough money. But

David never believed want of money could cause families to live apart.

Clara asked to accompany David on his afternoon jaunts along the shore of Long Island Sound. At first he was wary of her company and would purposely go patrolling right after his third-grade class let out. He knew this was the part of the afternoon when Clara stayed glued to her black-and-white television, watching a series of three soap operas, which she called her "stories": "The Edge of Night," "The Raging Tide," and "The Guiding Light."

The times she did accompany him, however, he discovered she was able to identify most of the beached sea animals and seaweed. As she peered at the Sound and sniffed the salty air, she was able to predict a low or high tide, and whether or not the fine weather would hold for the weekend. She often told David the Sound was a pit of sewage in comparison to the Caribbean.

It was on one of their first walks that David first asked Clara about her family. He was in particular wondering about her husband, whose image he had studied countless times in its picture frame: a coffee-colored man with a proud head and a dark smudge of moustache, who was standing half in profile next to a palmetto tree. "Don't you miss your husband, Clara?" David asked, picking a stick and dragging it in the cold, murky water.

"Of course I do," Clara said, taking a stick of her own and using it like a cane.

"But then why are you away from each other?"

She let loose a musical sigh. "A lot of money is to be made where he is working on the naval base in Guantanamo Bay. More even than up here."

"Do you have other children besides your daughter?"

Clara was silent a moment, looking far out over the water. Gulls taunted from above, and she glanced up at them for a moment before answering, "No, Eustace is my only. She lives in Kingston, the largest city of Jamaica."

"And she's the mother of the boy who made the pictures?"

"Yes, the mother of Derek."

"And is he your only grandchild?"

"She is due to have another—by end of summer."

"But you won't be there when the baby is born."

"As fate has it," Clara said. She picked up a flat stone, wound up, and pitched it in an amazing low arc. Fifty feet out over the plane of water it grazed the surface, bounced up, touched and bounced eight more times. David stopped, watching the stone fly. He was amazed. He had never seen anyone skip a stone so many times.

"You should challenge dad to a throw," he said after a moment.

Clara drew the air through her teeth disdainfully. "Him wouldn't throw against me."

"How do you know?"

"Too much pride. Him would lose, too. In my day, I was champion thrower of my form, even of the boys."

David imagined a youthful Clara in a pinafore. He looked up at her small dark eyes and thought he saw wildness in them.

"Clara," he said, "will you go back to Jamaica? I mean, will you go back soon?"

Clara frowned at him. "Of course I'll go back."

"But when?"

"When I'm tired of you."

In speaking to David, Clara was careful to pronounce each word and to add articles and pronouns she tended to leave out. However, he noticed that when she was speaking to friends she had known from Jamaica who lived in Brooklyn and the Bronx, or when she got angry, she clipped some words and changed the order of others. Phrases blurred together. Her patois took him some time to get accustomed to, but soon it became like music, music with rainbow colors.

He was thrilled by all these new sounds she had brought with her from Jamaica. There was a telephone extension outside her bedroom and Clara would take the receiver into her room in order to speak privately. David would creep up to her door and listen to her speech patterns, more for the pleasure of hearing the beautiful sounds than to eavesdrop. Soon, a few phrases and then whole sentences made sense. He tried mimicking her. After a while he even grew bold enough to lift up another phone extension in the house to hear the full round of her conversations. She'd get furious with him when she heard him practicing phrases she had only used on the phone with friends, expressions such as "yes, mu dear" and "cha, man, ya too lie!" But she was also amused by the idea of a little white boy trying to talk her patois.

On her weekends off, Clara would often stay with friends in Brooklyn, and they in turn introduced her to other Jamaicans. She slowly grew acquainted with many of her countrymen living in the metropolitan area, some who worked at hospitals, others who worked for families out on Long Island. Leona encouraged her to invite both old and new friends to visit her in Rye during the week.

One of these afternoon visitors, a woman Clara had known since her childhood, was named Icey Darden. David would always remember the first time he ever saw Icey Darden. She was getting out of a Rye taxi and bickering with the driver over a fixed fare. Icey was thin and regal-looking and wore rhinestone cat glasses. She whirled into the house with a pout on her face, and her glittering, bespectacled glance passed over the front foyer and the kitchen as though they were nothing in particular. Clara proudly offered to show Icey around, but unlike the rest of the Jamaican visitors, she had no interest in taking a tour. In fact, she made a quick beeline for Clara's bedroom, as though being anywhere else in the house made her feel compromised.

"How old you are?" Icey asked David after he had followed them upstairs and she was settled in Clara's tattered easy chair.

"Me na know. We na have birthday in dis house. Where ya live, a Brooklyn, Bronx, Miaahmi?" he asked.

Icey's small, delicate head jerked back, her eyes blinking with fright. "But stop," she sputtered. "So rude." Then she recovered herself. "Don't you talk that way! Where him learn patois?" she accused Clara, who was busy ironing, trying to keep a serious, innocent expression.

Clara shook her head. "Me can't help it if him clever as de devil. Him don't miss even a croak." She drew the air through her teeth. David tried imitating this, but only managed to make sounds like water gurgling down a drain.

"You mustn't talk like that," Icey Darden said, momentarily speaking more clearly, as Clara would have done in her stead. "Only low-class people talk like that."

David couldn't understand why Icey would claim patois was low-class when both she and Clara spoke it. Especially when they gossiped! Maybe it was just intended for gossiping—since they both could speak fairly normally when they chose to. He scrutinized Icey Darden, who certainly seemed to be the most distinguished of Clara's visitors. He'd once overheard Clara telling another of her friends that Icey owned and lived in her own brownstone.

"I bring you some candied currants," Icey told Clara as she reached into her blue patent-leather handbag.

David took a few steps closer, anticipating that he would be included in the treat.

She scowled at him. "Open your mouth. Let me look 'pon de state of your teeth," she ordered.

Wishing he had brushed them better that morning, David complied.

Icey was completely dissatisfied with what she saw. "I seen sea cow with nicer teeth den you," she told him sternly. Then a little smile wiggled her lips.

Clara was shaking her head. "Stop teasing and give de child some. I will worry about his teeth. 'Sea cow,' " she mocked Icey, who then broke down and laughed.

If ever Clara wanted to ensure that David would not overhear or eavesdrop upon her more private conversations with friends, she spoke in a language called Gypsy. Gypsy, she explained, was a mixture of African and Spanish. At first David thought it was just gibberish and that Clara was putting him on. But when he lifted the phone extension in the library, he heard identical sounds and inflections from the other party. Gypsy sounded dark and guttural, and David wondered if it was the language spoken by the Jamaican wanderers: people who wore ruined clothing and spent their lives around smoky campfires drinking moonshine. Gypsy words were too difficult for him to pronounce and he was forced to stop listening in on Clara. After repeated begging, however, she finally consented to teach him one phrase: *Na sa ru, ka ku, ma ma tu,* which more or less meant "I know it sounds crazy, but that's what my mother told me."

In no time at all, David could speak patois well enough to impersonate Clara and was even able to fool some of the people who telephoned

her. Whenever he answered the phone and heard a Jamaican voice
asking for Clara, he muffled the mouthpiece with his palm, acting as
though he were summoning her. He allowed thirty seconds to pass
before he spoke to the party again.

" 'Ello," he said once to Blanche Larkin, a friend of Clara's who
ran a beauty parlor in Flatbush.

"Clara, sweet darling, Blanche here. Wha happen?"

"Nadda thing. Wha gwan wid you?" David asked.

"No, me just waiting between customer. What is new up dere?"

"De little boi is too much, I'm telling you. Him is getting me out,
getting on me nerves terrible."

"Listen na, him is all right," Blanche said. "You not work wid some
children I have. Dem is notorious. So tell me, you watching the
story?"

The stories aired before David got home from school. This part of
the conversation usually tripped him up.

"I'm telling you, the whole thing just getting on me nerves so that
I not gwan trouble it for a while."

"But stop!" Blanche had gotten a little suspicious by now. "Up till
yesterday you were telling me how things get exciting and how Jocelyn
Martin gwan get what the bears get."

"Cha, man, what happen her today? She kill somebody or what?
Me too busy wid ironing fe watch her."

"But wait, Miss Clara, you do ironing in ya room. Don't I see you
when I come? What happen? Miss Hart stop giving you ya rest
period?"

There was a long pause and then David heard a loud click, a sound
Clara and her friends used. "Wait, who talking over dis phone?"
Blanche exploded. "David, if is you, I gwan come up dere and beat
ya backside. You know how Miss Clara don't like it when you get so
nasty." She immediately began speaking more properly. "You should
have more respect for me, after all."

"Get outside, get outside!" Clara screamed at David when she
found out what he had done. She grabbed a broom from the utility
closet in the kitchen and chased after him. "Dishonesty is a terrible
thing," she kept barking at him, finally throwing the broom, whose

straw head hit David in the small of the back. Startled more by the broom's impact than actual hurt, he began to cry.

"You is no good and further on too nosy," Clara said angrily, folding her arms across her chest. "I don't have no use for you."

Crawling over to where she stood, David tried to embrace her legs. Clara pulled away. "Don't you come suck suck around me wid ya damned crying," she admonished him.

"I told you, David, that you can't infringe on Clara's privacy," said Leona, who had been drawn by the commotion.

Clara turned to her. "Cha, Miss Hart, you think him will remember such idea next time? You must tump him and tump him until he minds what you say. "Don't it, David?" She smiled sweetly at him.

The cross yet compassionate look on Clara's face caused David to stop faking injury. He picked himself up and shut his eyes, and now Clara allowed him to hug her waist.

One afternoon two months after her arrival, Clara caught Leona in the nursery refolding Edith's rompers and stacking them in the closet. Leona froze in the act, muttering what she knew was a stupid excuse for being there. Clara drew nearer, her face clouding with pity, and gently took the clothing away. She led Leona downstairs to the bar and poured her a tall glass of bourbon. Her eyes searching Leona's, she suggested it was time they dismantled the nursery. Leona protested bitterly, but Clara told her she knew what was best.

Leona collapsed into sobs. Clara made her finish the drink, led her to the master bedroom, and made her lie down. She drew the shades, banishing all light from the room, and then hummed a gloomy lullaby about Blue Mountain. As soon as Leona fell asleep, Clara crept into the nursery. She looked at each article of furniture, each plaything, warding off tremors of her own misery. She began to take apart the wooden crib, hoping that in doing so she'd finally help Leona escape the imprisonment of grief. She collected the stuffed animals and put them in plastic garbage bags, pulled the neat stacks of Edith's clothing from the closet shelves and stuffed them in cardboard boxes. She brought everything down to the cellar, scraping her elbows in the process, and then called to have it hauled away.

But Leona could not get used to the empty nursery, a place where she had been able to go and conjure up memories, a shrine to her departed child. There, somehow, she had felt more at ease. Now, without any tangible remnant of her daughter's interrupted life, she grew depressed again and lost her appetite and favored the comfort of a dark, shaded bedroom.

She began to suffer the same sailboat nightmare she'd had in Jamaica. The dream always started and ended exactly at the same place: out in the middle of the Sound with Edith, and the boat capsizing. The only part of the dream that ever changed was Clara's presence: Sometimes she was flailing her arms at the shore and sometimes she did not exist. Leona would wake up in a sweat and be unable to fall back to sleep for the rest of the night. She was afraid to tell Bill about the dream, certain he would misunderstand and think she was skidding back into a depression. Perhaps Clara, having suffered her own mysterious tragedy, might be able to divine what was causing this sudden unrest.

After one particularly brutal night, half drugged on Valium, Leona staggered from her bedroom down to the kitchen, where she found Clara sitting at the table, making a fervent attempt at a *National Enquirer* word game.

"Help me a minute," Clara said when she came in. *"Blank* of my existence. Four letters."

Leona's temples were throbbing and as she reached up to rub them, she had a moment of clarity, able to suggest the word *bane.*

Clara studied the column for a moment. "Yes," she cried happily. "Good cigar!" She finally sensed Leona's need to talk. She carefully folded the newspaper around her black pen and thoughtfully listened to the description of the nightmare. By the time Leona finished recounting it, Clara was grinning. "Well, if we go by my Pella, the Gypsy's law, when you dream something repeatedly, usually means the opposite of what you dream might come true—in other words, probably you'll have another child."

Leona shook her head. "That's the last thing I want to hear."

"What you talking?" Clara exclaimed.

"I don't want any more children."

"Perhaps *now* you don't."

"I'll never have another child." Leona looked keenly at Clara, searching for a sign of recognition. But Clara's eyes were lusterless, her own misfortunes locked deep within.

*   *   *

At first David couldn't understand why his mother suddenly was feeling worse again. He had expected her to return to the old routine of running around town, working for politics or giving dinner parties. Suddenly, he would come home from school to find her wearing a bathrobe and watching "Jeopardy" in her bedroom. By the sleepy greeting she gave him, he knew she had been taking nerve pills. He realized that with Clara in control of the household, it would be even easier for his mother to do nothing.

And so the day David arrived home to discover the nursery had been dismantled, he immediately felt relieved; he was certain this would mark the end of Edith's hold over his mother. He went down the hallway and stood at the doorway of the master bedroom. The television was blaring; he could hear shrieks of glee and bells ringing and applause. There were blue shadows ringing his mother's eyes. With a frightened smile, he waved to her, and she trilled her fingers at him and blew a kiss. It was as though she were trapped behind an imaginary bubble. He mumbled and she asked him to speak up. He took a few steps closer.

"Aren't you going to be better now?" he asked.

"I hope so."

As David crept closer, he noticed her eyes were looking more crinkled than usual. Their color was dull and her pupils were large dark drops. "Don't just sit there," he told her impatiently.

"What should I do instead of sitting here?" she asked, somewhat amused.

David thought for a moment. "You could bake for me," he finally suggested, noticing the hint of a smile.

"Your father would love that," she said.

"We don't have to tell him."

She chuckled. "What do you want me to bake?"

"Oh, anything. Date brownies would be okay."

She grabbed the remote control and clicked off the television set. David took a deep breath, watching the perfect white smile of the game-show host fading into gray oblivion. He listened to the crash of quiet. Leona got up from the bed, pausing with a bowed head as she adjusted to standing abruptly, and then walked by him, rubbing the top of his head as she passed. Her bathrobe smelled of perfume and sleep as she moved toward the door, the back of it filling with air like a queen's train. He didn't follow her at first, just stood there in the post-television stillness. Her vanity table with its braided flasks of perfume and slender translucent bottles of white lotion was more elaborate than Clara's own collection of toiletries—as were her moods. Amid the array of glass, camouflaged by yellow dust in a plastic cylinder, was the Valium.

David's reverie was shortly interrupted by a terrible clattering in the kitchen. He ran to the top of the main staircase. Down the corridor, Clara rushed out of her bedroom and yelled, "Who de ras troubling me kitchen?" She obviously thought it was he. He heard sluffing sounds of her house slippers descending the wooden steps. "Jesus, love, how you pulling up de place so?" Clara remarked once she arrived in the kitchen.

"I'm sorry, they all just fell out."

"But what going on?"

"David wants me to make brownies."

"Hiii." He heard Clara laughing. "You is something, Mrs. Hart, let me tell you. Lock up all day and den get a cookin' spirit. Never see anybody like you."

"I want to do something nice for him."

"Him needs to have his checkup at de doctor and a new pair of shoes if you well want to do something fe him. Further on, who is going to answer to Mr. Hart-who-detest-fat?"

"We'll hide 'em."

"But don't you see him weighing de child every week?"

"I didn't know that."

"Psss. Don't get me stink out today. And who will take de flogging for it?"

"Me, I'll take it." Leona started to giggle.

"Might just wake you up."

That night David waited until his father was alone in the library before going in and asking what was happening to his mother. Bill's face was newly flushed with a tan; he had gone to Panama on business the previous weekend, during which Leona had begun to brood. He was wearing half-glasses, which he wore when he needed to pore over long documents finely printed in two languages. David watched how his question immediately wrenched his father out of the dilemma of these endless pages covering the antique desk. He began to nervously comb his steel-colored hair with large, callused fingers.

Bill tried to explain that David's mother was having trouble sleeping. This made her feel tired and unhappy during the day. David reminded his father that he had promised she would be fine when they returned from Jamaica. His father shrugged and said that his mother might go through such periods of feeling worse until she became her old self again.

"But how long will it go on?" David asked.

"It's hard to say. She might even have to go to a special doctor."

"You mean a psychiatrist?"

Bill winced. "If worse comes to worst."

David hated running up against this feeling of uncertainty in his father, something he had never seen before. His father used to have explanations for everything, and even though David might not understand them, he knew he could put his trust in his father if he told him something was so. He began to resent Edith's death. Once he thought he'd miss the baby sister he used to feel jealous of, but now, even in death Edith was robbing him of his mother. It was as though his mother loved him less than she once did. How long could her brooding last? Death wasn't just vanishing suddenly or being permanently out of contact; David was beginning to realize someone could be alive and dead, too.

Meanwhile, Leona listened to Clara and tried busying herself with chores such as taking David to the shoe store. But as she drove through the winding roads of her neighborhood, the first time she had driven in many weeks, she realized that being alone with him actually made her nervous. Her trembling hands could barely grip the steering wheel; and as she approached heavier traffic, she grew more and more convinced there would be an accident. She kept glancing over at David's placid, unsuspecting face, feeling hot surges of anxiety, a loss of control. Potential traffic hazards kept thrusting their way into her overactive imagination, which then spun visions of David being hurled through the windshield, his body mangled, his face unrecognizably gashed. She ended up braking the car in order to shatter the illusion.

David turned to her, concerned. "Mom, you okay?"

"I'm sorry," she said. "I guess I overreact."

Hunkering his shoulders, David stared down at his sneakers and was quiet for the rest of the ride.

"When will you feel completely better?" he asked the next day when they were on the way to the doctor. Traffic had bottlenecked and she was wriggling behind the wheel, fighting off an attack of claustrophobia.

"Soon," she said.

"By the time it gets warm?"

"Sure, I imagine." She would say anything to silence his questions.

He turned to her with wounded eyes, as if he wondered whether she would rather he had died instead of his sister. But Leona couldn't find the words to reassure him.

When they got home later that afternoon, she wandered into David's room while he was mounting butterflies. They were perfect specimens he had taken care to preserve, their wings powdery and silken. She showed him which colors she thought would look best together under glass. He murmured thanks and kept pinning wings to white matting, his hands as steady as a surgeon's. Admiring his skill at laying out his specimens, Leona resolved to buy him some exotic butterflies the next time she went to Manhattan.

That night she tucked him into bed with a tender kiss. But then, later on in a suburban loneliness between ten and eleven o'clock at night when the house was still and Bill was calling other continents from the library, she ventured from her bedroom and wandered through the hallways. She stood in the doorway of David's room, her shadow stippling his walls. She looked at his face turned toward her in the fathoms of sleep, realizing sadly that part of her love had died with Edith.

Leona was sitting on the New Haven local, the budding spring a blur outside her window. She was wearing a black skirt and a red blouse. Earlier that morning she had deliberated over whether or not to wear her rope of pearls. Her friend Stella had told her she should bring something she had worn for many years to the psychic, something that would have acquired the vibrations of her body. A ring, Stella had suggested, but Leona didn't want to use anything Bill had given her for fear that the medium might confuse their signals. The pearls were different. She had been wearing them since her mother died.

Before she left for the train station, Leona had found Clara sitting at the dining-room table, polishing the silver with a pink abrasive fluid. She made an attempt to voice her fear of harming David.

Clara stopped polishing and glanced up at Leona with a look of shock. "For shame," she said. "You almost talking devilry now."

"Devilry?"

"A child is a woman's greatest miracle, don't care how much she succeeds in life. God has given you another. You should pour ya soul into him. Be amazed that a boy has come from your woman's body."

"Then why am I afraid?" Leona asked.

"Mrs. Hart," Clara said, "fear is life, I'm afraid. But if you start neglecting your child, only his ruin will come from your neglect."

A few tears dripped down Leona's cheeks; she stifled the rest of them. "At least he has you."

"But him should have closeness wid you. I'm not his muddar. It's not proper for him to turn to me."

"I'm trying to tell you I have trouble," Leona suddenly wailed.

"Then you must go into yourself and learn why," Clara said solemnly. "And you *will* understand. Then it certainly shall change."

At that moment Leona realized she could not confide in Clara about visiting a medium and concocted a story about taking the train to New York to see her and Bill's accountant. It sounded like a lame excuse and Clara was probably clever enough to sense something was afoot. But Leona knew Clara's opinion of her seeing a psychic, whatever it was, would have clouded her openness toward the experience.

The address Leona had written down led her to a large transient hotel for dancers and actors on the Upper West Side of Manhattan. In the busy lobby she passed people of all ages dressed in black tunics and leotards. She took the elevator to the fifth floor, walking down several hallways on her way to the psychic's apartment. There was a strong smell of fresh paint. Some of the apartments she passed were in the middle of renovation, their doors wide open, with scaffolding and workmen inside. Along the way, Leona heard several operatic voices singing scales.

An old Russian woman in a housedress with a brocaded turban on her head opened the door to an apartment with enormous windows and a dim western view. Her living room was filled with hanging ferns and cobwebs. As Leona was led inside, she saw that every square inch of the walls was filled with reproductions of mythical icons. Beneath the gold headwrapping, the medium had a craggy face caked with orange powder, and amazing deep blue eyes. A polished onyx dangling from a pewter chain hung around her neck.

"Sit down, be comfortable," the woman said in a heavy Russian accent as she motioned Leona to a high-backed salon chair opposite a deep armchair in which she then sat down. "Will you have some tea?"

"No, thanks," Leona said. "I'm just fine."

"Okay, then we'll get started," the psychic said, crossing her legs, which were riddled with blue varicose veins. She took off her chain and swung the stone before Leona. "This is the instrument of Guiding

Spirit," she explained. "He was my first husband, Leonard. He answers all questions from other side." She looked carefully at Leona.
"It does not take psychic to see you are troubled. Right, Leonard?"
she asked the stone.

Without any seeming movement on her part, the onyx swung
dramatically on its chain in Leona's direction. "This means yes," the
psychic said. "The opposite way means no." Craning her neck, the
woman shut her eyes. "You don't live in Manhattan, do you?" she
murmured after a few moments of silence, during which she had
whispered to herself.

"No, I live in the suburbs."

"I see house. Green, no?"

"It's white."

"Oh, big house . . . I see fence around it?"

"No fence," Leona said.

The psychic's eyes popped open. "I'm going to get things wrong at
first. This is my test pattern," she explained. "Okay?"

Leona shrugged. She was surprised at how quickly her heart was
beating. She looked around the living room, noticing a cut crystal dish
filled with bright empty candy wrappers, the colors heightened by her
buzzing anxiety.

"Oh," the woman said suddenly. "You lost child."

Leona was surprised. "Yes, I did."

The medium was shaking her head. "But I see why. Your child die
. . . because in previous incarnation was born twin with other soul.
This time, though, was born without a mate. And wanted to be with
them . . . right, Leonard?"

The stone began to swing in the yes direction.

The medium leaned close to Leona. Her breath smelled of wine and
onions. "Did you ever have severe pains in hands when you first get
pregnant?"

Leona thought a moment and then shook her head.

"You might have had and don't remember. That is sign child might
die."

It all sounded preposterous. Even so, it was soothing for Leona to
consider a different approach to what had happened. The psychic's

explanations dealt with external forces. Then again, Leona realized she could never have proof whether or not Edith had a twin on the other side.

"You have other child?" the woman asked.

"A son."

She paused for a moment and then she smiled. "Funny boy, your son. Not many friends. He will have difficult life. Never will he grow tough skin."

To Leona this sounded like a generalization, the sort of prediction that could be aimed at many mothers. She was about to dismiss the whole experience when suddenly the Russian woman found real inspiration. "I see dark woman close to you," she whispered. "Do you know who this should be?"

"I have a housekeeper."

The medium focused her deep blue eyes upon the peeling vault of her living-room ceiling, as though some sort of invisible tableau were drawn upon it. "I see her surrounded by beautiful sea. Tropic. Waves. But wait," she said, frowning. "She is very sad. I see people gathering. She is torn." The psychic now peered myopically at Leona. "She is good for you . . . to a point. She is very forceful and will try to influence you. So be careful."

Leona told the psychic what she had heard from the little girl in Port Antonio. The woman reflected on this, her jaw quivering as if she were tasting the words. Then she shook her head. "That is very sad, surely, but I feel it's something more than what you say. But I can't tell. I don't get it clearly."

The reading turned to the subject of Leona's marriage. "That will be your trouble for next few years," the psychic warned.

"What do you mean by trouble?"

"You will have to work hard so it doesn't end. But I don't know if you will be successful."

When the reading ended, Leona paid the woman $50. As she was leaving the apartment, the psychic recommended she read the teachings of Edgar Cayce, particularly a book called *The Sleeping Prophet.*

Leona was feeling rather light-headed when she got out into the street. The air smelled of greening and of seasons shifting. She felt

a new burst of optimism. She decided to go directly to a nearby
bookstore she knew on the Upper West Side and buy *The Sleeping
Prophet.* While she was there, she picked up a diary of ghosthunting
written by Hans Holzer. She then hailed a taxi to Grand Central.

She bought a train ticket back to Rye, and with a half-hour to kill,
began wandering around the station, finally deciding to have a bowl
of fish soup at the Oyster Bar. But just as she was about to go in, she
glimpsed Bill out of the corner of her eye. He was sitting inside with
an Oriental woman whose slender legs were crossed tightly, one
hooked provocatively under the other. He was smiling and she was
sucking on a long cigarette. Leona held her breath. For a moment she
didn't know whether to stand there until Bill noticed her or turn
around and walk out. After several moments of uncertainty, she
decided to confront him.

Fixing a hard gaze on the pretty, moon-shaped Oriental face, she
tuned a smile to her own lips and walked into the Oyster Bar. Leona
relished her momentary power to provoke the bewilderment that
slowly grew on the woman's face. Sensing something amiss, Bill
swiveled his massive body around in his chair, blushing deeply when
he saw that it was his wife.

"Hi, honey," he said—somewhat darkly, she felt.

"What a coincidence." Leona was amazed at the even sound of her
voice. "Is this—an occasion?"

Bill glanced at his lunch date and a moment of awkwardness si-
lenced them all. "You remember Ching," he said. "I introduced you
at the Italian Trade Commission's Christmas party."

Leona smiled tightly. "I'm sorry, I don't."

"Hello, Mrs. Hart," the woman said. "Nice to see you again."

"What brings you to the city?" Bill asked, still blushing.

"I had an appointment with the accountant," Leona said, beginning
to feel a little faint."

"Have you had lunch?"

Leona nodded. "On the—yeah, I did." Her head now was reeling,
but she forced back her composure. "In fact, I'm just about to catch
a train. I'll see you at home." She then turned to the woman. "I really
don't recall meeting you. Which surprises me. I think I would remem-

ber such a pretty face," she said, and quickly left the Oyster Bar.

Her mind plagued with relentless suspicions, Leona made her way to the train. She kept picturing Bill's acute embarrassment, which she felt clinched her assumption that he and the Oriental woman were more than just professionally involved. The bag of books in her hand got moistened from the sweat in her palms as she dejectedly walked along the platform and then entered a train car.

She felt the eyes of businessmen following her movements. She suddenly imagined herself sitting next to one of these suburban commuters, allowing their legs to press together. Then she felt ashamed. It was the first time she had been stirred by sexual thoughts for many months. But why had the feelings suddenly surfaced? She began to chide herself; this woman could very well be a client Bill was meeting for lunch. He did have lots of women clients. She had seen them in the waiting annex to his office: Greek widows with silver combs in their hair; soigné Argentine shipping brokers; dark-eyed, fidgety Italian beauties—heiresses, all of them.

Leona replayed her old inner pep talk: Sex with a stranger was not making love. Then again, why not? Lunch at an oyster bar and then do some sport-fucking herself. But if she was ready and willing to cheat on her husband when the opportunity arose, wasn't she just one step away from behaving the way Bill behaved? She lived in the suburbs, where it was difficult to meet men. Or maybe this was just her excuse. The Italian carpenter who did the bedroom last summer had stared at her. Leona remembered his large, paint-flecked hands, his shiny dark hair and olive skin that turned a deeper chestnut color after each of his lazy beach days. Once he had asked her for a beer, and after finishing most of it, he boldly offered her a sip. She remembered where the ice-cold bottle was made warm by those large hands.

Midway between Manhattan and Rye, she turned her face toward the bright oblivious world outside her window and sobbed. She wept for a long time before she could collect herself. Then she opened *The Sleeping Prophet* and read about an ordinary man with a great psychic power that could be put to use only while he was asleep.

By evening she had finished the book. She was suddenly eager to read more about such things as trances and ghosts and faith healing.

The next day she went to the Rye Library, where she found a whole shelf devoted to Edgar Cayce, including his own writings. She checked out several other books on subjects ranging from contacting spirits to astral projections to home cures. Over the next few days she tried concocting these remedies: lotions made of olive oil and yeast; cancer preventives made of crushed almonds; healing salves of sardine paste.

Clara was amused by such strange culinary preparations. "Cooking like Gypsy now," she muttered to herself. At least Leona's new interests would keep her occupied enough to stop moping around the house all day long in self-pity. But when Leona enrolled in an astrology course at the New School, Clara began to grow concerned.

By summertime, Leona was gone much of the day at seminars. On a Saturday afternoon at the Waldorf-Astoria Hotel, she learned how to read auras. She attended various one-day marathon courses in organic cooking. On a Friday in late June, she packed an overnight bag and took the train to Southampton for a retreat with Swami Munishri Titubani.

One day Leona returned from Manhattan before David got home from school. She climbed the stairs and locked herself in her bedroom. Clara, busy ironing while watching the stories in her room, could feel something eerie going on. Finding it difficult to concentrate, she finally set down her iron. "Wonder if Leona getting breakdown," she mused. "Wouldn't surprise me after all dis running up and down." She went and listened a moment outside the locked master bedroom. She could hear absolutely nothing. She rapped loudly.

"Oh, fuck, what?" Leona cried out.

"Me well want to know what you doing in dere, Mrs. Hart," Clara cried indignantly.

"I'm busy."

"Listen na, if me must call Bellevue to pronounce you crazy, I will to let you explain."

Clara heard sighing and then a burst of muffled laughter. She clucked her tongue. Either she amuse or taken leave of her sense, one or de oddar.

"Come open de door," she insisted.

A moment later Clara was sitting on Leona's bed. Leona had put on her black satin eyeshade and was lying there giving a detailed explanation of astral projection. "Oh," Clara said. "Sort of like taking whirlwind tour without paying ya fare."

"Come on, don't mock me," Leona complained.

"Let me tell you one thing," Clara said gravely. "If you get stuck somewhere between here and dere, they certainly not gwan serve you lunch."

"Rice for breakfast?" David objected. "Can't we at least have the whole-wheat pancakes?"

"And with vegetables yet," Bill agreed.

"I'm just doing a little experiment," Leona said cheerfully. She was standing over them at the kitchen table, holding a Teflon pan filled with brown rice lightly fried in sesame oil with carrots and zucchini. She was wearing a purple smock and white drawstring pants. She had no makeup on.

It was Saturday morning and the three of them were about to go sailing. Clara's departure for Brooklyn was imminent; she was just descending the wooden steps, her arrival in the kitchen preceded by an aura of Touch of Fire. She was dressed in a blue serge suit and was wearing her braided wig. When she saw David sitting glumly before his huge plate of rice, she dropped her red suitcase and slanted her eyes like a Chinese. He wondered if Clara's gesture was meant to mock his mother. "Eating like coolie now," she remarked. "You like me braid?" She whirled in place so they all could see.

"Me na fool, fool Chinee man." David broke into a Jamaican song she had taught him.

"Me na come from foreign land," Clara said.

Still hovering over the stove, Leona began to pout. She was overly sensitive to Clara's lighthearted ridicule. "You want some breakfast?" she asked, despite herself.

"No, sir," Clara said.

72

"Last call before I sit down."

Clara turned to face Leona. "Look ya, me na interest to eat ant's nest."

"Ant's nest!" David shrieked.

"All right, simmer down," Bill told him.

Clara had been the only one of them to make it perfectly clear she thought such meals were pitiful. A car honking shattered the mood in the kitchen. Clara hurried to the side door and peered out the window. "Taxi here," she announced. "Goodbye, everybody. Sweet weekend. Don't get indigestion," she joked, grabbing her red suitcase and squeezing through the door.

Leona went to the window and watched the taxi drive away. David, meanwhile, felt forlorn. The house always had an empty feeling when Clara left. He had eaten little of his breakfast, his stomach already swelling from the food. He watched his mother sit down and help herself to a double portion, which she then consumed down to the very last grain of rice. In the past month she had gained several pounds.

The previous evening, David had helped his father score hardened barnacles from the white prow of their Sunfish to ready the boat for its first excursion of the season. On this beautiful cool morning in late June, they would be sailing around the bend into the next harbor, where a mansion had been bequeathed to a spiritualist society Leona had recently joined. Family lectures were being offered all day long. Normally it would have been impossible for Leona to get David and Bill to accompany her, but Bill was curious to explore the house, with its antique paintings and furniture, and David was looking forward to the noonday feast. However, in case the food was entirely macrobiotic —which meant tasteless—Bill had instructed him to bring along potato chips, Wonder bread, and Velveeta cheese.

While they were shoving off from the dock, David and his father briefly argued over who would hold the mainsheet. The wind was light and tricky; Bill didn't want the boat to drift too far off course with a less experienced hand at the sail. Leona remained quiet, refraining from taking sides. Bill kept looking over to where she sat in the bow, trying to guess her mood. She was still wearing her purple smock but had changed into cutoff shorts. Her fingers dangled in the cool water, tendrils of her auburn hair tickled by the breeze.

At first Bill suspected the lectures Leona attended were part of a scheme so that she could go off and have an affair. Perhaps he only wished Leona were having an affair—and that he could find out about it without her knowing—so he'd feel less guilty about his own duplicity. But he soon realized it was not a man who engaged her those afternoons she spent in Manhattan. She had come home with paperbacks about Edgar Cayce and the sixth sense and would spend her weekends poring over self-instruction books on astrology.

From her straw bag, Leona took out a plastic bottle filled with a skin-lotion concoction she had learned from a manual of organic remedies. As she rubbed the mixture over her hands, Bill got a whiff of olive oil and oregano. She smelled like an Italian restaurant.

"What's that?" David asked her.

Leona tried to rub some on him.

"No." He shrank back. "Why are you putting it on me?"

"It's a natural sunscreen."

"What's the purpose of a sunscreen?" Bill asked.

"It blocks the sun from tanning," she explained. "Tanning isn't good for the skin."

"You mean to tell me you're not going to get a suntan in the summers anymore?"

She shook her head.

"You're not going to sit out by the pool at the club?"

"When am I going to have time for that?"

"Weekends."

Leona shook her head. The wind was dying suddenly. Bill bit the mainsheet, reaching forward and hauling it in with his right hand. The line tasted salty.

She went on to say she had too much reading to do on weekends. Then there was the Loudon House, their destination, where there were always plenty of lectures. She already had begun arising at six o'clock some mornings to go there for yoga class. She went with her friend Stella, a divorcée who lived on a nearby Tudor estate with three kids and eight dogs.

As they rounded the bend and began to sail toward the adjacent harbor, Bill got chilly and asked David to pass him his windbreaker. Just as the jacket was changing hands, the wind shifted suddenly and the boom swung. "Watch your heads," Bill cried out as everybody ducked. The garment was swept up in the process and skittered into the water. It looked as though a purple membrane had been strewn upon their blue wake.

"Just come about, stay in the wind, and I'll swim after it," David offered.

"Isn't it still a little too cold?" Bill asked.

"I swam in it yesterday."

"All right, go ahead."

David quickly peeled down to his bathing suit, his flesh shimmering as he got ready to dive in. Bill looked over his son's bell-shaped physique, wishing he could lose more weight—he'd be such a handsome kid. After David dived in, Bill steered the boat into the wind and sculled the rudder, which hampered their progress. David, meanwhile, sprinted twenty-five yards back toward the floating windbreaker. When he reached it, he treaded water while he took one of the sleeves and looped it through his bathing suit. With the windbreaker trailing behind him like a loose towline, he started back to the sailboat.

"Jesus, he can really swim," Leona remarked.

"He'll make the swim team this year," Bill said proudly.

"Just don't push him," she warned. "He's only nine."

"What are you going on about?" Bill asked, his eyes still on David.

"The reason he didn't make it last year was that he was so worried what you'd say if he didn't and how disappointed you'd be."

Bill looked dolefully at Leona. "I don't think that's true."

She brushed straying hair out of her eyes. "You don't realize you put pressure on him. He has enough pressure."

"So, I should do what you do. Not come home at all. Leave him completely alone."

Leona shook her head and looked off toward the ever-so-faint shoreline of Long Island. Moments passed. "I have to do this right now," she said. "It's a change and I need it." Her voice quavered.

"I'm trying to understand that, Lee. I'm even going to one of your lectures."

She heaved an exasperated sigh as she turned back to him, squinting. "Bill, you're only going because you're curious about the house."

The Loudon House was a Newport, Rhode Island, type of mansion fancifully supported by neoclassic columns that would have better suited a courthouse or a post office. Bill, Leona, and David glided up to the dock on a run, the sail let out to its full extreme. People roving about the vast clipped lawns and formal gardens turned to stare at their arrival, a few of them applauding when the boat made a perfect kiss up to the dock. David and Bill cast the moorings and stepped ashore, standing together in a self-conscious huddle. Leona saw a young woman she had recently met at a ghosthunting society in Manhattan and began an animated conversation with her. As they were talking, the woman reached into a canvas bookbag and took out a pile of flyers, which Leona soon began distributing among the other visitors strolling around the property. She handed one to Bill.

"Why are *you* handing them out?" he asked her.

"I like to volunteer," she said.

Bill read the mimeographed sheet. A $25 fee was required of each person attending the festivities. This included a forty-five-minute lecture by Swami Munishri Titubani, whom Leona had gone to hear in Southampton—she could have waited another month and saved herself the trip. Next on the schedule was the noonday feast. Bill could see long white banquet tables set up on the north lawn of the estate. Following lunch, Peter Thurmond, a professor of philosophy and religion at Columbia University, would be lecturing on "Self and the Life of the Spirit." Bill looked at long-haired men in their mid- to late twenties, their wives in peasant dresses, their children unkempt and raucous. Among them he noticed a closely cropped white shock of hair belonging to a frail-looking man wearing a business suit.

David, who had been staring with awe at the steady parade of people, turned to his father. "I can tell you right now we're going to get bored."

"Too late. If you had refused to come, I would have."

"Mom said there'd be lots of good food."

Bill scowled at David. "Which you don't need."

"But I thought this kind of food was less fattening."

"Why is that?"

" 'Cause it tastes so yucky."

"Con artist," Bill remarked pleasantly.

His father fell asleep in the sun during the first lecture, while David found a boy and a girl to play with. They wore drawstring pants and had dirt caked in their fingernails, smudged in the hollows behind their ears, as though they hadn't taken a bath in weeks. The little girl's name was Gemma and the boy's name was Dudad. They were taller than David and scrawny. Gemma was the more aggressive of the two; her brother was subdued and he stammered. Gemma had crooked teeth, her eyes were tawny-colored, and she smelled of patchouli. When David was close to her, she made strange, drawn-out gestures, as though she were trying to act grown-up. At one point she took a handkerchief out of one of her drawstring pockets and wound it around her brother's eyes. "You stay here," she told him as she took David's hands. They went running off into a grove of oak trees.

"Where are we going?" David asked.

Gemma said nothing and kept tugging at his arm. "There's a garden shed I want you to see," she whispered.

"How do you know?" David asked.

"We come here all the time."

They eventually found a half-caved-in structure that looked like an evil cottage from a fairy tale. Gemma pried open a broken window and clambered inside. David followed her. The sun shivered in the dusty room, where there were three rusted lawn chairs and a table. She sat down on one of the chairs and hiked down her drawstring pants. As she gazed at David, her tawny eyes caught a glimmer of sun and shone. David felt an excited shriveling in his stomach. Gemma asked him to put his face close to where she peed; he was afraid she would pee on him, although she didn't. Then she told David to sit where she had sat and made him pull down his pants. She put her mouth on his penis, explaining that she had seen her parents doing this. It was the most amazing, slick gliding sensation David had ever felt. Abruptly, Gemma stopped. He asked her to continue, but she refused. She ordered him to pull up his pants and then hurried to climb back out. Silent, they both walked back to the mansion, an air of dissatisfaction between them. The lecture was just ending and David felt that his father was staring at them suspiciously.

The lunch was endless mound after mound of vegetables and grains. The vegetables were cooked several different ways: in broth, stir-fried, or ratatouille-style. There was steaming bulgar wheat and brown rice with soybeans and raisins. Leona was helping with the serving, assuring people who were strict vegetarians that the ingredients had no meat. David and his father managed to find something that resembled hamburgers, which turned out to be tofu-burgers. David noticed Gemma and her brother eating them, but when he tried one it made him feel ill. He ended up going to the sailboat for the bags of potato chips, Velveeta cheese, and Wonder bread, which he and his father ate by the dock.

"We should've come here ourselves in the sailboat and had your mother drive," Bill said between bites of his sandwich.

"How much longer do we have to stay?" David asked as he plunged his hand deep into the bag of potato chips.

"An hour-and-a-half lecture," Bill said. "Now, not too many of those."

"If you didn't want me to have them, you shouldn't have had me bring them," David complained.

"*I* wanted to have them," Bill said.

David looked at his father with exasperation. "Can't we leave when we're done eating?"

"Your mother won't like us pooping out on her."

"I'm going to ask her if we can," David said, and went looking for his mother among the groups of picnickers. He spied her holding a plate heaped with untouched food, talking to a middle-aged man with thick snow-white hair. David was struck by a strange and overpowering feeling. He thought it was due to the sheer color of the man's hair. He slowed his walk, studying him carefully. The man's complexion was very clear, his features were fine, his nose was sharp. His eyes were large and slate-colored and they looked extremely calm, as did his delicate face. David had to wait a few minutes until they allowed him to interrupt their conversation.

"This is Peter Thurmond." His mother finally introduced them. "He's going to be lecturing this afternoon."

"Mom . . ." David stared at the ground, embarrassed but determined. "Dad and I want to sail home now. Can you get a ride from someone?"

Leona stiffened. "It's the wrong time to be asking me this."

"Ah, Leona, maybe you should let them go," suggested the man in a soft, reedy voice.

David looked up and caught him touching her arm as emphasis. The man's hand was small and white with tiny liver spots and prominent veins. The gesture bothered David. Leona seemed to realize this, because she flicked her arm away as she said it was okay for them to leave. But now David was reluctant to walk away; he wanted to ask her how she'd get home. He was afraid this man would drive her and he didn't want that to happen.

He finally went back to his father and told him they were free to return home. His father looked skeptical. David watched him walking over to where his mother still stood talking with the lecturer. He watched the two men shake hands, his father's hulking frame physically diminishing the man's presence. His father then took his mother's arm and led her away. He could tell by the way their lips curled that their conversation was flooded with angry words. Finally, his mother wrenched herself from his father's grasp and walked back to where she had been standing previously.

They had to zigzag back and forth across the harbor several times in order to break out into the main body of the Sound. His father kept strangely quiet, his gray eyes riveted to the horizon. David kept looking at his father's rugged, handsome profile. Something troubled him. The sun was a blistering pocket above them and on the water floated a million quicksilver razors. Had his father seen the man touching his mother's arm? Perhaps—but then, could he have known what he and Gemma had done in the shed amid the dust and the splinters? David kept remembering the strong woody scent of patchouli blending with the smell of Gemma's pee, the feeling her mouth had given him, then the man's white fingers closing over his mother's wrist. These lectures and foods did things to people, he decided, made them want to fondle each other. He was afraid his mother and Peter would end up visiting the shed. The wind rushed past him, tousling his hair, salt spray making his clothes and fingers gritty. There was so much David wanted to tell his father, but he was too frightened of what his father might say.

When they had finished hosing off the boat and stowing the sails and mast, his father insisted they go hit golf balls. His father usually went to driving ranges when he was upset or angry. David asked to be left at home, promising he would stay inside. It didn't take much coaxing before his father consented to this and drove off alone.

David spent the afternoon drawing pictures of the Loudon House, of the sailboat heeling with the wind, trying to re-create the silver web the sun had thrown upon the water. When his father stayed away longer than he'd promised, David began to worry. He finally went down to the dining room and sat nervously in one of the high-backed chairs, which, through a mullioned window, allowed him to keep a vigil over the entrance to the property. Finally, he saw an unfamiliar station wagon pulling into the driveway and his mother getting out. The person who had driven her home was the person he dreaded.

Clara began to write long letters to Jamaica around the same time David's mother began going to lectures in Manhattan. Sometimes, from far down the hallway, he would spy Clara standing at her bedroom window with a look of puzzlement as the daylight faded. In the midst of describing a thought on a piece of her scented stationery, she would have to leave her bridge table in order to think about what she wanted to say next. She would look out to where shadows crept across the formal shrubberies of the garden, a pink glow licking the stone pathway that snaked back toward Long Island Sound. She soon returned to writing, her dark thoughts gushing into a torrent of further scribbling. David moved closer and closer until he could see her lips forming the words she wrote, her nose twitching as feelings poured forth. He wondered whom she could be writing to, realizing that a whole life in Jamaica lived within her memory, years of happy and sad events. He felt belittled by her unknown past life, even jealous of it.

He felt sure Clara was writing about how his mother suddenly started taking classes in Manhattan, night classes that would keep her away from the house until well after he was asleep; how she was learning to make smelly lotions, to rub him with sandy medicines, and cook food that tasted rotten. His mother told them this was the food and medicine of the future, but his father called it all a hoax. When David asked Clara her opinion of his mother's claim, she peered at him with the face of a skeptic. And although she refused to speak

81

against his mother, David knew what Clara's mind was saying to her voice that refused to answer him.

It was the summer David made the swim team, the summer men walked over the moon. He often wondered if the moist, swollen wheat his mother fried in the black skillet, or the bitter-tasting syrup she made him swallow for headaches instead of taking aspirins, or the lotion she dabbed on his poison-ivy rash, were the secret food and remedies the astronauts had brought with them to space. He would always remember that she was at a psychic fair at the Sheraton Hotel, his father on the way to Singapore, the afternoon he and Clara watched the moon landing. David got a ride to swim practice from the next-door neighbor, and Clara had arranged for his swim coach to let him out early and for a taxi to bring him home from the country club so he could see the event as it happened.

She waited for David at the front door and ushered him upstairs to her bedroom, which she normally liked hot and humid, but which, that afternoon, she had kept air-conditioned so he'd be comfortable. Clara was trying to catch up on a backload of his father's laundry while he was out of the country, so she had set up the iron and ironing board. There was a plate of totos waiting for him next to a stack of pressed blue and white shirts. She was deliberately going against his father's "No totos" mandate, and David wondered if this had something to do with the importance of the occasion.

He took his plate of cookies and a cold glass of milk and sat near Clara's legs beneath the ironing board. The room smelled fresh with the scent of newly laundered clothes and toasty from the heat of the iron. He heard the iron planing on the roof of the flimsy structure above him, which creaked like the house did when wind blew. He listened to bleeping conversations at Mission Control and fuzzy replies resounding from the moon. He felt proud that his father, winging across the stratosphere, was one of the few humans who were closer to the astronauts. David pictured his mother learning how to make new salves with other mothers in the ballroom of a hotel.

"Imagine a Sea of Tranquillity," Clara said, echoing voices on the television. "Too bad no such place can be found close to Rye. I'd call us a taxi quick and fast and we'd take us some lunch and go right there now to wet our toes."

Clara's words of dreaming made David feel insignificant. Men were preparing to walk in space, and here he was sitting beneath an old ironing board stuffing himself with totos. He told Clara about this feeling, and at first she couldn't answer, just gazed at the televised image of the *Lunar Eagle*. It was the first time she'd had to think about anything he asked her. David wondered if watching the moon and thinking about travel had given him the power to ask unanswerable questions.

"Child, it's good to know where you stand," Clara answered finally. "Just because them up in de sky dressed like clown don't mean they won't come back and not be human. Walking a dirty moon not gwan change a thing. Dem will come back to earth, sit right down, and eat they toto."

And yet, despite what Clara said, that important afternoon the world did seem to change. David figured that his mother being in New York and his father on the way to Asia gave him license to be closer to Clara. While they listened to the astronauts, he began to rub her toes and feet and then her calfs. She never told him to quit, so he assumed she liked his touch. He remembered overhearing Clara telling his mother that her legs were naturally hairless and that she never needed to shave them.

Then David got bolder, his hands venturing a bit higher up, to her thighs. Clara suddenly reeled back, as though his touch had branded her. The iron fell to the floor, making a Gothic burn on the carpeting. "Don't you touch me like that!" she shrieked. "Leave off my person!" She grabbed for the nearest weapon, a newspaper, and slammed David in the nose. "What are you trying to do me, child? Why you not respect me?" She had a wild yet defeated look on her face he had never seen before.

His nose burned the way it did when pool water sneaked in during his flip turns. His eyes brimmed with tears and the television screen looked blurry. "I'm sorry," he sobbed. "I didn't know it would upset you. Please don't be mad."

Wringing her hands, Clara began pacing the room. "No, sir," she insisted, "you must never do me that again. You hear what I telling you?" she shrilled.

"But what am I not supposed to touch?" he cried.

"Everything! Lord have mercy, everything!" Clara shouted, by now in a scary state. "My two-cent tootsie, my breasts, everywhere!"

"Okay, okay."

"Get out of me room now."

"I'm sorry."

"I said go to your own room," she insisted.

"Please don't send me out. What about the moon?" David pleaded.

"Go watch ya parents' TV."

"I don't want to."

"Look here," Clara said. "You and I not romantic."

Silence plummeted in her room and voices radioed between the earth and moon were bleating over the television.

"Roger, Tranquillity, we copy you on the ground."

"You're looking good here."

"A very smooth touchdown."

David heard whoops of cheering. He turned to Clara. "Then what are you?" he asked softly. "Are you my mother?"

"Lord have mercy in heaven," Clara groaned, unprepared for such a question. She shook her head and mused and muttered for a while. Finally she said, "I can't be anything more to you than a good friend."

"But why—if she's gone so much?"

"Because that is how the world has made.it. And there is nothing we can do about it."

David went to his room. He turned his air conditioning to high and lay on his bed until it was too cold for a T-shirt. He got up, took his ski parka from the closet, and put it on. He lay back down again and wished himself to the moon the way his mother tried astro-propelling herself to such sacred places as India and Istanbul. David willed himself into a clear capsule that hurtled through space and helped the astronauts. His good deeds up there would make Clara forgive him. He knew where he had touched her had something to do with what his parents did together when they slammed their bedroom door in the middle of the afternoon, which they hadn't done for the longest time. But then his parents took off their clothes and pressed their bodies to one another. And that did not happen in Clara's room.

But what did happen that afternoon dimmed David's appetite in the evening.

"Come and eat something," Clara said, referring to the pork chops and the ear of corn that were getting cold on his plate.

"I'm not hungry," he told her. "Besides, my father keeps telling me I'm too fat."

By now Clara had recovered from her frantic mood of earlier and was feeling guilty about reacting so strongly. "Your father prejudice against fat people," she told David. "In Jamaica fat don't mean bad the way it do up here. Fat mean you rich and have plenty girl-friends."

"Then we should go there," he said glumly.

Clara smiled. "I was just remembering when I was into school and used to sit what they called 'back bench.' There sat all the tough girls, who listened to whatever I did tell them. We have a teacher, Mr. Jordan. Him was very strict and if him found you talking you'd get quick lashes with cat-o'-nine-tails. Sometimes old Jordan get so vexed with me, him came running with cat-o'-nine to lash me at my legs. But I jumped right over the damned thing."

"You did?" David squealed.

"Yes, papa, I certainly did." Clara laughed. "Of course, him get to me eventually. Red stings all over my little black legs." David watched as a thought slowly occurred to Clara. "Perhaps I should send to Tichfield School in Port Antonio for cat-o'-nine."

"No!"

"Of course I should. To lash at your legs the way Jordan lash at mine. Then I'll learn you to be a good boy and not touch two-cent tootsie when it don't ask you."

It was a Monday evening, and Clara owed David a Jamaican story. He made several passes by her room, but she was busy writing blue aerograms. He wondered if she was writing about how he had put his hands where her legs were warm and secret. He knew she would place the letter on the kitchen table early the next morning, that it would vanish by the time he returned from school. He imagined that a magic hand stole into the house, spiriting away Clara's correspondence thousands of miles to an island surrounded by the coral and the silvery abalone shells his mother had brought back.

"What about my story?" he said finally.

"What time is it?"

"Eight-thirty."

"All right, get outside so I can make myself comfortable."

"I'll just turn my head so you can change."

Clara looked at him incredulously. "After this afternoon, you think I going to trust you? Get outside and don't come back till I call you."

David waited a few moments outside Clara's door. Bursting into giggles, he rushed in unannounced. She was just pulling on a faded blue nightgown with tiny red hearts. He got a glimpse of her dark, gourd-shaped breasts; she had on a pair of mustard-colored panties.

"Knew you'd try to do that." Clara laughed with him this time. "Seems when it comes to my privates, you not yaself enough to know respect. But all you get to see is a couple of old jugs."

"Your body is so young-looking," David told her. "How old are you now?"

"Flatterer. You know I'm fifty-six."

David perched at Clara's feet, staring at toenails that were painted a peach color, as she began her story.

"Once there was a wicked city in Jamaica called Port Royal. It was full of wicked people."

"Full of swindlers?" David asked.

"Them and more," Clara said. "Anyway, all sorts of bad business and buildings and houses built right on top of each other. One day about lunchtime the earth started to shake. A lot of earthquakes were in the world at de time, and people didn't worry so much at first. But it got worse quickly, and the whole city start to heave. Buildings tottered and most of them fall. It was like Babylon. Then people saw huge cracks forming in de street. Everybody selling fruits in the market, fish and so, tried to pack up their wares and run. But cracks open into a big crevice and den de town got swallowed by earth." Clara's eyes opened wide and she swept her hands in jerky motions through the still air of the room. "Boats in the port thrashed against their moorings. Fires broke out everywhere. In Jamaica dem call it a latter-day Sodom and Gomorrah."

"What are they?"

"Story from Bible. I will mark de pages and let you read. Anyway, to de point of de story. There was a good man living in Port Royal. Some people claim he was as good and pious as a saint. And to him happened a miracle that makes the whole story have significance. Him was actually swallowed up into the ground along with most other people who died. Him was falling into its bowels just like it happen into a nightmare. Then suddenly he heard a sound like God belching and the earth delivered him back up to de top. Him land in de sea and nearly drowned, but was able to survive. So, in Jamaica him is called 'the man who was buried twice.' First during the earthquake, and second, years later when he finally did die. Him was the one person who lived to chronicle the true story of the disaster."

Telling the story seemed to have a calming effect on Clara. As soon as she finished speaking, she settled back on her bed and shut her eyes. A while later her whole body quivered. Her breathing grew more even and soon she was snoring.

Her closet door was ajar and inside it David could see the red vinyl suitcase where he knew she kept all her personal letters. She normally kept it locked; he had seen her put the key in one of her blue envelopes, hidden somewhere in the night table. He climbed off the bed and tiptoed over to the closet door, opening it further. The dark cavity was instantly flooded with light cast by Clara's bedside lamp. The clasp on the suitcase was open!

Just as he was about to reach into the closet, Clara woke up.

"What you think you're doing?"

He whirled to face her. "Just looking around."

She shook her head. "Today must be about the worst-behaved I ever did see you. I wonder if it mark a new cycle, like reoccurring decimal?"

"No," David groaned, wondering if Clara was suggesting the moon landing had something to do with his behavior.

"But, David, is the same thing I telling you today," Clara insisted. "About my person. You musn't touch where you don't concern.

. . . I losing patience now. Since you don't seem to understand this room is my privacy. So let me tell you, if I ever catch you into my things, your backside will be red for months. Redder than de suitcase." She clapped her hands. "Story time is over now. Go to your own room."

David trudged to the door, then turned around again and peered at Clara. "Don't ever leave me," he whispered.

PART
TWO

1971

Life began to change during a heat wave in early September, the week David's air-conditioner broke. Leona called a repairman while he was at school, and David came home expecting the trouble to be cured. Switching it on, David heard the air-conditioner making the same sounds he had heard the night before: sounds of sparrows being slaughtered. His mother came hurrying into his bedroom, yelling, "How dare you turn it on without asking my permission?" For once she hadn't gone to a lecture in New York City. She looked unkempt and frazzled.

That night the air-conditioner stood mute in his stifling room while David slept on an old couch in the cool basement near the unused pool table. He slept with a plastic jeroboam of cream soda cradled in his arms. The next morning his mother began calling one repairman after another. All of them shook their heads over the air-conditioner as though it fatally ailed. David's mother blamed him for turning it on during winter; she claimed he had worn out the motor. She called the Salvation Army to have it hauled away. Finally, a smaller air-conditioner with less power was delivered. It had buttons instead of dials.

From lack of sleep, David felt weary those first few days of sixth grade. Teachers were introducing the x powers of algebra, handing out textbooks twice as thick as the ones David had learned from the year before. Boys began whispering about girls who had come back from summer wearing training bras. It was on one of these afternoons

when classes recessed into an unbearable, syrupy heat that David
forgot to lock his bicycle at the school fence.

That day he had been wearing a brand-new plaid shirt Clara had
not yet washed. The fabric felt stiff and was sticking to the small of
his back when he walked out into the schoolyard. A humid wind was
worrying girls' hair ribbons and mimeographed pages of homework
assignments as David approached the place where he thought he had
left his bicycle. It was empty. He looked around frantically, hoping
he had just forgotten where he had parked it, and then realized the
lock was still in his bookbag. At that moment he wanted to die; the
bicycle had been stolen.

As David trudged home, he decided to cover his blunder with a lie.
He decided to tell his mother that someone was going around school
with a hacksaw and cracking bicycle locks. But as he got closer to the
house, he realized he did not have the nerve to face his mother's anger
and decided to wait until his father got home from work, no matter
how late it was, and lie to him first.

He spent the rest of the afternoon in his bedroom, listening to the
quiet whir of his new air-conditioner, drawing pictures of crushed
flowers in broken vases and of wingless butterflies. When he grew
tired of drawing, he paced back and forth between his window and
the door. He would not leave his room until the moment he heard his
father coming through the kitchen.

When he finally heard his father's heavy footsteps, David took a
deep breath and made his way downstairs. Bill was standing at the
refrigerator, rummaging for food. His large fingers pried between
half-drunk bottles of milk and jars of hamburger relish, containers
clanging amid the silence. Seeing David, his face lit up. David looked
down at his feet. While his heart pounded, he quietly explained that
someone had picked his bicycle lock.

There was a buzzing moment of quiet. "Jesus Christ!" his father
snapped. The strong spotlight in the garden was burning into the
kitchen, making a momentary welt on the back of David's neck.
"Look at me," Bill said, and David peered up into his bewildered face.
"Are you telling me the truth?"

David gulped. "Yes, that's what happened."

His father's eyes narrowed. "You're lying!" he said in a low voice.
"You're trying to con me."

"I am not."

"You forgot to lock your bicycle, didn't you?"

David shook his head.

"Come on, admit it."

"All right, I forgot," David confessed.

"That's it," his father said. "That's the last bicycle you'll ever get."

David ran from the house, out across the dewy lawns. His heart felt
frozen, his ears blistered with shame. He went down to the boathouse
and shimmied up into the rafters with the Sunfish sails, the center-
board, and the rudder, and looked out the dormer window toward the
house. Level with his parents' bedroom, he could spy their shadows
on the drawn shades: gesturing hands and the shape of his father's
head. He wondered if they were discussing the fate of his bicycle.

Up there in the rafters, David began reckoning that lately there had
been abnormal politeness between his parents. They had been saying
please and thank you to one another; they even whispered when they
were in their bedroom. For a while he had been hoping that after so
many months of bickering they were finally growing closer again. But
such hope had recently dissolved when David saw his mother leaving
a hushed bedroom talk, her eyes rimmed with tears. He was shocked;
tears usually followed an argument. He slowly realized that speaking
civilly and politely to one another did not necessarily mean his parents
were in love.

The kitchen door opened and a dark figure sprinted across the lawn.
David's heart stood still. He felt sure that he was going to be hit with
the belt. He began to tremble. It had been so long since he had been
hit with the belt. His father's footsteps fell on the floorboards of
boathouse, and soon he was standing below David.

"Come on down," his father coaxed. "I'm not angry anymore."

To his amazement, David saw that his father had been weeping. As
he began to climb down, his father babbled about how the Sunfish
needed a new sail; perhaps they should take it to the boatyard together
on Sunday. His father did not mention the bicycle—only that on
Saturday they would play golf. David groaned. He was feeling guilty

about the bicycle and knew he would have to submit to a game of golf.
But he just couldn't understand why his father would be acting as
though it were *he* who had done something wrong.

"I wonder if Pella dead down there," Clara said over the phone to
Blanche, her friend who ran the beauty parlor in Flatbush. David was
at home, so Clara spoke mostly in Gypsy.

"I don't believe so," Blanche said.

"But I write her twice asking to put some hex into things up here.
From first time Harts grow farther from happy, den de lady come to
tell me dem thinking 'bout separating. Wonder if Pella not get de
letters or do de wrong thing."

"Better call her," Blanche suggested. "It could be dat Obeah don't
carry well from Jamaica."

"Wouldn't dat be devil," Clara said.

"Unless like Pella get her power working contrary."

"Dis no joke, you know," Clara said. "Divorce would certainly
bring round a terrible state. Especially for me child," she said in a
whisper, though she was speaking a language unintelligible to David.
"Me last hope is Mr. Hart refuse to accept it."

"Mayfield," Blanche said, "wha happen? You don't speak ya mind
again? Don't de woman rely 'pon you?"

"Not a question of dat, Blanche. Me can't tell her stay when she
determine to go. Anyway, she don't ask me piece so much now since
she gone to Gypsy school. She know I don't agree wid dat, so she
reluctant. Further on, when she told de news, I thought must careful
not to step between de two o' dem."

"Yes, you right about dat," said Blanche, who then managed to
steer their conversation to what was happening in the stories. For a
while they relaxed into chatter about television love and death and
their favorite character, Jocelyn Martin.

"Oh, Lord, Clara," Blanche suddenly interrupted. "Me forget to
tell you Bertha gone home to Jamaica."

"No, sir! What a way. Gone quick and fast," Clara said. "Cha, man,
you lost a good beautician," she remarked.

"Her apartment want to let," Blanche said.

"Which one, dat above the cemetery?"

"Eh-heh."

"How much dem crooks asking?"

"Cheap, man. Since she have lease another three years. She want sublease for one-fifty a month. But no girls here will take it because of looking down 'pon de broken tombs."

"Is that so?" Clara said. "Well, I'd rather be looking down 'pon broken tombs than be under broken tombs looking up." In the meantime, she had been making some inner calculations. "I'm thinking, Blanche, me make five hundred a month up here and have me meals provide. Could easily afford to take apartment instead of staying at Icey's weekends so much as I do. Then if me daughter come up here, she'd have a place to stay while I working."

"You de first one me think of fe it."

"And also you know me must prepare for dis divorce business. Dem could pitch me out into de street straight, straight wid no place to go."

"Dem wouldn't pitch you out," Blanche scoffed.

"You don't know dis Leona like me know dis Leona. She craven fe new interest all the while. She might decide to sell dis place tomorrow and gone to Backpack land or wherever she wan' go when she lie on her bed and pray."

Blanche shrieked with laughter.

"Cha, stop de laughing. Watch how she will buy up a house on some island near China and force de child to turn coolie, since she have dat look o' Chinese. . . . Anyway, better I get back to me iron," Clara said. "Me will see you when I come to de shop."

As soon as she could get away, Clara went to look at the apartment, and was satisfied that it was a good deal. On her way back to Rye, she stopped at Western Union and wired Bertha in Kingston. Bertha phoned her in Rye the following day to settle the details of the sublease.

That Saturday morning was hazy and hot. On the previous evening, before she left for Brooklyn, Clara had picked out a turquoise polo shirt and a pair of tan slacks and laid them over the back of David's desk chair. She normally never bothered picking out his clothing. His

mother was still sleeping when he and his father left in their BMW.
Since his father had bought the car, David had rarely ridden in it, and
as they sped past the estates that edged Long Island Sound, he felt
as though he were driving with a stranger. At different points in their
ride, he was afforded a view of the water, calm and mother-of-pearl
in the early morning. He turned to his father.

"This car smells like the train," he said.

"What does that smell like?"

David thought a moment. "Like cigarettes and metal." He touched
the leather on the bucket seats, which were hard and cold. He studied
his father's hands and legs, then his own, searching for similarity in
their shape and size. If he was a replica of his father, he was a fleshy
one. Some boys at school already were getting veins popping out of
their arms. Their voices flickered with lower tones; dark smudges
appeared above their lips where moustaches were coming in. They
were already turning into men. David felt hairless and naked by
comparison.

They reached the country club, turned through tall stone gates onto
a straight two-mile drive lined with maple trees. Bright fairways
unfolded on both sides of the road, the putting greens hazed by a misty
blue veil. "Remember, I get to drive," David reminded his father, who
immediately stopped the car and put on the parking brake. "Okay."
Bill got out of his side, they traded places, and David drove the rest
of the way to the parking lot, carefully steering the car between the
parallel lines of empty spot.

"Good job," his father commended him.

They went over to the nine-hole course because it generally stayed
empty and they could stop and practice shots if they wanted to. David
loved the clipped beauty of golf courses; they looked like endless
sheared carpets with a razor line where the fairway ended and the
rough began. He loved the waving flag at the putting green hundreds
of yards distant. Next to the golf course was a ruined windmill, an
eight-sided structure strangled with wild shrubs and weeds. A caddy
had told him it dated back to the Revolutionary War, when it was a
hiding place for British soldiers in retreat across the state of New
York. David had long since given up asking his father if they could

scour the inside of the windmill for bullet shells and coins. His father had promised that they would, but whenever they finished golfing together, he always pleaded weariness.

His father stood on the level tee, taking a few practice swings. "Dad," David asked him, "do you mind if I follow you around and just watch?"

Bill nervously combed his fingers through his flyaway hair. "Come on," he said. "It'll probably be the last time this season we get to play."

David looked toward the other side of the country club, where he could see one end of the twenty-five-meter swimming pool, which shimmered aquamarine. "But it's the last time I have swim practice," he said. "We're having races today. I don't want to get too tired before."

Bill looked at him sadly and said, "Just tee it up, okay?"

David's first shot was perfect. He knew it would be when he heard the whirring whup of the driver and the golf ball's thwoking takeoff. He watched as it cleared a high wire and then dropped a few yards before a creek. "Good play!" said his father as he teed up his own ball, which ended up going a hundred yards farther. David wondered if he would ever get good enough at golf to drive as far as his father or play as consistently. He resisted golfing because he knew how expert his father was at the game. But he also didn't like playing golf because it was never his choice of activities: His father never liked to do things David liked; his father got bored fishing out of a rowboat or bicycle riding.

"Gorgeous day, huh?" Bill said.

David turned his solemn face up to the sky. "It's okay. It's nice."

"Maybe we'll stop and get ice cream on the way home."

"All right."

"You don't sound so thrilled with the idea."

"I am." David tried to sound enthusiastic.

For his next shot, David selected a three iron from his golf bag and took two practice swings. "Remember, keep your eye on the ball," his father told him. Breathing quietly, David focused, but when he finally swung, the ball veered off sharply to the left.

His father put another ball down in front of him and said, "Try again. Don't take your eye off it this time."

"I didn't," David protested.

"You did. I saw you. You're always too anxious to know where the ball goes. Now, remember to follow through."

This time David missed completely. He cursed and threw his club.

"Hey, hey, hey," Bill said.

"What do you want from me? I *can't play.*"

"Just be patient."

David shook his head, picked up his golf bag, fetched his club, and walked until they reached his father's lie. His father took a five wood from his bag and, without any practicing, addressed the ball. It soared until it almost disappeared, and then fell a few yards short of the putting green. They began to walk again and had gone ten yards farther when suddenly they heard honking sounds and looked up at the sky. A V of Canadian geese was flying overhead, their shadows dappling the golf course. Although it was blazing hot, the noise of the geese threw David a chill. He remembered the scratchy feeling of wool sweaters, the crackling pyres of autumn leaves. When he glanced over at his father, he was surprised to see that he had suddenly dropped his golf club and was rubbing his forehead as though he were in pain.

"What's wrong?" David asked.

For a moment his father would not answer.

"Are you okay, dad?"

His father nodded. "Your mother and I . . . " he began. "We're having problems." He spoke in that aching voice David remembered hearing over the phone from Jamaica when Nipper died.

"How bad?" David managed to ask.

"We're in trouble," his father said, words he had spoken once when he and David had sailed halfway across the Sound and there was a squall following them that was turning the water black.

"Does that mean . . . " David drew in his breath. "Are you going to get divorced?"

His father nodded miserably.

The dread began as a small prick beneath David's ribs, and quickly blossomed into a pinwheeling pain that dug into his muscles until it was hard for him to breathe. His mind filled up with crazy notions: his parents shredding checkbooks that bore both their names; his mother yanking apart the gold chain and locket his father had given her during their engagement. He pictured each of them clinging to opposite sides of the bed, yards of quilts and sheets and pillows separating them. He saw a big knife cutting through the house, dividing everything in half. Then he looked down at his red-and-white checkered golf bag, his shiny clubs, whose heads were muddied and grass-stained from summers of unwanted play. He had never hated golf more than he did now. He even blamed it for what was happening to his parents. He swore to himself that he would never play golf again.

"Okay" was all he could say.

His father began to walk on toward his lie, as though David had just given him permission to get divorced from his mother. David wanted to say it was not okay, but his father was too far away.

He desperately wanted his father to miss his next shot. Divorce should at least disturb his father's ability to concentrate. But when Bill took a nine iron out of his bag, approached his own golf ball, and swung, the ball flew up in a high arc—David felt himself shrinking as he watched it fly. It finally descended from the blue altitude and landed on the green, with little movement afterward. He groaned. It just couldn't be true.

Slowly, as they played the next hole, his father began to talk of changes David had heard of only on television: "custody" and "visiting privileges" and "alimony," a new language that would punctuate the next few years of his life, the ideas of divorce.

"How about Clara?" David asked. "What's going to happen with her?" He was afraid that in all the arrangements she'd be taken from him.

"With me gone, Clara will be needed more than ever in the house," his father explained. David took some consolation in the fact that she, at least, would not get divorced from him.

There was a long silence as they walked between the hole they just finished and the one that lay ahead. David's mouth was dry and his head felt as though it hovered a foot above his shoulders. The beauty of the golf course only lent an absurdity to the strange churnings inside him. Several times his father tried to put a comforting arm around his shoulders, but David shrank from the affection. He suddenly felt a need to be alone, in order to think about what was about to happen. He let his father walk ahead toward the next tee, and then sneaked back to the first hole and ran down an embankment, ending up by the creek.

After a while he could hear his father calling. He crouched lower so as not to be found. Then, out of the corner of his eye, he noticed an enormous black bullfrog. It was the largest one he had ever seen. He grew determined to catch it.

His father finally discovered him. "What are you doing?" he demanded.

"Shh," David told him. "You'll scare him."

"Scare who?"

David bit his lip and puffed air into his cheeks. "There's this enormous frog."

Bill tried to be patient. "Come on, let's finish our talk. Let's finish the game."

David crouched down and slunk forward like a cat. Then he sprang. The frog jumped a few inches into the air and he pounced on it with both hands. At first a dark diamond of a head protruded between his fingers and then the rest of an enormous bullfrog squeezed through until David clamped down on it firmly at the hip, while two large, muscular legs kicked frantically behind. With his free hand, he took off his sneaker and sock and then put the frog inside the sock.

"That's cruel, David," his father said. "Let him go, or he'll die."

David looked up at his father. A single-engine plane was sputtering along above their heads, writing a wisp of exhaust between two clouds. "If you make me let it go, I'll never play golf with you again."

"You're being ridiculous."

"Golf is the biggest bore in the world."

"Glad to hear it," his father said.

David turned the sock upside down. The frog took enormous frantic hops back toward the creek, jumped off the embankment, and landed

with a great splash. David picked up his clubs and stalked off the golf
course.

"You little fuck," Bill whispered.

David felt too upset to face the swimming team and ended up waiting
for his father by the car. He dreaded going home, dreaded hearing
what his mother would say about the divorce. He knew whatever she
had to say to him would only aggravate his disappointment. His only
hope was that when Clara came back from Brooklyn, she might take
his part and help convince his parents to change their minds.

He finally noticed his father walking toward the car with his clubs
on his shoulder. As he got closer, David refused to make eye contact.
His father threw his golf bag in the trunk, the clubs making a hollow
clunking; unlocked the car; and they both got in. He turned on the
ignition, put back the sunroof, and drove off without a word.

David looked up through the sunroof at the canopy of maple trees
that lined the county-club drive. He heard his father sigh. "You have
every right to be angry," Bill said, "but eventually you're going to
have to try to understand."

"I don't want to understand," David answered in a cold voice.

"I'm afraid you don't really have a choice."

They drove on in silence, David looking out the window at the last
blaze of summer green. Humid wind was rushing through the car and
he smelled dandelions and mown lawns and tried to imagine how
things would have changed by the time it got cold. As they neared
home and were driving on an overpass above the New England Thru-
way, he gazed down at the whirling procession of weekend traffic.
Suddenly, he spied something red and familiar at the grass shoulder
of the road.

"Stop!" he shouted. "Stop the car!"

His father slammed on the brakes so hard that David had to brace
his hands against the dashboard. "What is it?" his father cried.

David shaded his eyes against the brutal sun and squinted. "My
bicycle is down there."

Bill pulled over to the side of the overpass. They both got out and
stood at the hurricane fence, meshing their fingers among diamonds

of chain metal. Down below, sticking out of the weeds, was David's bicycle, tires deflated, smashed and bent into itself like a dead insect.

David tried not to cry. "I have to go get it."

Bill grabbed David's arm and held him fast. "Leave it there," he said. But David persisted. "Okay, I'll get you a new one." They could hear endless rhythms of cars riding the lips of concrete. Highway wind was buffeting the fence, and the overpass was swaying from the weight of two-way traffic. "Your bicycle can't be fixed," his father said. With a rough hand he wiped the tears from David's eyes. "Some things get that way."

When they got home, Bill sent David inside to talk to his mother and then drove off so that the two of them could be alone. Leona was in a leotard, sprawled out on her bedroom carpeting. She had just returned from the beauty parlor, her hair stained a deeper tint, neatly coiled into bouncing corkscrews. She smelled sickly sweet like hairspray and grunted as she put herself through a whole series of yoga exercises.

Unlike Bill, Leona felt it necessary to give all sorts of explanations for why they had chosen to separate: Edith's death; her new spiritual interests and activities; his father's constant traveling. Her words sounded more like excuses dreamed up on the spur of the moment. Why couldn't she be like his father and simply say they were "in trouble"? David resented his mother, resented her bright-red leotard. And these exercises only seemed to be limbering her up for being unmarried.

"But this house is so big," he finally told her. "And you don't really bother each other. Look how much time dad spends downstairs in the library."

"People only live in the same house if there's something to keep them together," his mother said.

"I don't think that's true."

"Unless they're old and it's too late to go out and meet new people."

"Does dad have a girlfriend or something? Is that it?" He voiced his worst fear.

His mother clutched her knees to her chest, gazing at him sadly.

"I wouldn't know. But he's taken an apartment. And he's buying furniture for it."

David blinked as those words tried yet failed to take shape. They formed a circle and pressed against his throat until it was difficult to speak. "Do you have a boyfriend?" he stammered.

"Nope."

She had looked away slightly when she said this and her voice rattled.

Neither spoke for a few moments. "But will you love me the same?" His voice suddenly sounded squeaky, tremulous, the frightened voice of the child he was trying not to be.

"Of course we will," she said. Not *I* but *we*. After that she rested her chin on her bent knees and was very quiet. Then her shoulders began to quake.

David ran from the bedroom out into the hallway. He stood there for a moment, not knowing what to do. Finally, he went downstairs and out the kitchen door. He ran to the boathouse, where, hanging on a hook next to a half-dozen orange life preservers, there was an old bathing suit. For a while he just stared at the bathing suit, and soon he shut his eyes. The well-woven security of his world seemed to be unraveling, leaving him with nothing but a knot of confusion. He needed to do something powerful that could somehow disarm his parents. And so David decided to swim to Long Island. All twenty miles across the Sound.

He kicked off his shoes, walked gingerly over the pebbly sand, and tested the water, which hadn't quite chilled down to autumn temperatures. By now his heart was pounding. He took off his shirt, his pants and underwear. He slipped on the bathing suit. It was stiff from being left outside and smelled of hay and mildew. He began limbering up the way he did before going into the pool, then stepped to the lip of the Sound. He hesitated a moment, knowing the swim would be a great undertaking, and then dived in. He immediately jumped up, gasping from the shock of the cold, but forced himself to continue. Pretty soon, a warm numbness came over him; for a while he completely shed feeling in his churning arms. While David swam, he watched the murky bottom slowly turning darker and soon shafts of sunlight plumbed deep into the water. When he breathed on the right side, he spied the vicarage and Tudor mansions that commanded the shoreline gradually shrinking away. He swam past Lightnings and catamarans at their moorings. People scrubbing the hulls of their boats paused to stare at the brave swimmer.

For a while David felt powerful, untouchable, as he tirelessly propelled himself through the great mass of water. He kept listening for motorboats, detecting them from far away. Two came close enough to make him nervous. He treaded water and splashed so they would know someone was swimming. He looked back at the shoreline and saw the low skyline of Mamaroneck and its threads of rising smoke. He was surprised no boats stopped to ask if he was okay or if he needed a lift, and wondered whether in the water it was difficult to tell how old he was. This strange idea was able to penetrate through the mind-blanking exertion that came from already having swum a quarter-mile.

He rounded the last bend of the harbor, following the black cans out toward the center of the Sound. Periodically he would stop and tread, looking back over the incredible expanse of water he had crossed. The bottom seemed miles below him, the sky a curving palpitation of blue. By now everything was simplified. There was his body, the cold water, and the sky. He swam on, aware, however, that there was something strange going on inside his head. He thought of his mother continuing to do sit-ups back inside the house that suddenly seemed so safe and warm. If only she knew where he was.

David's breathing gradually grew more labored. Soon he began to feel stabbing aches in his arms. He swam farther than this in workouts, but never felt so exhausted. Then in the middle of a stroke, he gasped, realizing that he was scared. He heard some sort of mute explosion and stopped swimming. He had never thought such terror could exist: a feeling of being frozen in motion, his thoughts frantically jumbled up and pricking him. "Help!" he heard himself call out. "Help me!" But his voice would not carry and thudded into the swells. It was as though he were crying out from inside a closet.

He felt dizzy, close to fainting. There was a voice as soft as the wind in his ear, telling him to just let go, inhale the water and sleep. In a moment he was ready to give up and be nothing. But then something told him to turn on his back and focus on one of the beautiful cloud banks that were crossing above. While he was floating, he saw green spines of evergreens on his limited horizon. He realized there was a tiny islet only a few hundred yards to the left. He turned on his stomach and did an easy crawl stroke. Then he began to sprint. He would outdistance this fear. He picked up his head and looked toward the grove of trees, which kept getting closer. This calmed him. When he finally got to the small piece of land, he stood up unsteadily on the shoals. He felt a warm wind. There was a lot farther to go; he knew he had no choice but to swim. But he felt more relaxed, knowing he was heading home. Once he was swimming again, whenever he'd feel panic creeping over him, he'd turn on his back for a while and look up at the clouds.

For a month his parents let the news sink in. They gave him time to get used to it as the weather grew colder and the trees turned. He would come directly home from school in the afternoon and go strolling alone along the Sound. He'd find piles of wet leaves amassed just beyond the tideline. From afar they looked like dead animals. There was a strong smell of brine.

In his bedroom David made sketches of the building on East Fifty-seventh street where his father was moving. His father had taken him by there once, wanting David to make a mental picture of the place where his father would be living. It would make the transition easier, Bill said. In his father's new neighborhood, there was always a sharp breeze whipping off the river, where tugboats and barges moved sadly against the currents. His father's new building was neither old nor new and seemed the sort of place in which grandparents would live.

It was decided that the weekend his father moved out, David would be treated to a few days away with Clara in Brooklyn at *her* new apartment. His mother said this would help ease the strain of the separation. They would leave Friday morning; David was to miss a day of school. On the following Monday, his mother would write a note saying he had been ill. It was strange that what went on at home and what was demanded of him at school suddenly did not coincide.

The weekend fell in the beginning of November, during which there was a spell of Indian summer. Lately his father had been spending a few nights a week at a hotel in Manhattan, and he was not at home that Friday morning. Clara was sitting at the kitchen table spooning condensed milk from a tin into her coffee when David came down to breakfast dressed in white tennis shorts and a torn blue T-shirt. As soon as she saw him, she stopped stirring and her face turned sour.

"You not going dressed like that," she told him firmly.

"But it's so hot."

"Don't care. You saw how I put out your nice tan slacks and madras shirt. You must dress properly. You'll be waiting for me whilst I am at Blanche. I certainly don't want my friends to see you dressed a ruffian."

"Blanche's Beauty?"

"Having my hair and wigs done."

"Why can't I wait for you at your apartment?"

"And let Blanche and all the girls be disappointed? They've been waiting to meet you for all this time. Get upstairs now and change your clothes."

When David came downstairs again, Clara was standing by the dining-room window, presumably keeping an eye out for Rye Taxi. "Go say goodbye to ya muddar," she ordered David.

He had turned around and was heading back upstairs again when Leona met him at the kitchen entrance. She was wearing the red bathrobe she wore around the house when she got depressed, although this morning her face looked tranquil. Divorce seemed to take an easier toll on her than death. "Hi, honey," she said. "Ready to go?" and took David's hand, ushering him back into the kitchen. David suddenly wished she had not come down to say goodbye; what had been his excitement at visiting Clara's new apartment suddenly shifted into a dread of the change that would invade the house while he was gone. Clara was still standing her taxi sentinel by the side door, her red suitcase resting next to her dark ankles. The two women exchanged a boding look while his mother involuntarily tightened her grip on his hand. There was an awkward silence. "You must be making the 10:10," Leona said.

Clara nodded and then looked out the window. "If de taxi would get here."

"You know how much I appreciate this," Leona said, her eyes crinkling with feeling.

"I'm glad to do it. For him." Clara indicated David with her head.

Leona grimaced. "Well, it makes it easier for me, too."

Clara broke into a disarming smile that glimmered with gold teeth. "Me can't concern wid what makes it easier for you who have de choice. Me must concern for him who don't."

Leona shrugged, and focused on David. "Then take good care of him," she said.

"Of course!" Clara said with soft incredulity.

Leona bent down and kissed the top of David's head. "I'll see you Sunday."

On the way to the station, Clara chattered merrily about the racetrack with the gangly, red-haired driver; David figured he must have taken her to the train on other occasions. After Clara paid the fare, she led David to a news kiosk inside the old, red brick station. There, she picked up a copy of the *National Enquirer*. David was about to buy a *Playboy* when she snatched it away from him.

They waited on the platform. When the train was delayed, Clara pursed her lips and glared impatiently at her gold-plated Timex. Finally the square face of the engine came into view. "Duhty crooks," she muttered scornfully.

They wandered through two stuffy, smoke-filled cars until they found a no-smoking compartment. People they passed peered at them curiously, as though trying to figure out what their relationship could be. On the worn seat of the New York–New Haven train, a seat large enough for four people, they stayed close together. The bumpy ride caused Clara's soft flesh to jiggle against David's. It made him tingle.

He watched the bright green cloak of the suburbs slowly turning gray and desolate and urban. He kept remembering that his father's books and clothing were being carted away, afraid the house would be different when he got back. He glanced over at Clara, who was busy reading about wonder diets and secret love affairs between celebrities and strange murders where the killers were still at large. Her lips moved faintly as she followed the printed words. David felt different

from other kids his age who might ride the same train, most likely
with their parents on the way to matinees or to visit relatives—but
never on a Friday morning, and never with a housekeeper to spend
a weekend at the housekeeper's apartment.

David looked out the window and was awed by the burned-out
tenements of the South Bronx. Pollution was spiraling up from smoke-
stacks. He told himself he was going to Brooklyn because of Divorce,
picturing Divorce as his parents sitting alone in vacant rooms with
boxes of belongings, living a life of sadness that was something close
to mourning the dead. Divorce was the sort of thing other kids at
school whispered about with a mixture of fascination and pity, the way
they did when one of his classmates began to see a psychiatrist. It was
strange for there to be problems outside parents' control.

Once they left the train at Grand Central, Clara held David by the
elbow with one hand and her red suitcase with the other. "I'm not a
baby," he insisted, but soon felt foolish for complaining. People were
pushing at them from all angles. There were many directions they had
to take as they hurried down flights of dirty concrete steps, smelling
stale popcorn and grilled food, the underground as hot as an oven. At
one point Clara gave David a brass coin and told him to put it into
a slot, but he missed the hole and the coin dropped to the ground. In
a moment, people already had piled up impatiently behind him,
making him feel as though they were in a race. Clara bent down
quickly and picked up the token. She put it in the slot for him this
time, and he was able to get through a shiny metal turnstile.

They waited until a number 4 train came, and stepped aboard a
subway packed with people who had mean looks in their eyes. The
train went what seemed to be a hundred miles an hour, the sound of
its flight blasting through the open windows. Beyond the windows
serpentined a black world sewn with sequins of light. People were
complaining about the November heat wave and how the train was
blowing heat through its ducts instead of air conditioning. It was as
if the weather were betraying everyone. At one stop someone stamped
hard on David's foot and he cried out.

After twenty minutes went by, the train climbed aboveground and
the crowd began to thin out. David had never been to Brooklyn before,

and was surprised to see that it was made up of many two- and three-story buildings, like a dense surburban town that went on and on. Most of the buildings were solid brick with black metal grillwork. They got off the train at Atlantic Avenue and walked down a quiet, tree-lined street. Finally they came to an old white stucco building. At the ground level was a black script sign that read "Blanche's Beauty." The window glass had been hit with a rock and shards fanned out into a glittery spider's web.

The moment they walked into the shop, there was a commotion.

"Miss Clara! Miss Clara!" cried a half-dozen hairdressers as they crowded into the anteroom of the salon. David wondered why they used "Miss" to address her. The ladies all wore identical floral smocks, and some had teased-up bouffant hairdos. "You bring him after all," one woman said. "You bring de boy who speaks patois."

"David, meet Felicia, Lydia, Bobs, and Doris Williams." Clara went from one wide-eyed hairdresser to the next. He smelled Touch of Fire on one of them. "Where Blanche is?" Clara asked.

"Wid customer," Lydia said.

David followed Clara and the other beauticians into the salon. They passed a glass display case full of hairbrushes, tortoiseshell combs, and clear bags full of colored plastic curlers. Two gashed vinyl chairs were pulled up to a chipped glass coffee table that was covered with back issues of magazines. The salon was decorated in wallpaper with red and yellow tulips. The wallpaper matched the smocks worn by the beauticians. David smelled hairsprays and setting lotion, but there was also a distinct odor of burning hair. He suddenly realized he was the only white person in the place.

Several customers were lying half-reclined in retractable chairs, their hair sticking straight out in identical disarray. They looked as though they had just been electrocuted, like the brides of Frankenstein. David was captivated. The beauticians he had just met now returned to these clients, shuttling back and forth between them and a white enamel kitchen stove in the rear, whose gas flames heated thick brass combs. They would remove the metal instruments, run them under a fine spray of water, and do a test strand on the customer's hair. David heard sizzling when the comb was first applied; then smelled burning black hair. He watched Doris Williams dip her fingers into a gold jar of hair-straightening cream and smear it on her customer's hair before using the hot comb to melt its unruly kinks. Once the wild hair relaxed, she tamed it into waves.

"Jamaicans love having straight hair," Clara explained. "Afro never did go over well with us. Except wid Blanche." She turned around. "Blanche, come and meet my David. Him asking for hot comb this afternoon."

"Am not," David argued.

A short, muscular woman working quietly on a wash-and-set in the corner turned toward them with a lingering smile. She had nervous, flitting black eyes and a tiny pug nose. Blanche was five feet tall, the same height as David, but wore an Afro that made her look six inches taller. She left her client to come and meet them, and in so doing gave David the once-over.

"You lost some weight since de picture Clara showed me," Blanche remarked.

"Don't I tell you him swim in summer?" Clara asked her friend. "Dat reduce him good."

"Could still lost some." Blanche winked as she looked David over again. "Eyes pretty green so till," she said.

He began to squirm with embarrassment.

"Favor his muddar," Clara remarked.

Blanche now came even closer to David, who tried to pull away. Clara grabbed his arm while Blanche picked up a strand of his hair and began studying it. "His father bald?" Blanche asked Clara.

"No, sir. Still holding on."

Suddenly, Blanche took David's shoulders and began shaking him roughly. "After all this time I finally meeting you," she exclaimed. "Though I should be slapping your backside fe all the trouble you did give me over de phone."

"Sweet darling, dat was years ago," David told her in patois. "You talking when I was a bebe."

Blanche chuckled, biting her lower lip with tobacco-stained teeth. Then she cuffed David on the shoulder.

"Don't listen dat boy," Clara warned her. "Him will try to charm everybody."

"Him done long ago when you first talk him," said Lydia, who had overheard. She suddenly clenched her fists, gyrating her hips back and forth while she jerked her arms overhead.

"Lift it up, baby, lift up ya beef!" Doris Williams cried, clapping her hands.

"All right, stop de ramping now." Blanche raised her voice. She turned to Clara. "What we gwan do here today?"

Clara dropped her red suitcase. She reached up to unpin the braid-wig she was wearing and soon held it in her hand, uncoiled like a captive snake.

"Take this, na, Felicia," Blanche told a matronly woman who had gray hair and a gold front tooth. Felicia walked over from her unoccupied station, took the braid, and set it down on a plastic marbelized counter. Clara, meanwhile, dug in her red suitcase for the beehive wig.

"You want us groom both o' dem?" Blanche asked.

David suddenly squealed with laughter.

"What is troubling him?"

"Him always get funny over me wigs," Clara explained. She looked sternly at David. "Now I have something to tell you."

"What?"

"I arrange for Blanche to cut ya hair."

David gulped down his shock. "Forget it," he managed to say.

"Your hair too long and well want to cut," she insisted.

"I'll go to a barber."

"But them wouldn't cut it so professional."

"They're good enough for me."

"Sit down in her chair," Clara ordered.

"No!"

"Listen me. If you don't sit down and let she cut ye hair, I putting you back onto de train. I will never take you to my apartment. I will never let you come visiting wid me."

"That's blackmail," David said.

"But she only will cut it a bit shorter, shaping it nice," Clara promised him. "Don't it, Blanche?"

"Miss Clara," Blanche said, "if him so reluctant, let him stay."

"No, sir, I well want his hair cut. I even tell his muddar."

Blanche heaved her shoulders and cast David a glance of sympathy, as though she wanted to tell him it wasn't worth arguing with Clara when her heart was set on something. "Come sit down," she cajoled. "I'll gi' you a nice schoolboy."

"What's that?"

"Will suit you just fine."

"Oh, schoolboy is something lovely," Clara appended. "And it's not something dat she give everybody. It's a special style. Takes plenty of care."

Although David was furious that Clara was trying to manipulate him, he was afraid to confront her. With much regret he sat down in Blanche's chair.

He squeezed his eyes shut. His heart thrummed. He shuddered at first to hear the disturbing sound of scissors shearing through his hair. A few minutes into the ordeal, he ventured to look at Blanche's progress, but as she had been working on the back part of his head, the overall effects were not yet noticeable. He relaxed a little, though he continued begging her to leave as much as possible. He soon began to feel a cooling breeze on the nape of his neck, noticing how Blanche's mood brightened as she clipped away more hunks of hair.

Suddenly, there was a loud hoot. David glanced toward the entrance of the salon, where a squat woman with broad shoulders had just waddled in. She had a tough-looking face with hard-boiled features. She was wearing a beautician's uniform.

"Hello, Dora," Felicia said.

"Wha gwan?" said Doris Williams.

By now Dora had fixed her attention on David as she wended her way back toward Blanche's station. "So where you get this white charge?" she asked Blanche quickly.

"She get me from church bazaar," David answered. "Me was left in de manger."

Dora squinted her cold eyes at him. "Jesus, Father," she remarked.

"Is Clara's boy, de Hart child," Blanche explained as she began to snip the hair around David's ears.

"Where she is?" Dora asked, looking around.

"See her dere." Blanche pointed her scissors at Felicia's station, where Clara's head was tilted back into the sink, her hair saturated with suds.

"So where you go this morning?" Blanche asked Dora. "When you were supposed to be here working," she added tactfully.

"Just come from a sale at Macy."

"What you buy?"

"Couple o' brassiere." Dora glanced at David. "And some hot pantie."

Blanche was frowning as she cut David's bangs. "Don't talk so in front of de child," she warned Dora.

"Him na understand."

"Yes, me do," David said.

"What is hot pantie den?" Dora asked him.

"Red pantie," David said.

Dora clucked her tongue and then glanced at Clara, whose hair was now being rinsed. She turned back to David and fixed a steady gaze upon him. "So, did ya black mama tell you 'bout Ralfie?"

Blanche started violently. "What trouble you trying to concoct today?" She whispered angrily to Dora. "If you must talk so, go back to ya station!"

David was about to ask who Ralfie was, but Blanche sensed this. Cutting shears meshed in her fingers, she managed to put her hand over his mouth. "Forget what she say, child." Then to Dora, "If she knew you talk this, she'd tump you to ya grave."

"Me na 'fraid of her."

"You professional liar."

Intent upon figuring out the meaning of the conversation between the two women, David had lost track of Blanche's progress on his hair. Now, when he looked in the mirror, he was horrified to discover it had been fashioned into a bowl cut, one length all the way around. His bangs were too short to be swept aside with a comb. His face looked fatter and rounder.

Bellowing, he glanced down at the floor where his shorn hair lay crisscrossed over itself like a loose pile of harvested hay. He had the urge to bend down, gather it up, and press it back to his scalp. "What did you do to me?" he cried. "You made me look like a goon!"

"What you talking?" Clara barked from across the room. She was sitting upright in Felicia's chair, her hair in the midst of being combed out.

David twisted around. "Look at this!"

"I'm quite sorry it don't suit you," Blanche said sarcastically. "I personally feel it looks lovely."

Clara hurried over to Blanche's station, her head dripping spit curls. She yanked David out of the chair and led him over to a vacant spot beneath a hair dryer, where she made him sit down. "If you fret so about a stinking haircut, you nothing but a bebe," she scolded him.

"I'm having a heart attack," David yelped.

"Well, if you dead in here, at least we won't worry to cut ya hair again." Clara flicked his temples. "She cut it just fine."

David spied Dora mocking him. She used her first two fingers to imitate scissors and was hacking away at her own hair. He nudged Clara and showed her what was going on. She let go of him, walked to the middle of the salon, and shrilled so that the entire beauty shop could hear. "You know something, Dora Cambridge? Ya sense of humor is about as foul as your crotch. Dat is why no man on this earth could ever want you."

Dora turned her back. David hated her.

Clara stood there glaring after Dora. She left David to stew under his hair dryer and went back to sit in Felicia's chair.

David was so angry and disappointed in his haircut that for a long time he hung his head, unable to look up. When he finally did, Blanche was waiting to catch his attention with a smile.

Five minutes later, Clara got up to use the ladies'. Meanwhile Felicia sprayed powder shampoo on the wigs, which she combed out and restyled. Blanche waited until Clara was out of the room before opening up one of her marbleized drawers and bringing out a stack of girlie magazines. David's eyes bulged when he saw them, and witnessing this, all the beauticians giggled wickedly. He was thrilled to be in their favor once again.

"Mind Clara don't see them," Blanche warned him. "Don't want to cause her no distress. She and I been friends too long. Wait a while. Put dem b'ind de seat. After she gets back, you'll see how she falls asleep under her dryer."

Blanche obviously spoke from experience. No sooner did Clara sit next to David and pull the plastic dome back down on her head than she fell asleep. David quietly took the magazines out from where he had hidden them. Delighting in all the pictures of naked women, he nearly forgot about his rotten haircut.

"You like them? They sweet you, darling?" Blanche cooed to him from her station, where she was teasing up a new head of hair.

David nodded eagerly, glancing over at Clara every minute or so to be sure she was unaware of his activities. Her lips pouted while she slept, her cheeks shuddering their nervous response to dreams.

As they rode in a bus down Nostrand Avenue, David observed an unfamiliar Flatbush of old, decrepit, prewar buildings and run-down stores blurring beyond the windows.

"Who's Ralfie?" he asked after several minutes.

Clara lurched forward in her seat, alarmed. "Who call dat name to you?"

"Dora was talking to Blanche. I couldn't hear very well." Something told David to play everything down.

Clara clenched her fists and beat them together. "Already it start," she said angrily. "Already, already. Can't even take you to beauty parlor without you gossiping."

"I didn't say anything, Clara. That lady, Dora, was talking."

"But Dora is no friend of mine," Clara insisted. "She's a notorious character. And she well want to control Blanche." Clara puffed out her lips, continuing to look out the window with her head tilted at a peevish angle. Her eyes seemed to take in so much that was not even there. "I gwan to call the shop when we get back to the apartment. Me will tell Dora Cambridge where to get off at."

The bus was passing a billboard advertising Coppertone: a dog pulling down a child's bathing suit to show the contrast between the white of her behind and a red invasion of sunburn on her lower back and legs.

"Let me warn you something," Clara said, pointing toward the billboard. "If you ever try discuss my business wid any o' dem mine, I will lash your skin as red as that."

117

"But I didn't do anything," David protested. "Except get a lousy haircut." He probed the strange nakedness of his scalp, feeling blamed and put out for people and events outside his own life.

"Stop ya brooding now," Clara warned him. She had calmed down somewhat. "And ya hair looks—well, it's a bit one way, but at least she don't gi' you cane row."

David looked at Clara. "Cane row?"

"In Jamaica if you'd get bad haircut, dem would call it dat because it favor broken rows of sugarcane."

"Cane row." David tried out the expression. He spoke it louder, and a few people in the bus turned to look at him.

"Me have something to show you now," Clara said. She turned over her left hand and for the first time David saw a faint scar that began below her thumb, ran jaggedly across the slope of her palm up to her wrist. The flesh had healed over with a foamy pink tissue. "Me get dis whilst I was working a cane row," she explained. "I was swathing one fine afternoon and de blade did break and cut me. Dem sew me up right 'pon the field. Even passed out for a while," she said.

"Did you quit working after that?" David asked.

Clara looked at him strangely. "No, sir, went right to work out de Copra factory. See me fingertips." She showed him tiny crosshatch gouges. "Those scars from dere. Honey, you no conception what it's like to worry for ya every meal. Me couldn't quit from anywhere. Who would feed my children?"

As the bus carried them along, the shadows of the afternoon thickened into dusk. Flatbush ebbed with moody light that flared as the sun reflected off windows, jumping from story to story, building to building, like the relay of a secret code. They got off the bus and strolled down a wide, tree-lined boulevard, one side of which was occupied by a cemetery, a vast field of white tombstones, mausoleums, and granite angels unfolding behind tall wrought-iron gates. David almost forgot about being grumpy as he looked at the decaying cenotaphs and tall nineteenth-century headstones with rounded crowns and corners carved into sharp ridges. The main gates to the graveyard were wound with thick chains and fastened with ancient rusted locks. Just beyond the cemetery rose a thirteen-story building like a solitary sentinel. This was where Clara lived.

They walked into a dim entryway, passing shiny brass mail slots, one of which Clara pointed to as her own. David looked at the factory-produced letters that spelled out Mayfield. Clara lived in 11H. "You will always remember which apartment mine since its letter begins your last name," she told him.

Clara's apartment had a long entrance hall that led to a living area and sleeping alcove that were divided by a narrow kitchen. The plaster walls were veined with cracks and each was a slightly different shade of green. In the living room, a threadbare orange love seat had been moved flush to the far windows; alongside it was a brown Formica two-drawer end table. Unlike Clara's bedroom in Rye, her Brooklyn apartment brimmed with souvenirs. Every available space on the countertops and bureau was covered with beaded trinkets, carved wooden boxes, silver hairpins. There were coasters on the coffee table imprinted with "Jamaica Reef," a hotel Clara had worked for in Port Antonio. A blue pennant draped from her bedroom wall advertised Frenchman's Cove. The place smelled of tangerine peel and potpourri.

They put their things down near the love seat. Clara went immediately to a beige phone kept next to a chipped blue vase on one of the end tables. She dialed quickly. David was anxious to hear how she would deal with the beauticians, but she ended up speaking only to Blanche, and the entire conversation took place in Gypsy. David watched her gesticulating, heard the name Dora uttered at least a dozen times during the angry speech. Clara opened her mouth as wide as possible and made savage, throaty sounds. To pronounce certain words, she had to bare her white teeth all the way to the gums.

"Everything okay now?" he asked once she put down the phone.

She smiled crookedly at him. "For the present."

He noticed two of her grandson Derek's drawings, framed in bamboo, hanging on the wall near the kitchen. The first was of a pair of sandpipers, the second a row of peasant shanties in a poverty-stricken quarter of Kingston. He asked why she wanted to look at such an unhappy scene of her country.

She smiled. "So I remember it's not just pretty beaches and lovely sights."

Clara walked over to the window and looked out right and left before peering down on the graves. She turned to David and flicked her head back toward what lay beyond. He came to her side, scanning the stretch of cemetery below. It was like a field of deathbeds, stretching many blocks far and wide. He had never seen such a large graveyard before. It was old, not like the new and well-kept cemetery where Edith was buried. Half of the tombstones were cracked or fallen down, akimbo. Directly next to the building, eleven stories below, a massive hole had been dug, into which all the broken stonework from the ruined monuments was being dumped. It was getting dark outside, the tombs beginning to gleam like blanched, weathered bones.

The warm November wind rushed in Clara's window. David blinked his eyes and tried to think of death and what it was like to be buried under tombs. Death was something Clara could not explain. He thought of Edith; he thought of all the times his parents dragged him to temple, when the rabbi said a prayer for the dead; and how his father had lit fat candles in glasses when David's grandfather died.

David thought of that time his grandfather had died. When he was four, his parents took him to Florida. They had only been there three days when the phone call came. His father answered the phone and David watched as he stiffened and fell into a shaking heap on the bed. His father had been dressed in bright golf clothes, and David remembered thinking that he was wearing the wrong clothes to hear bad news in; he should have been wearing his dark business suit. His mother led David from the room, out of the hotel, and they stood near a grove of palm trees. There was a tepid tropical wind blowing that smelled of pineapple drinks, the sea so clear when she told him his Poppy had died. David had looked up at scalloped pink clouds racing above the flapping flag of the hotel, trying to see his Poppy. But all he could see were black crows circling the building without flapping their wings.

His father had left by plane that night for New York; David and his mother returned the following morning. He remembered how much his parents comforted one another; how people came to the house with baskets of perfect oranges and plums wrapped in amber cellophane; how he sneaked some sweet wine and fell asleep in the living room, lulled by the heavy fragrance of roses and chrysanthemums. After all the mourners had gone, his parents woke him up with bitter sips of coffee. He was pleased by the concern they were showing one another; now, he even hazarded to think that death might not be so strange and scary. At least for those afternoons when the house filled up with visitors, death made his parents care for one another.

He turned away from the window and looked at Clara. "Why do my parents have to get divorced?"

"Come ya and sit wid me," she whispered.

He sat down on the love seat and leaned against her. He could smell her Touch of Fire, and with his back could feel her bosom heave. She reminded him he would still see his parents as much as ever, it was just that they would be living in different places. "Your parents not been happy together for quite some time now," she tried to explain. "Though I for one always felt dem should stay together for your sake. But I hail from Jamaica. People in my country try to stay marry unless one of de parents get dangerous. But, darling, marriage always pain and compromise; sometimes too much pain and compromise. People part out o' dere own misery, despite children. Makes it easier if dem have plenty money as ya parents do."

"Does that mean if they didn't have money they might not be getting divorced?" David asked.

"No, sir. Don't twist up what me telling you. Just dat money makes plenty difficult things easier. Your muddar don't have to worry about getting herself a job to keep you in food and housekeeper."

But David was already wishing he were poor like the kids at school who lived above the storefronts in Rye, large families crowded into only a few rooms that smelled of cooking fat and spices. The poorer kids walked to school in groups. They were happier and more athletic than the rich kids who lived on the estates along the Sound. Maybe he could convince one of his school friends who lost a brother in Vietnam to take them in. They would sleep in the bed of the soldier who was killed. Clara would help the family get over their grief by speaking her Jamaican sayings. She'd contribute to the washing and cooking and they'd be a lot happier. He wouldn't even mind sharing her with other children.

"It seems so weird," he said to Clara. "When you get married, you must love the person you marry a lot. But then if there is so much caring in the beginning, how does it change so people want to live away from each other?"

"Well, now you talking the strangeness of life," Clara said ominously. "People meet and love each other so hard and for so long believe they will love this person their whole life. Then bai, bai, dem speak one word and the other gone like hummingbird."

They were both quiet as the evening slipped into place. David rested his head against Clara's shoulder, drifting off into a doze. The world suddenly seemed so fragile, life threatening to go wrong, the way it did when he got sick with a fever and the bedsheets felt crumpled and crooked and crazy words and ideas stirred in his head.

"Looking out is my favorite part of living here." Clara finally broke the long silence.

David picked up his head from her shoulder and peered at her. "You don't get sad staying above a cemetery?"

"Not usually. Reminds me to make the most of my life before it's too late."

There was another protracted silence. "I'm hungry," David told her, which wasn't true exactly. He just felt anxious about Clara; eating always brought them together.

She looked at him wearily. "All right. Let us go to my Greek coffee shop. Just around the corner."

The brightly lit restaurant was filled with cigarette smoke. Along one wall was a hand-painted mural of a rocky island surrounded by the Aegean; the sea had been colored an unnatural electric blue. The place was crowded and noisy with black and Hispanic families squabbling among themselves.

Clara was on first-name terms with the Greek waiters, who kept nodding to her as they hurried through the cramped narrow aisles, their hairy arms burdened with several plates at a time. She ordered tripe and hot sauce, which David could barely look at, much less taste when she offered him a forkful. He ordered rice pudding with grenadine syrup, figuring at first that Clara would protest such an unwholesome meal. But Clara seemed oddly preoccupied; she hardly noticed what he was eating.

"Do you ever wish you had a job in Brooklyn?" David asked. "So you wouldn't have to do all that traveling back and forth?"

Clara frowned and then carefully put down her fork. "Funny. Often on the long trains between here and Rye I ask myself the same thing."

"And?" David filled with momentary dread.

"Brooklyn recalls too much Port Antonio. Too many my countrymen here in Flatbush, too many people know me from de past, reminding me of old troubles. In Rye no one but ya muddar knows me from former times."

David had been stirring his uneaten rice pudding. By now the grenadine syrup had bled through it evenly and had turned the color of pink Pepto-Bismol. He looked up at Clara. "Why did you get so upset before when I asked you about that guy, Ralfie?"

She pinched her shoulders together and muttered, "You too damn nosy."

"No I'm not."

David heard a sudden crashing of plates and then a furious reaction in Greek. He and Clara glanced toward the counter, where one of the waiters had dropped a platter of fishburgers and french fries.

Clara turned back to him. "Always you looking for details. You almost make me sorry I brought you wid me this weekend," she muttered.

David was hurt. "Why? I haven't done you anything."

Clara shook her head and groaned. "What a way, what a life this turned out to be."

"What are you saying?" David asked, looking at the mural, which momentarily portrayed Jamaica in his mind's eye.

She looked fixedly at him. "Ralfie was me son."

David swallowed. "Your son? But I didn't know you had a son."

"I don't—no more."

"You mean—he's not alive?"

Clara nodded.

"You never said anything about him."

There was silence as they listened to dishes clattering and bursts of laughter and argument around them. "Because me keep such things deep into me heart," Clara finally said.

David swallowed. He tried to understand this, but found he could not. Clara, meanwhile, had signaled for the check.

They left the restaurant in brooding silence and walked by the cemetery on their way back to Clara's building. Streetlamps were frosting the tombs. The night was cooling down with a sharp breeze, and David felt clammy.

When they got back to the apartment, he sat down on the sofa, watching Clara pulling sets of sheets from a closet near the kitchen. "Get up," she told him. "This makes your bed."

David helped her remove the bolsters from the love seat and then watched how a double bed was magically ejected from its belly. "You'll have to sleep without a real pillow," she told him, "but I'll stuff some towels into a case." After they made up a suitable pillow for him, Clara went into the bathroom.

David sat down on his bed and gazed out the window. He wanted to ask Clara how her son died and how old he had been, but he knew she would not answer these questions. Rice pudding gurgled in his stomach as he looked far beyond the black and white quiltwork of the cemetery. In the distance he could make out the Verrazano Narrows Bridge, whose twinkling lamps ascended the suspension cables like Christmas ornaments.

David undressed and got under the covers. He listened to the tinkling sounds of water coming from the bathroom, peered at the hieroglyphic cracks on the ceiling, thought he smelled a cheap perfume, the body odor of a stranger. Clara came into the living room wearing her nightgown. She had removed her wig and fixed her natural hair into dozens of plaited pigtails. She turned off the overhead light. "Goodnight, sweet darling," she said, passing through the kitchen on her way to the bedroom. She left her door open and David could hear her rustling between the sheets. Her pigtails stuck out straight when she lay her head down. He smelled a lingering winter-

green scent of her nightcream, a fume of bay rum. He listened to the
short panting of her breath lengthening until she finally fell asleep.

David lay awake for the longest time. He thought of the brooding
cameo of Clara's husband. He tried to imagine a child who would be
a mixture of their skin tones lying in bed, smothered with rum-soaked
washcloths, Clara tending him dutifully throughout the night, calling
a preacher toward morning, her keening voice overpowered by the cry
of the sea.

She hadn't bothered to draw the curtains together; they were still
fully parted, the glossy windowpane separating them. David watched
the muslin billowing softly with the breeze, swelling into hoop-skirt
shapes and deflating.

It seemed he had been asleep for only five minutes when he awoke
suddenly, wrested from sleep by the explosive revving of a motorcycle.
Outside, the sky was blessed with pink light. It was nearly dawn. He
smelled something burning.

Faint flickering lights drew David's eyes toward the kitchen. What
were they? he wondered. Were they candles burning? Making as little
noise as possible, he crept out of bed. He tiptoed toward the kitchen,
practically stumbling over Clara's red suitcase, which was lying wide
open in the middle of the floor. In the dim light, he could make out
several bundles of aerograms inside it. Three of these letters had been
removed from the pile and were opened up until they became a single
sheet of paper.

Wondering why Clara would bring letters with her to Brooklyn,
David continued to creep toward the kitchen. At first he saw quivering
shadows and then could make out her face bathed in yellow light. He
moved closer until he could see her clearly, and what he saw disturbed
him deeply.

Clara had lighted a green coil that seemed to be made from a pulp
of crushed straw, which was burning slowly like incense. Three stubby
votive candles flickered next to it. From a cupboard above the refrigerator, she took down a small amber bottle and unscrewed a dropper.
She squeezed drops of fluid over the candles, which flared up dramatically. Then she did a horrifying thing: pinched the burning orange
center of the coil until she winced in pain. She grabbed a washcloth

that had been lying on the counter and pressed it to her forehead. Her cheeks were moist with tears.

"Is it your migraine?" David blurted out involuntarily.

Clara jerked around to face him. "What you doing up?" she demanded with the same breath that blew out the candles.

"I—I couldn't sleep."

There was an embarrassed silence. A letter lay on the counter next to the candles.

"What were you doing just now?" David asked her softly.

"Reading something." Her voice was hoarse. "Didn't want to disturb you wid kitchen light."

"Why are you reading?" David asked.

Clara was staring straight ahead as though hypnotized. "Well," she said, "me have things in me mind juking me so till me can't sleep."

David had begun to smell a new burning odor, which grew so powerful it turned his stomach. He was afraid he smelled Clara's injured skin. "What things?" he asked.

"Private things." she said.

"What about that?" He pointed to the coil. "What is that for?"

"Old Jamaican remedy for headache," she told him. "De smell drive devil of pain away."

"Can I get you anything?"

Clara sighed. "Sweet of you to care, but is all right. Go back to your bed now, David."

On his way back to his bed, David stared for a moment at the suitcase full of letters. He wondered whom they were from and what they said and why Clara would deliberately wound herself. He began to imagine she had to do such things to keep herself from being driven crazy by the voice of the dead. He imagined there were other Jamaicans, thousands of miles away, enduring similar torments in houses edged by jungles of quiet. He imagined them looking out on an ivory moon, down limestone cliffs where the ocean lay black and swirling beneath that Cyclops eye of light.

The temperature began to plummet the next morning, and by the time Clara and David got back to Rye, the weather had grown chilly. Leona had arranged for a taxi to meet their train when it arrived at the station. She was peering myopically out the kitchen window when they drove in the driveway, and David knew she was anxious about his arrival. It was frightening to think his father was not inside, and that in the last two days he had carted away everything that belonged to him. David could feel Clara stiffening next to him in the seat, and he wondered if this was crossing her mind, too.

As soon as they walked into the house, David smelled garlic and spicy cooking; his mother had obviously gone out of her way to prepare a meal. She was wearing an Irish knit sweater and tweed pants. Her auburn hair was freshly washed and set and tumbled voluminously around her shoulders. Her green eyes were bright and anticipating.

"Did you have a good weekend?" she asked.

"I had fun."

David stopped and listened to the muffled booming sound of the central heating system. Summer was definitely over; it would be many months before the weather turned warm again. And his father was gone.

"I like your haircut," Leona said.

"You're the only one who does," he told her.

Clara clucked her tongue, and David cast a cold eye in her direction.

127

"I made you lasagna and steamed asparagus."

David was suspicious of his mother's gesture. Now that his father had left, was she going to try harder to be a good parent? "I'm going upstairs for a while," he told her.

"Don't be long," she called after him. "Dinner's been waiting.

"Him did enjoy his stay," Clara told her as David left the kitchen. A silence followed as they waited for him to discover how the house had changed.

David's breath quickened as he passed through the living room and entered the library. What he saw there made him momentarily shut his eyes. The tall shelves—once lined with his father's lawbooks, golfing journals, and sailing manuals—were empty. The antique writing desk was gone; there were circular brands on the carpeting where its legs had rested. A large framed map of the world on which his father had drawn red and black vectors, tracing ships over the high seas, had been removed from the wall.

Dreading the state of change in his parents' bedroom, David climbed the main staircase. He trudged down the hall, glancing for a moment into the empty room that was once Edith's nursery. The door to his parents' bedroom was shut; he opened it to a cloying atmosphere of his mother's Estée Lauder perfume. The first thing he noticed was the absence of his father's wooden valet that had always stood sentinel next to his side of the bed. He went to the low mahogany chest of drawers that his father used as a night table. He opened the top drawer. His father's reading glasses were gone, as well as a picture book of submarines that David had given him for his last birthday. Wincing, David opened the bottom drawer, which he discovered to have been emptied of his father's thick cotton socks and underwear.

He continued to the narrow closet his mother had had specially built for shoes. The shelves of his father's dark brogans and oxfords and white bucks were vacant. Finally, David went to the bathroom and opened the medicine cabinet. He discovered gaping spaces in what were once overstocked shelves. His father had left behind a bottle of Aqua Velva, a white styptic pencil, an old two-sided razor he had long ago abandoned. It suddenly dawned on David that his father would no longer manhandle the cold cuts in the refrigerator before sneaking

into the library; he would no longer meet his taxi at the edge of the
long driveway and catch a commuter train. He would no longer return
home.

David closed the medicine cabinet and peered at himself in the
mirror. He studied himself until he got scared that he was actually
trapped inside the silvered glass. His heart raced as he tried blinking
away the sensation. He ventured to look at himself once again, trying
to decide which of his parents he more closely resembled. He needed
to be allied with one of them; it was too painful, confusing, to be
caught in the middle. It was easier to blame someone for the divorce.

David finally returned to the kitchen, but with little appetite. After
he and Clara and his mother sat down to dinner, he had to be cajoled
into eating something. Lasagna, his favorite meal, looked heavy and
indigestible, the tomatoe sauce reminding him of blood and guts. He
wondered where his father was eating tonight. He tried picturing him
in a new apartment that smelled of fresh paint and was filled with
cartons and new furniture still wrapped in plastic.

He looked at his mother. "Do you know if dad's home?"

"Why don't you go call him?"

"I will later."

"It might make you feel better if you called him now," Leona
suggested.

"Why would talking to him make me feel any better?" David asked
angrily. "Don't act so stupid."

"Shut up ya mouth!" Clara scolded him.

"It's okay," Leona said. She was gazing at David with a crooked
face, and her eyes shone with tears.

"No, sir, don't care how upset, him will behave."

David turned to Clara. "Then she shouldn't tell me I'm going to feel
good talking to my father in his new apartment."

"He's right," Leona said. "It *was* a ridiculous thing to say."

"Look 'pon me, David," Clara said, and David turned her way.
"You must try to get used to dis."

"How?"

"You must . . ." Clara paused.

"Must what?"

"Know dat ya parents care for you and will do their best. And further on"—Clara pointed to herself—"you have dis old sarcophagus."

David looked meaningfully at his mother. "It was nice in Brooklyn," he told her. "I liked Clara's apartment. I wouldn't mind going back."

His mother lowered her head, pinching her forehead with her fingers, but said nothing.

He could have asked her for his father's new telephone number, but he wanted to see if it was already listed with Directory Assistance. Sure enough, there was a new listing for William Hart on East Fifty-seventh Street. The fact that his father's number was already on record and available to people proved to David that he had begun to live a different life.

He took a few deep breaths and dialed. When a woman answered the phone, his first thought was that he had taken down the wrong number. "I'm trying to reach William Hart," he said.

"He's here, hold on," the woman told him.

David groaned when he realized he *had* dialed correctly. Who was this woman? He heard the phone being muffled.

"David?" His father got on.

"Who answered the phone?"

"That's Deena. My decorator."

David was quiet for a moment, taking in the idea. "Weren't you expecting me to call?" he said.

"Oh course I was. Why do you ask?"

"Then why did you have that lady answer it?"

"Because I was up on a ladder trying to hang some drapes."

It amazed David that his father was suddenly doing domestic tasks. "Your *decorator* is there on a Sunday night?"

There was a silence. "I needed help, David."

"Come on, dad."

"Okay. Okay. Dave," his father said uncomfortably, "it's hard for me to be here by myself. I need company."

The idea of his father needing company made David feel threatened. He was uncertain how to respond. "But is she just the decorator?" he asked.

"Yes, that's all she is."

Then the conversation lulled. "Well, do you like your new apartment?" he finally asked his father.

"Yeah, it's coming along," Bill said. "You'll see it next weekend when you come to see me."

"I have to go to see *you*?"

"Don't you think it'd be easier than my coming up to the house?" David said nothing.

"There's more to do in the city, anyway," his father told him.

All during that week in school, David was plagued by the thought of his father carrying on with the decorator. He imagined them working closely together, flipping through fabric samples, her hands touching his by accident, then purposely, until they were making love.

That weekend David rode the train to Manhattan and took a taxi from Grand Central to his father's apartment. The doorman sternly refused to let him proceed to the elevator until he checked with Bill on the house phone. As soon as it was established that David was the son of Mr. Hart, the doorman smiled artificially and became uncommonly polite. David's father answered the door wearing a black silk shirt with tiny white polka dots and gray gabardine pants. The style of the shirt made his shoulders look less broad. Up until then, David had seen his father wearing only two kinds of clothing: business suits or casual golfing and sailing attire. As he said hello and walked into the apartment, he tried to categorize what his father wore. Lounging clothes, he finally decided. He's a bachelor now, isn't he? Bachelors lounge around, don't they?

"Where'd you get that haircut?" Bill asked.

"In Brooklyn."

"Some job they gave you. A little severe, don't you think?"

"Don't rub it in."

Bill shrugged. David could see flakes of dandruff on the silk shirt. "Guess you'll just have to wait until it grows out."

Expecting to find an empty apartment, David was surprised to see how finished the place looked. The decor was modern and geometric, unlike the antique mood of the house in Rye. The dining-room table was a glass square supported by an egg-shaped cement pedestal; the dining chairs looked like fabric-covered waves. The dining area was divided from the living room by an Oriental screen. Two enormous yucca plants flanked the couch, which looked hard and streamlined like the couch in the waiting room of the law office.

Bill led David to the windows, parting the large vertical blinds and pointing left to a partial view of the East River. He seemed proud to be able to see a slot of water. As they walked away from the window, the blinds were trembling; they made snapping sounds as they struck one another. Suddenly remembering his phone conversation with his father the previous weekend, David got a pang when he realized there were no curtains.

"What happened to the drapes?"

"His father smiled wearily at him. "They're in the bedroom."

David nodded stiffly.

"You didn't believe me, did you?"

"I did and I didn't," David said.

There was an even deeper silence as they walked toward the master bedroom.

"That's authentic fur," his father remarked of the bedspread covering his king-size bed.

"Must've been expensive."

"I can afford it."

They retraced their steps and went through the narrow kitchen to the guest bedroom. In one corner stood a magnificent, six-foot-tall Prussian toy soldier. Bill had recently acquired it at an art auction. "That's really beautiful," David remarked, admiring the look of commitment carved into the soldier's expression.

"I got it for you, David," his father said. "And this is your room. I hope you'll stay the night."

"I didn't bring any clothes, or a toothbrush."

"I have everything you need. Even an extra toothbrush. I went to Brooks Brothers and got you some stuff. Look in those drawers."

David opened the drawers of a natural-finish Scandinavian bureau.

His father had bought him a pink and a white oxford shirt, a blue argyle sweater, Izod socks, and three pairs of cotton boxer shorts. In the closet hung a pair of gray flannel trousers and a pair of chinos, both of which still needed to be altered. David realized his father had never before bought him clothing.

"That was nice of you," he said. "How did you know my size?"

"Your mom told me."

A pall was cast upon David's momentary delight. It seemed as though together his parents had planned out this installment of wardrobe so that he would feel more comfortable in the new environment of his father's apartment. It was as though they were bribing him to get used to the idea of their living apart and his having to shuttle back and forth between them.

"What's wrong?" Bill asked.

"Nothing . . . I guess I have to get used to being here."

They went back to the living room, and David sat down on the office couch, finding it hard and bouncy and rather uncomfortable. "You want a beer?" his father asked.

"A *beer?*"

His father threw up his hands. "Don't question me at every turn. I feel as strange as you do. You'll be twelve in six months. I had my first beer when I was twelve."

"Okay," David said. "I'll have a beer." He shut his eyes and fought against the clot of crazy feelings that were trying to get out.

David drank his beer and then sat next to his father on the fur bedspread in the bedroom and watched television. A golf tournament was being broadcast from Pebble Beach, California.

"I played there once," Bill murmured. "One of the most beautiful courses I've ever played. Right along the Pacific."

"Looks great," David said, giggling. There was a warm buzzing in his head. He imagined it to be the way a man felt when he returned home from a long day at work and had a drink before dinner. Inadvertently he began to caress the soft fur of the bedspread with his hands. Suddenly he felt stinging in his eyes and recoiled. He knew the sensation the bedspread gave him was something people wanted to feel against their bodies when they had no clothes on. He knew his father had spent thousands of dollars on this bedspread not so he could watch golf in comfort but so he could bring women here, unzip their dresses, and make love without closing the bedroom door—there would be no one else in the apartment who needed to be shut out.

But why did the fact that his father had sex suddenly seem so apparent, when for all the years of David's childhood it was something he hardly knew about, always going on behind closed doors, when he was asleep? He realized why he didn't like the apartment. It was not a place to be comfortable; but rather like a place that made it easy to find new love. His father no longer struck him as being like a father, but more like somebody who was going to college.

By six o'clock that night, David was hungry. Bill, who had already made plans to take him to a fashionable restaurant at eight, reluctantly called to make the reservation earlier. "There will be only a few people there then," he told David, his voice tinged with annoyance.

"What difference does that make?"

"Part of the fun of going to a swanky restaurant is looking at all the swanky people."

"Then why don't you cancel the reservation and we'll go to a coffee shop," David suggested.

"I wanted to take you to this place. Besides, I don't go to coffee shops."

"What do you mean? We always go to coffee shops when I come to your office. Chock Full o' Nuts. And the automat."

"I don't eat in those places anymore," Bill tried to explain. "Not at night, anyway."

David put on his new pink oxford shirt and blue argyle sweater, and at 6:30 they went to an Italian restaurant called Il Cornuto. On the way over in the taxi, his father explained that it was impossible to book a table for the same day unless you knew the management. And yet, as soon as they walked in the door, David noticed the place was practically empty. Did that mean that if you didn't know this smiling, swarthy maître d' now warmly greeting his father, you would not be allowed to have dinner at one of these many tables that otherwise would remain unoccupied?

The restaurant had a cozy feeling—dark oak walls and white table-cloths, exposed beams hung with empty Chianti bottles. They were led to the restaurant's middle bay, squeezing through a tight formation of vacant candlelight tables. No sooner had they sat down than a bottle of Chianti, a replica of the ghosts on the ceiling, was placed before them. A drop of its dark fluid licked down the green glass. Suddenly, sitting across from his father in the empty restaurant, David got a feeling of being closed in. He was afraid he would have nothing to say, that they would sit there like dummies. Bill poured himself a glass of wine.

A tall, slow-moving waiter brought menus that were written in Italian, and David had to ask his father to translate everything to him.

"My son is in from the suburbs," Bill said to the waiter. David cringed; he and his father were now from different places, and it was as if his father wanted to publicly disassociate himself from Rye. "I think I'll have oysters on the half-shell. My son can try them. And then the veal chop. Do you know what you want?" he asked David.

"You have to tell me what there is first," David answered with embarrassment.

Looking down his nose at David, the waiter proceeded to rattle off a list of twenty things in heavily accented English, all of which David forgot the moment they were uttered. He wished his father had taken him to a French restaurant; he was studying French, already proving to be one of the best students in class, and would have been able to read the menu. He always believed learning patois had primed him for learning French. Now, however, he was too nervous to trust his ear.

"What about the scampi?" Bill suggested. "You love shrimp."

"Fine."

In the silence that followed, David listened to insistent tinkling of water glasses striking one another, sounds of stainless steel pinging against china, drifting over from where a handful of dinners were being served in the less desirable bays of the restaurant. His father was looking at him shrewdly. "That haircut is really remarkable. You look like Prince Valiant. Maybe we should try taking you to my barber and see if he can fix it up."

"I'll leave it the way it is, thanks," David said.

Bill arched his heavy eyebrows. "I haven't even asked you—how was it at Clara's?"

David turned wistful. "I only wish she could take me with her more often."

"But then you wouldn't get to see me," his father pointed out, nervously raking his fingers through his steel-colored hair. The candlelight was staining his scalp yellow.

"We're going to see each other every weekend?" David asked.

Bill looked momentarily miserable.

"That's what your mother and I agreed upon."

"Can't we see each other sometimes during the week?"

"You have school."

"I could take the train to the city after school and have dinner with you."

"But then you'd have to go back."

"So?"

"I'd like if you stayed with me on weekends, David. It'll be the only time I get to see you."

"I'm saying if I wanted to go spend the weekend with Clara, then I could see you sometimes during the week instead."

His father was silent, looking hurt.

The waiter brought a plate of something wet, gray, and shivering served on what looked like barnacles and a dinner salad. He then took a carved wooden pepper mill and sprinkled the lettuce with chunky grounds. Bill speared an oyster with a cocktail fork and held it out for David to taste.

David gritted his teeth and shuddered. "Why's it so wet?"

"That's the brine," Bill said. "Come on, kiddo, try it."

"I don't want to," David said, suddenly feeling terribly sad.

"They're wonderful once you get used to them. But you have to acquire the taste."

David closed his eyes and took the oyster, which tasted like a sour noodle. The flavor of brine was like tears in his mouth.

No sooner has his father finished the rest of the oysters than the main course arrived. David was glad; eating was giving them something to do. Bill, however, seemed annoyed. "What's the rush?" he asked the waiter.

Shrugging his bony shoulders, the waiter explained, "Senor Hart, the kitchen has nothing very little to do at this early hour."

His father looked at David, disgruntled, as though David were responsible for the overly efficient kitchen. "Okay, put' em down," he told the waiter, and then leaned forward and said confidentially, "I've got to take you here one night when it's busy so you can see what it's really like. It's much more fun when there're people around."

"But *we're* here," David pointed out.

"That's true," Bill conceded.

Conversation had lapsed into several minutes of silence when suddenly there was a blond woman standing at the table. David looked up at her, confused. She was saying hello to his father and then extending a long slender hand to him. His father seemed embarrassed.

"This must be your son," the woman said. David immediately detected a foreign accent.

Bill smiled nervously. "Deena, meet David," he said.

Deena, the decorator, thought David. He threw a murderous glance at his father. Why did he have to invite her?

"How about having some dessert with us?" Bill asked, pulling a chair away to let Deena sit down.

"I'm just going to stay for a few minutes," she said, aware that David was looking at her carefully. Her skin was perfect and taut. Her fine light hair was twisted into a knot. After an uncomfortable silence, Deena turned to David. "So, how is dinner tonight?"

He stared down at his uneaten shrimp scampi, then across the table at his father, who was nudging an enormous veal chop with his fork. "I'm not very hungry tonight," he said.

"You were before," Bill said.

"It's hard for me to eat when strangers are watching me," he said, looking directly at Deena. "It makes me nervous." She now struck him as so much prettier than his mother, which was hurtful. He felt ashamed of her extreme loveliness. He doubted he would ever have such a beautiful girlfriend for himself.

"Go ahead, eat," Deena said, reaching forward to touch David's arm, but he drew it quickly away. "How do you like your father's apartment?" she said, continuing to smile at him.

David thought of the rabbit skin. He shrugged. "I guess it's okay. How much did my father's bedspread cost?" he asked.

Deena shot a look of complicity at Bill, which David resented. "The rug was your father's idea. It was very expensive."

"I think you should get rid of it," David told her.

"Why?" Deena now smiled as though her cheeks were wound back by strings.

"It's ugly. And it feels ugly."

Deena laughed. Bill tried to laugh along with her, although he was clearly disturbed. She reached over and tugged on the lapel of his silk shirt. David suddenly noticed that his father unbuttoned his shirt lower than he had while he was living with his mother. By emphasizing his chest, was he asking to be loved by a different—perhaps younger—kind of woman? It made David feel so helpless. It made him feel lost.

"Well." Deena stood up, once again extending her hand, which David grudgingly shook. "It was nice to meet you," she said. "Goodnight, Bill." She kissed his father. "I'll see you tomorrow." And she disappeared into the depths of the empty restaurant.

Several uncomfortable moments passed, Bill looking sadly at David. Finally, he winked. "Pretty, don't you think?"

"She's okay."

"Just okay?"

David drew in his breath. "She really likes you, doesn't she?"

Bill smiled. "Why not? I'm not such a bad guy—am I?"

There was a pause. "I just didn't like it that she had to answer the phone the first time I called you. God, dad, you and mom just got separated—I didn't have to know you were there with someone."

The candle had burned low and its weak light was doing funny things to his father's face. However, David was sure he was witnessing the flush of anger. "At least I'm not trying to hide from you who I'm seeing," Bill suddenly snapped.

A sudden chill settled through David, gripping his stomach so that it felt tight and nauseated. "What are you talking about, dad?"

"I'm talking about your mother."

"What about her?"

"I'm talking about that she's been carrying on with somebody."

The news seemed to resound from every corner of the restaurant, and David thought the few people there could hear it clearly. "How do you know?" he managed to whisper.

"How do I know?" Bill shut his eyes, massaging his face with his right hand. "How do I know?" he repeated. He opened his gray eyes wide and then looked into the distance. "I've seen them together— myself. It's not as if they're doing it in secret."

David was aghast. "Mom has a boyfriend?"

His father nodded.

Who?"

"You could answer that question as well as I could. You met him —that afternoon, two years ago. . . ."

Bill didn't have to finish. David was already recalling the serene, white-haired man he'd met when they visited the Loudon House. His father was so well built and youthful; how could his mother prefer someone so frail, someone who looked older? David grew skeptical: How could she have been seeing this man all this time; he would've guessed, he would've known somehow. Then he remembered the time he and his mother first discussed the divorce and how she bristled when he asked if there was someone else in her life.

The restaurant had grown completely still. Waiters, busboys, and diners seemed to have stopped moving. David looked painfully at his father. "Why didn't you tell me any of this before?"

Bill could not hold David's stare and looked away. "I shouldn't have said anything," he said. "It was stupid of me. I should have let her tell you."

"Is that why you're getting divorced—because mom's had this boyfriend?"

Bill shook his head. "That has little to do with it."

"But why didn't you try to stop her?"

His father shrugged. "I don't know." He looked at David with moist, dejected eyes. "Maybe it's good she has somebody. In a way I'm glad. Your mother deserves to be happy."

The restaurant lighting suddenly seemed to pulse. "But what about me?" David cried. "I don't have anybody. Don't I deserve to be happy?"

His father was absently nodding his head. "Yes, David, you do deserve to be happy." He raised his right arm and flagged wearily for the check.

When David returned from Manhattan the following evening, he found his mother in the master bedroom reading a thick paperback. She was looking owlish in a pair of large round reading glasses as she highlighted paragraphs with a yellow marker and took notes at the margin with a sterling-silver Cross pen.

When he confronted her about what his father had said, his mother took off her glasses. The color drained from her face and she smiled with acute embarrassment. "I already know about what your father told you. He called me this afternoon after you left, guilty as hell."

"I'm so glad the two of you are keeping in good contact," David said nastily.

"We're supposed to keep in contact, David. We're not supposed to have one-way conversations with you about each other. Your father had no right to tell you something that was my responsibility to explain. He even admits it. He says he drank too much and got out of control."

"He didn't drink too much," David objected.

"All the more reason," Leona said.

"Well, then, you should have at least told me about Peter, so that dad wouldn't have to," David complained.

"David, your father led you to believe that Peter and I have been involved for a long time. And that's just not true. In fact, it's been such a short time that I haven't even had enough time to think about how I want to explain everything to you."

Leona promised that neither she nor Peter wanted to get involved until after she had signed the separation agreement with David's father; they had basically been friends for the past two years and seen each other mainly at lectures. She said Peter had influenced her to read philosophy, which had gradually replaced her interests in psychic phenomena. She claimed he had been her platonic "mentor" for a long time and that their relationship only recently had changed.

"But dad said he saw you together places."

"For your father to report to you like that was really cruel. And unfair. Let me tell you, David, if I ever saw *him* somewhere with someone, I'd never let *you* know."

"You probably never saw dad with anybody," David challenged his mother, who smiled confidently at him, although she said nothing. The response, nevertheless, bothered him.

"Okay, so now I know you're in love with someone else," David told her unhappily.

Leona nodded slowly.

"But knowing there was someone else made you want to get divorced?"

She shook her head. "You keep wanting to believe that something on the outside made things between your father and me change. It was our own lives, David."

"Why should I listen to you? Why should I believe what you tell me about not being involved with Peter until when you said?"

"I don't know, David. Why should you?"

"I mean, you still haven't been around for the past few years. It's like if you didn't take courses or go to the Loudon House, you would've gone crazy."

Leona fell into troubled silence. "I did all those things because I was looking for all sorts of answers to questions. Peter made a lot of things fall into place. I've learned a lot from him. I think when you're older you'll understand that people can go through phases like this. Maybe later on things will happen to you and you might not be able to get beyond them until you can figure them out. Sometimes you have to put all your energy into understanding so you can save yourself. Even if it means neglecting other people around you."

"Sounds like the most selfish thing I've ever heard," David told her.

"I never said it wasn't selfish," Leona admitted sadly. "But we're all selfish in this family."

The selfish Harts, David was thinking as he left his mother and wandered down the hall. He passed Edith's room, its few scant pieces of furniture covered with dusty sheets, a room that had long since ceased to be a focus of importance. She had been dead two and a half years. To think that at one time the house had been so infected with her tragedy. His mother mentioned Edith only seldom, could now discuss her without being overcome by grief. Was it this new love that finally had cured her of mourning? Had she learned something from this frail, colorless man she had not learned from the gurus or the lecturers, something that allowed everything to "fall into place"?

David trudged down the stairs, sliding desultorily in his stocking feet across the cold marble of the foyer, and entered the dining room. In the dimness there was a tremor of silver light coming from sterling chafing dishes and tureens Clara had polished on Friday but had neglected to put back into the dining chest. He took a chair and faced the window, deciding to wait in the dark for her taxi. He had drifted off to sleep when a pair of headlamps shot through the glass, their light inflaming a pair of modern figures in an oil painting his father had given his mother last Hanukkah. Wondering if his father had purposely given his mother something extravagant to appease her for the preceding months of unhappiness, David pushed the chair back under the dining table and went to the kitchen door. Clara hurried in wearing her knitted coat, arms laden with shopping bags and her red suitcase. He tried to relieve her of the suitcase, but she held on to it, handing him one of her shopping bags instead.

"How was your weekend?" he asked as they climbed the wooden steps.

"Lovely. Was at Icey all day today. Thinking of you. Good labrishing. We girls can get fast, let me tell you."

"Who was there?"

"Blanche, Lydia, and meself."

They stopped at the landing outside Clara's door. She dropped the suitcase, rooting through her handbag for the key to her room.

"Since when have you been locking your door?" David asked, hurt.

"Since I decide."

"But why?"

"Me have some rubies in dere protecting fe a friend."

"Come on."

"Listen na," she said, as she opened the door and switched on the light. "Me just come from Brooklyn. It was nice not to be answering your questions every minute. If you want bug me so, I'll just ignore you."

"All right, all right," David said, helping her carry in the packages."

"How was it at your father?" Clara asked as she hung up her coat in the closet.

"That's what I want to talk to you about."

She now gave him her full attention. "Wha happen, baby?"

David was about to speak when Clara said, "Ssh, hold on. Let us go to de kitchen and put up some tea for me. You want cocoa?"

"I don't know."

"Nice for you to have cocoa when I have me tea," she coaxed him.

David followed Clara downstairs to the kitchen, where the fluorescent lights were bright and her eyes looked strained and tired. As she put on the kettle, he began to recount his dinner conversation with his father, which involved the news of his mother's new boyfriend.

Clara waved him off. "Me know everything already."

David's mouth dropped open. "Why didn't you tell me?"

She drew the air through her teeth. "Me na chat."

"But how did you find out?"

"Mouth shut, ears open."

"But don't you think it's terrible?"

Clara frowned. "Compare to what, David? Is it de first time you realize ya muddar quick and fast? Dis would happen sooner or later. But wid ya muddar is always sooner since her dust never settle."

They went back upstairs with tall, steaming mugs, Clara's room gathering the moist smells of cocoa bitters and orange pekoe tea. She switched on the television, keeping the sound off; and for a moment before they talked, they both observed a Sunday-night police drama unfolding silently in the endless sunlight of southern California.

Clara plopped down on her bed, took off her shoes and stockings, and began rubbing her feet.

"I'll rub them for you," David offered.

She looked at him wickedly. "Mind where you put dem duhty hands."

As David kneaded Clara's toes and ankles, he told her his mother claimed that for a long time she was just a "friend" of Peter's, but that he didn't believe her.

Clara, who had shut her eyes and was rocking her head in obvious euphoria to be given a foot massage, now peered sadly at David. "So why you must know what is what?" she said, surprising him. "Better to adjust to what is. Let me tell you something, child, so you know where I stand. I'd have left this place long ago if it weren't for you. But I feel is my duty to make sure you don't end up a sideways sort of a person. So just know you can always depend on me."

"Even when you're in Brooklyn?"

"Yes, sir."

"Does that mean I can still go there with you?" David asked with the small bit of hope left in his heart.

"Whenever you like. But try not to worry so much about what momma is doing. You know from long ago can't stop she who have such a strong mind. But is all right—you and I will trundle, get our acorns in, and pitch our camp through winter."

Together they laughed at Clara's image of them as two squirrels and she took him into her arms. Her caring immediately soothed his confusion. On her dress he could smell subways and cloves; she had attended church before visiting Icey. Slowly, a secret wish made itself known to David: that Clara would adopt him and they would then live in her small apartment above the cemetery, talking about the odd ways of life while thumbing their noses at death. They would be buried together in adjoining graves, roots of trees drawing nutrients from their bodies so that eventually they would become part of the same thing.

It was still quite a shock to David when, a week later, his mother told him Peter was coming over to the house. To inaugurate the occasion, Leona went to a gourmet grocery and bought Jaffa oranges and sweet Italian sausages. She also picked up a coffee-grinder and a bag of freshly roasted beans—Peter, apparently, loved good coffee. She spent much of the afternoon in the kitchen preparing what she called a "late-afternoon brunch" that she planned to serve at five o'clock in the evening. David came home from school just as she was folding egg whites into a yellow ceramic bowl of waffle mix. She told him he would be expected to eat with her and Peter.

"Is this supposed to be like dinner?" David asked.

"No, it isn't." His mother's voice rose to a semiwhine. She was obviously anxious about Peter's arrival. "This is supposed to be exactly what it is: light food served in the late afternoon. If you get hungry later on, you can make yourself a bologna sandwich," she told David as she began milling the coffee. The screaming sounds made by the new appliance unnerved him and the kitchen filled up with nutty smells of fresh grounds.

Whoever heard of brunch at five o'clock in the afternoon? David wondered as he walked over the black and white diamonds of marble in the foyer and began to climb the staircase. "What kind of time schedule is he on, anyway?" he yelled down the staircase.

Leona immediately popped her frazzled auburn head through the swinging door that led to the kitchen, gaping until she found him staring at her through the bars of the stairs. "He's got papers to

146

correct and lectures to prepare. He likes to eat early so he can work late."

David continued up to his bedroom, overwhelmed by his mother's concern for a man who just a week before had been a vague impression left over from the past. David felt excluded; he felt he needed some immediate activity. He cast his eyes about his bedroom. The mimeographed questions from his science homework lay wrinkled on his desk. He would wait until after they ate to do his work. Then it dawned on David that Peter might do his own work in the very place where his father used to watch television, scribble in his yellow legal pads, and look at pictures of submarines. David could smell warm bread and hear a faint sizzling of frying sausages.

He wandered into Clara's bedroom and found her ironing a linen tablecloth and napkins. "Mom going to use those for the meal?" he asked.

Her face convoluted into an ugly frown. "You think I'd break me ass fe just any man ya muddar bring in here?" she asked. "You must be getting crazy amongst all de craziness going on in dis house."

"God, are you in a bad mood!"

Clara put down the iron and turned off the steam. David noticed she was wearing a ratty dress and there was no wig on her head.

"What you think ya muddar ask me?"

"What?"

"She ask me to help her in de kitchen."

"Like a maid?"

"Don't you use dat word to me!" Clara scolded him.

"You obviously refused," David said.

"Of course. See how me dress is dreadful, how me drag off me wig so to look a shanty lady?" Clara pulled at one of the perennially plaited pigtails of her real hair. "So she will leave me out of it."

"But what will you eat for dinner?"

Clara narrowed her eyes. "Rather 'gnam' de garbage dan eat dinner wid her consort."

Peter arrived punctually at 4:30, carrying a briefcase and a black overnight bag. He gave Leona a kiss on the lips. She tried to act casual about the fact that David was seeing another man besides his father show her intimate affection—although David noticed her stiffen slightly. Peter looked even older than David remembered; the older a man was, the harder it would be to accept him as a possible successor to his father. Peter's pale face was drawn tightly over its bones and rippled into tight lines whenever he smiled. Indeed, if he laughed, it looked as though his whole face could break apart into hundreds of delicate pieces. His eyes were large and inquisitive.

"Hello, David," he said quietly, extending a small, bony hand. "It's good to see you again." He turned to Leona. "He's getting to be a good-looking fellow." Then to David, "I've been looking forward to this."

"How do you do?" David tried to be polite, feeling all the more strange.

"Will you be eating with us?" Peter asked.

"Yes, he will," Leona said.

Leona took Peter's overnight bag and led him upstairs to the master bedroom. "Before we go downstairs, let's go meet Clara," she suggested, and began leading the way down the hallway toward Clara's room. When they arrived, Clara was sitting on her bed, looking at television. She had snagged a pink teasing comb on one of her pigtails and the comb was sticking out straight from the side of her head. The television was blaring loudly and her face flickered with blue shadows.

"Clara, I'd like you to meet Peter," Leona said, frowning at the way she had dressed and fixed her hair.

Clara shifted her wan attention from the television, baring her teeth in a sinister smile, and with a flip of her hand saluted Peter.

"Are you going to come and eat with us?" Peter invited her.

"I not hungry now," Clara said.

"You sure?" Leona said. "It'll be delicious."

"Is all right," Clara said. "Me have some fish heads in me hatbox to gnam off later."

As Leona and Peter walked down Clara's wooden steps toward the kitchen, they began to talk softly, although David, who was sitting at the kitchen table, could hear them.

"She's really angry with me," he heard his mother say.

"You have to expect that."

"It's just so hard to talk to her now. She's suspicious of everything I do."

"She's seen a lot happen, Leona."

"I don't know—maybe when she gets to know you a little bit . . ."

"Don't count on it," Peter said.

Leona set the table in the dining room, which had been used only for elaborate occasions or entertaining while she was married to David's father. Before serving David and Peter the waffles and the sausages, she sat down for a moment. Peter extended one raspy hand to her and the other to David, asking them to join him in silent grace. David felt uncomfortable having to endure the lingering handclasp of a stranger.

Peter chewed his food carefully, savoring the waffles and the sausages. He asked David about school and what subjects he liked, nodding appreciatively as David spoke of his studies in science and art. In turn, whenever Peter talked to them, he did so very slowly, carefully pondering his words before uttering them. For emphasis he made small elliptical gestures with his hands. David noticed that under Peter's influence, his mother seemed to have improved her table manners. It began to disturb him that he could find nothing about Peter's personality to object to—only an anemic appearance, which he knew Peter could not help. He listened to them discuss philosophers, lectures they both seemed to have attended, and what Peter was preparing for his classes.

"How come mom is so familiar with everything you teach?" David asked as he carefully poured maple syrup on his waffles.

Peter put down his fork. "Your mother has a wonderful understanding of what she reads. She seems to understand principles that take most people a long time."

"Seems to?" Leona interjected.

Peter smiled at her. "Who knows? You could be faking it."

David loved hearing such teasing and laughed. His mother could only blush. Suddenly, he grew alarmed. "Does this mean you're going to start taking classes in philosophy?" he asked her.

"Why should she?" Peter said, his eyes twinkling. "She's got me."

David was relieved to hear this.

After the meal was finished, his mother and Peter went into the living room. Leona began reading a thick book of what David imagined to be philosophy, carefully highlighting paragraphs with her yellow marker. Peter, meanwhile, jotted down notes for forthcoming lectures. David sat opposite them and struggled with his science homework.

"I wonder if I should add Heidegger to my existentialism list?" Peter's soft voice interrupted after twenty minutes of silence.

At around 8:30 his mother and Peter went upstairs into the master bedroom and locked the door. David stood far down the hallway, staring after them, wondering if they were taking a nap or preparing to make love. He had liked Peter up until now. Now, he was feeling betrayed. He hurried to his room, slammed the door, and curled up in a ball on top of his bed.

David soon learned that there was a provision in his parents' separation agreement that forbade his mother to have a boyfriend stay over in the house more than once a week. At first he figured this would limit the number of nights his mother could spend with Peter; he didn't reckon that she would opt to spend them with him elsewhere.

The transformation happened quickly. At first his mother slept out at Peter's Manhattan apartment twice a week, returning home during the day to take Clara shopping and to accomplish any of the household chores that required driving. Each trip she made to Peter's she would take a few extra sweaters, blouses, and pairs of pants. David truly felt the pull of her other life when, on a reconnaissance mission to her closets, he found the chrome bars supporting empty garment bags. She deliberately left behind all her tailored suits and Italian shoes; Peter had influenced her to wear more casual dresses, billowing tops, and overlarge sweaters, sneakers instead of high-heeled shoes.

Leona repeatedly asked David to come and visit with her at Peter's apartment, but David felt afraid to see his mother comfortably settled in another man's abode. However, his refusal to visit only ended up making it more difficult to adjust to the idea that she was suddenly living in two places, dividing her time between a son and a lover. By Christmastime she was staying away four nights out of seven.

Despite the fact that she slept out many nights, Leona made it a point to be at home every day when David got back from school. She sat with him in the kitchen and they ate Clara's coconut-and-raisin totos. David couldn't help but notice that while his mother had been married to his father, involved in her psychic pursuits, she had often been too busy to pay any attention to him at all. Now that she was gone overnight, it seemed she felt her absence was far more telling. She suddenly wanted to condense the bit of time they spent together into something meaningful, so that she could return to Peter's believing they had made some sort of daily sense to one another.

On such a weekday afternoon, David came home to find his mother sitting at the kitchen table. She was wearing an oversize man's sweater and baggy jeans. Her hair was uncombed and dirty. She began asking him if he was making any new friends.

"I don't think I understand," David interrupted her.

"Understand what?"

"How you can be away so much and then come back and seem concerned. If things got rotten, you still wouldn't come back."

"That's not true, David," his mother said vehemently. "Anyway, there's no point discussing something hypothetical."

"I think there is."

"Look, David," Leona said, crossing her legs and folding her hands over her knee. "When your father and I first decided to split, I was too anxious to have the papers drawn up. When I agreed that no one could stay with me in the house, I was literally boxing myself in. I was preventing myself from having a full relationship with someone unless I went off to stay with him. It wasn't fair."

"So, what does that have to do with me?" David asked.

"Don't you think Peter would live here if we could do it? I don't like going to stay at his apartment. I'd much prefer to be here every night."

David was uncertain that he'd want Peter to live with them every night; it would saturate his life with formal dinners and philosophical discussion as well as his mother's submissiveness to Peter—she had acted much more exuberant around David's father—which wore on his nerves.

Leona uncrossed her legs. "You know, David, you're beginning to get a little older now, and I think you'd find things a lot easier if you weren't in the house so much. Got out more, especially after school, and certainly on weekends."

"You know I have to see dad on weekends."

"Still, don't you think it's about time you made an effort to spend more time with your friends?"

"I have a friend," David said loftily.

Leona blinked several times, considering how to say what she wanted to say next. "I think you need more than just Clara."

A moment later, as though telepathically summoned, Clara shuffled down her wooden steps and came into the kitchen. She stood there looking back and forth between the two of them.

"I was just telling David here, he should make more friends," Leona said to her.

Clara turned to him with raised eyebrows. "Well, we know she's right."

"This sounds like a conspiracy," David complained.

Leona began scratching her shoulder through the thick knit of the sweater. Then she grabbed her pocketbook and stood up. "You think about it, David, all right? I've got to go upstairs now and get some things to bring back with me."

A few minutes later, she entered the kitchen holding several hangers full of dresses and slacks.

Clara glared venomously at the clothing. "You mean to tell me you can't even wait until de child is gone for to take ya things?"

Leona slumped her shoulders. "I need some of this for tomorrow."

"But you have so much dere already."

"It's getting colder, Clara."

"All right, then stay a little while and talk to us."

"Let her go," David interjected.

"Shut up ya mouth," Clara told him.

"Sure, I'll stay a while longer," Leona said. "It's just that I've got some things to do before I get back."

"But you always in such a rush," Clara remarked. "Don't you see?"

"I'm not always in such a rush," Leona objected.

Clara's eyes widened as she dropped her head. "Tell me something, Mrs. Hart," she said softly. "Who blinded you?"

Leona winced. "I don't understand what you're saying, Clara. I'm in a hurry today because Peter's cooking tonight. I have to pick up some things for him on the way back."

"Must be him cooking you something fine this evening," Clara said sarcastically.

Leona looked at her sadly. "I don't know why you don't like him."

"It's not I don't like him. I don't like it when you bring him here to sleep into his father's bed."

Leona glanced at David. "I think we should discuss this some other time."

Clara ignored her. "Not in de matrimonial bed," she shrilled.

"Look, I've got to go," Leona said, grabbing the hangers of clothing and hurrying toward the kitchen door.

"Must be him cooking you shit on a palm frond," Clara muttered under her breath while she and David watched Leona walk across the gravel lip of the driveway that led to the garage. The wind caught the dry cleaner's plastic that sheathed her winter clothes and rattled it like paper. Meanwhile, a silence charged with dissatisfaction had invaded the kitchen.

David finally spoke up. "Peter really isn't such a bad guy. He's nice to me. He's always interested in what I have to say."

"What you talking now?" Clara scoffed. "Him just trying to win you over is all. What vex me is ya muddar insist to bring him here for you to know dem do more den read Gypsy books."

"I already figured that."

"Such a shame," Clara muttered as she went and opened the freezer door. "How about pizza for dinner?" she suggested, pulling out a frosty white cardboard package, squinting doubtfully at the printed directions on the back flap. "Boy-oh-boy, de whole world complicating right before my eyes," she complained. "Even frozen pizza can't simplify . . . turn back tinfoil, change down de temperature of the oven. Cha, man, dis worse than even cooking a damn chicken."

"You're just angry with mom," David said.

"No, man. It vex me dem don't make this easy for us who sim-pleminded." At this she opened the door of the oven and threw the frozen disk onto one of the metal grates, which made a loud pinging sound. "Orchestra start now," she said of the clamoring. She walked over to the onion-and-potato drawer and drew out a large convoluted pink yam. She opened the oven and put the yam in as well. David started laughing.

"Don't you laugh at me," Clara warned.

"You're not even going to wrap the yam in foil?"

Clara looked at him imperiously. "You ready to start in on cooking now?"

"No."

"Then keep ya shutters shut. Yam will cook nice if it don't trouble."

David shrieked with laughter.

"You must be getting crazy in here tonight," Clara said.

"You make the yam sound like it's alive," David told her.

Clara sucked the air through her teeth and then laughed herself. She took two glasses from the cupboard, filled them with ice, and then took a bottle of cream soda out of the refrigerator. She filled the glasses and bade David sit down with her at the kitchen table. The house was quiet except for the soda fizzing. Clara held up her glass. "To health and prosperity." She took a long draught, smacking her purple lips. A moment later she said, "To tell you quite truthfully, David, it's hard to believe your muddar is de same lady bawling and bawling at de hotel in Port Antonio. I'm so sorry things turn out this way, with divorce and dis man. I'd certainly be gone long ago if it weren't for you."

"I'm glad you stayed," David said, resting his chin on his hands. "I don't know how it'd work out if I didn't have you."

"What you mean?" Clara said. "She couldn't be drawing herself up like this, gone every night, if it weren't for me. She couldn't behave this way if—" Clara stopped, wanting to say, "if I were just a baby-sitter or an everyday housekeeper."

"If what?"

"Lose the train of thought."

"Sure you did."

"No, really, tell me something straight, David. You don't miss your mom?"

He sighed. "I do. But not nearly so much. I think it has to do with you."

Clara shook her head. "But, David, that is not good."

"But you're my friend," he insisted.

"Wait," Clara said. "Girls don't interest you as yet?"

"It's not they don't interest me. I don't interest them."

"Don't they start kissing round the bottle?"

"You mean spin the bottle?"

"Whatever dem call it up here . . . so, how about it?"

"Nobody's doing it as far as I know."

Keeping her lips closed, Clara stretched her jaw. "Probably them will start into it come spring."

"Probably."

David left the kitchen and went upstairs. When his mother was not home, Clara usually kept the master bedroom under lock and key—as though she didn't want David to be exposed to its overpowering feeling of vacancy—and opened it up once a week to dust and air things out. Whenever his mother came home, however, she usually left the door ajar on her way out.

The shades were drawn, the room ripening with the gloom of late afternoon. The bed was freshly made, the woolen coverlet pulled tight without a wrinkle. The nights Peter stayed over and David had caught glimpses of him and his mother in the master bedroom, he noticed that his mother slept opposite the side of the bed she had slept in while she was living with his father. Peter slept on her side. It was as though she wanted their sleeping bodies to form an X over the marriage, to cancel it out. David smelled a redolence of her many perfumes blending with a stale scent of talc. Her cabinets, particularly her vanity table, had a ghostly cast. She had left behind most of her cosmetics because Peter discouraged her using them. David imagined decades passing, her expensive moisture jellies interlaced with cobwebs. His heart beat faster and faster; his mother actually had gone and chosen another life for herself.

"What you doing in here?" Clara had come upstairs looking for David and had crept into the room.

"Nothing," he said.

"You know she na want you to trouble her things."

"Me na trouble her things," he answered in patois.

"Come into me room and watch de story. It's going to be exciting." Clara clapped her hands exultantly. "I can't wait to see what happen wid our own Jocelyn Martin."

"I just want to stay here for a little while," David told her.

"For what? To wish your muddar back?"

David turned to Clara, sensing her pity. "Don't you love me more, now that she's gone? Aren't I like your son?" he asked.

"Don't talk so," Clara said crossly, turning her head away to hide the pain afflicting her face.

"But you're my mother now," David told her softly.

Clara shook her head and moaned.

"Of course you are," he said, his tears falling into her dark hands.

Late one Thursday night when Leona was staying over at Peter's and Bill had gone to Florida for a long weekend, the phone rang. David awoke, but when he heard Clara answering it down the hall, he immediately drifted back to sleep. The next morning, he remembered having heard her exclaim, "Masse me God! Masse me God!" When he went down to breakfast, he found Clara perched at the kitchen table. She wore a pale green nightgown and was staring through the bay window to some indeterminate point out on the Sound.

"What's wrong?" David asked. But she wouldn't answer him at first, got up and began pacing with her head bowed.

"A lot of worries on me mind today," she said finally. "You can fix ya own breakfast, don't it?"

"What worries?" David asked.

Clara paused, as though debating whether or not to tell him. Then she sighed. "Not good to involve you. Moreover, hard to explain."

"But if you don't let me know something, it'll drive me crazy."

Clara looked miserably at David while muttering a few conflicting words to herself. "It was Blanche call me last night," she said finally. "To tell me Icey fall sick."

"How sick?" David asked as he sat down at the table.

"Bad sick."

"Does she have to go to the hospital?"

"What she have wrong wid her dem can't help at hospital," Clara said wistfully.

"How come?"

"Because somebody from Jamaica is venging her through obeah."

"Obeah?"

Clara paused. "It's our word for voodoo."

"But why· is somebody after her?"

Clara shook her head and then began clicking her fingernails against the wooden table. David pressed his back against the bars of the wooden ice-cream-parlor chair. "Icey come up here for a reason," Clara began. "Like all of us who come up here," she explained with ominous significance. "Down Jamaica she fell in love wid a rich man, a civil servant married to a crazy white woman. They were found out and it got so thick for Icey, she had to left and come here. Now it seems de white woman down there find an Obeah man to make revenge."

"Icey?" David threw his shoulders forward. "You're talking about Icey, the same lady who came here?"

"But what is wrong wid you?" Clara said angrily.

"Icey seems like such a goody-goody."

"Shut up, man, you don't even know her. She's just proud."

"But can't Pella help you?"

Clara drew the air through her teeth. "Listen how him quick and fast," she mumbled to herself. "Darling, Pella don't have dis kind of power. White women down dere have plenty money fe find somebody deep and power from back country. Pella not of dat order."

"But what exactly is wrong with Icey?"

"It first start wid hard drafts of pain into her stomach. Dem caused by pins sticking into a doll dem must be make down there. Den she gone for tests at de doctor's. Dem saying she have some form of leukemia—cancer—but dem don't know obeah. Obeah can imitate de worst kind of sickness," Clara said. "I would go to her right today, but me can't leave you."

So they left for Brooklyn the next morning.

Two weeks remained until Christmas. The weather had turned unseasonably cold and gray. Squat Italian housewives in Rye climbed up to their attics and brought down cardboard boxes of plastic shepherds and God-children and made nativity scenes on their modest front lawns. The cold air smelled of garlic and tomato sauce. The train station was festooned with tin bells and fake wreaths and smelled of pine spray. Silver beads of sleet fell intermittently on the people waiting for the weekend trains. Everyone carried bright bags overflowing with ski parkas and toaster ovens and sets of stainless-steel cutlery. Smiles and greetings were exchanged in billowing breaths, the cheery mood a contrast to the dark threat of illness that loomed over David and Clara's travel.

At the newsstand Clara laid down 50¢ for the latest *National Enquirer*. David noticed, however, that once they were riding the train, she kept getting distracted from her reading by inner thoughts. She ended up peering out the window and whispering to herself. David imagined her incanting against evil, cursing the jealous wife, defying the Jamaican Obeah man.

The train had stopped in Pelham to load passengers when suddenly Clara recognized a blond woman with a haggard, unfriendly face coming down the aisle. The woman's hair was cut bluntly and lacquered under in a pageboy. She was dressed in a dark wool suit and held a slim briefcase across her chest as though inside it was something valuable. By now, Clara had stiffened in her seat and there was worry in her eyes. "God in heaven," she exclaimed to David in a fierce whisper. "I gwan tump her," she warned when the woman ended up sitting down across the way. "Lord God, I so frighten me can't even tell you," Clara said aloud, glaring at the woman. "Dat is Jocelyn Martin from 'The Raging Tide.' "

David was skeptical. "Are you positive?"

"You could come to ask me? When me watch her every day, when *she* control me whole schedule?"

"She hasn't been on lately," he noted.

"Not for two weeks," Clara said confidentially. "Her husband went to Brazil and supposedly she gone look for him." She lengthened her face. "Looks as though she just get back."

"Clara, it's only a show."

The actress had noticed them staring and now smiled wearily in their direction.

"Might have gun wid her," Clara whispered to David. "Better we should move so not to catch any trouble."

David looked at Clara; he wasn't sure how serious she was being. Then he shrieked with laughter, startling the blond woman.

"Jocelyn Martin?" Clara suddenly called across the train. "You find ya husband or not?"

The woman shook her head as she opened her briefcase and rummaged for a cigarette. Then, realizing they were in a no-smoking car, she refrained from lighting it.

"Dem have nice smoking car down de way," Clara told her.

David nudged Clara. "Cut it out," he whispered.

The woman glared. "I beg your pardon?"

"Me have one thing to tell you, Jocelyn Martin," Clara said.

The woman rolled her eyes. "My name is not Jocelyn Martin. Jocelyn Martin is just a character I play."

"You must take me for a fool," Clara told her. "Me know you real name, Virginia. Virginia Crocket. But you is Jocelyn Martin, too. And to Jocelyn Martin me well want to say one thing. If you touch dat lovely lady just come on—you know, de one named Clarissa, sweet thing dat she is—I mean it, if you juke her, I'll break de TV. Me break three o' me TV already since I vexed wid you from first time."

"Listen, honey," the lady told Clara, suppressing an urge to laugh, "don't bother breaking another TV. You're not going to see me too much longer."

There was an incredulous pause. "They not gwan kill you off?" Clara asked.

The woman nodded.

"Jesus Father, dem will lose plenty viewers."

"I've been on the show for a long time," the actress explained. "Everyone else I started with has been gone for years."

Clara looked dismayed. The train rushed below a cut-stone bridge somewhere on the outskirts of Mount Vernon. From above, two teen-aged boys threw down an empty milk bottle, which shattered on the roof. A diamond shard got lodged in the crevice outside David's window.

"I gwan tell de girls at Blanche's to write channel two a letter," she said finally. "Boy-oh-boy, me friends will certainly be vexed. Jocelyn Martin," she went on in a grave voice, "everybody enjoys cussing you out afternoons. And wicked though you might be, you are the heart of the whole story."

As they rode the D train to Flatbush, Clara decided not to mention anything they had heard about what was in store for Jocelyn Martin. "Can't spoil all de girls' fun by letting them know she gwan kill off," she told David. It was late afternoon by the time they reached Clara's neighborhood. They had walked to within a block of the beauty shop when they noticed a shiny red Cadillac with a sunroof pull up, its enormous whitewall tires scraping against the curb. From the driver's side emerged a lanky black man wearing a blue patent-leather jacket. With his arms crossed tightly against the chill, he hurried to the door, opened it, and leaned inside, as if he were reluctant to enter a hair-dressing parlor.

"Which one o' dem could be carrying on wid such a pimp?" Clara remarked.

Her question was answered when Dora stepped outside the door of the salon, a pleased look on her hard face. She was wearing a fake fur that came up well short of her beautician's smock. She grabbed the hand of the fellow in the patent-leather jacket and they began walking down the block.

The shop had been decorated for Christmas. Five-and-dime-store reflecting balls hung from the fluorescent lighting fixtures; painted cardboard angels dangled from the knobs of marbleized drawers. One of the ladies had stopped in at a Hispanic variety store to buy a lamb piñata that was suspended from the ceiling in all its garishness. Next to Blanche's station rose a two-foot-high artificial Christmas tree, covered with blinking teardrop lights and white fiber-glass locks.

In contrast to this air of festivity, the beauty parlor seemed to be in a grim frame of mind that cold, gray Friday afternoon. The hair-dressers hardly reacted when David and Clara came in. Lydia and Felicia looked red-eyed and weary and turned out to be nursing severe head colds. Doris Williams was taking a break. A Silva Thins 100 cigarette stained with lipstick was hanging from her mouth; the dark fingers of her right hand wound like tentacles around the long stem of her pink teasing comb. David wondered if the ladies were unsettled by what was happening to Icey, whom he knew to be a regular customer. "Life is certainly a bitch," Lydia remarked as they passed her station. "Nicest people always get juked," Doris Williams agreed in a chortle of smoke.

Clara ordered David to go and read in one of the chàirs underneath a hair dryer. But now, in comparison to the last time he'd visited the shop, the idea of sitting beneath a hair dryer made him feel self-conscious. Instead, he went and sat on one of the gashed chairs out in the anteroom, allowing Clara and Blanche to plunge into a worried conversation about Icey's health. While they talked, Blanche set the russet-colored hair of a white lady—probably one of the Flatbush ladies who Clara claimed patronized the beauty shop. Blanche held a spray of metal clips in her mouth, jabbing her fingers into a jar of green holding gel as she worked. Clara spoke to her in Gypsy, unwilling to even chance anyone being able to understand them.

Through the large front window and thin voile curtains, David saw Dora and her boyfriend come to stand by the red Cadillac. Now that he could get a better view, he noticed that one side of the man's face had deep parallel cuts, which did not look accidental.

Moments later Clara strolled into the anteroom, surprising David by putting on her coat. She stood before him with an air of impatience. "Let's go," she said.

"What's the rush?"

"Me leave de wigs. Will pick dem up tomorrow. Me must hurry to go see Icey," she said.

As Clara and David left the shop, they both saw Dora and the man with the strange cuts on his face darting into an alley several buildings down the block. "Let's see where they go," Clara suggested as they automatically quickened their pace. She stopped abruptly when they got to the display window of a pet shop; inside they could hear muffled plaints of kittens and the shrieks of caged tropical birds. Clara turned to him. "Stay here for a minute while I go see what is what."

She crept forward down the block and peeked into the alleyway where Dora and her friend had gone. Edging closer, she was able to see them clambering up against each other, kissing deeply. In the meantime, David had followed behind and was able to hear what came next.

"Can't even wait to get him into you house, you must be pulling him up into the street," Clara interrupted them.

Dora and the man broke their embrace. "What the fuck you doing here?" he shouted. His lips were wet and turned out.

"But you see, Mayfield," Dora taunted, "some men *do* want me."

"You mean some men *do* want to sell you," Clara answered her.

"Shut your face!" the pimp told Clara. "Get the hell out of here!"

"You come shut me up," Clara challenged him.

David couldn't believe Clara was provoking them.

"Leave her," Dora told her friend. "She's liable to do something."

"Sheeeit," the man said. He was American. "She can't hurt me."

"She right to tell you not to fuck wid me," Clara cried. David had never heard her use the word before. "Let her tell you what I did people like you in Jamaica. What I did her."

The black man began stalking toward Clara, and David felt urgent flutters in his stomach.

"Bundy! I said to leave her!" Dora insisted. "Listen to me when I talking."

The man froze while Clara clenched her fists. They glared at one another for several seconds. Then he turned around and, sidling up to Dora, walked arm in arm with her toward the other end of the alley. Clara was left standing alone. When she turned and saw David standing there, she snapped, "Don't I tell you stay back?"

"I was afraid something was going to happen," he cried, warding off a deepening chill and digging his elbows into his sides.

"And so if something happen, what you would do to stop it?" she asked.

"Kick him in the balls."

Clara managed to laugh. "Perfectly right."

She turned and hurried out of the dark alley into the failing afternoon light. David followed her, wondering what she could have done to people like Dora in Jamaica: Was there a power Clara had that enabled her to defend herself against men?

"If de phone ring, mind you don't talk patois," she warned David as they continued to walk in the direction of her building.

"Can't I go with you?" he asked.

"Of course you can't come wid me."

"But I want to give Icey my best."

"Ya too lie. You well want to see what Obeah will do."

"I've seen sick people before."

"Yes, but in dis case different," Clara explained as she hustled David along. "We have her dressed certain way, burning things into the house to fight off the bad ways."

"Who's we?"

"Each of us taking turns looking after her," Clara said. "Don't you see some de girls looking hard?"

"I want to go," David insisted.

"I said no." Clara's angry breath mushroomed up into the darkness. They had just reached her building. She dug through her purse and handed him the key to her apartment. "Now get upstairs and behave" were her last words of warning before she proceeded to walk along the sidewalk that edged the cemetery.

When David got inside Clara's apartment, he found it oppressively hot. Not knowing how to turn the heat lower, he went downstairs and knocked on the superintendent's door. There was no answer. He went back upstairs and peeled off his shetland sweater and his shirt. He opened both windows. Though freezing, the air outside was still and the apartment cooled off only slightly. He knew Clara kept an old metal fan in one of her closets and with a little searching he was able to find it. He plugged it in. The blades whirred for a few seconds and then suddenly David heard clicking. The lights in the apartment blinked off. He must have blown a fuse. Clara had once said something about the apartment having bad wiring and how she had to turn off the refrigerator to run the iron or the hair dryer.

David found the circuit box in a kitchen cupboard and switched the circuit breaker off again. He went behind the refrigerator, yanked out the plug, and returned to the fan, switching it on high. The low-ebbing drone of the blades rose to a whine and soon a powerful column of air blasted him in the face. When he muttered to himself, he quickly discovered that the sound waves in his voice were minced by the fan's rapid revolutions, acquiring strong vibrations as though electrified. "Na sa ru, ka ku, ma ma tu." He chanted the one phrase of Gypsy he knew. "So deese is Brooklyn," he told the fan. "Me na like Brooklyn. Brooklyn have all sorts of bad ways. Gypsies. Obeah."

Suddenly, the phone rang. David picked it up and heard a dial tone. This happened several times, and he began to get nervous, suddenly afraid to be alone in the apartment. He considered the idea of surprising Clara at Icey's, but knew Clara would get angry. Then he realized he could always use the rash of phone calls as an excuse. With this in mind, he called Information and asked for Icey's telephone number, making up a street name in order to trick them into giving her address. Then he went downstairs and once again knocked on the superintendent's door. This time David found the man at home. The superintendent was able to give him directions to Icey's, which was only six blocks away.

David trudged through the penetrating cold along the fringe of the cemetery. He crossed the avenue and entered a quiet neighborhood full of single-family homes and town houses. When he got to the address, he noticed two cars parked in the driveway and two more out on the street. Icey's brownstone was four stories tall; he wondered if she really owned the entire thing.

For a moment he stood before the lighted house, watching dark shapes of women in turbans roaming past the upper windows. A few stray notes of mournful blues filtered out into the cold. There was certainly no spirit of Christmas here.

Lydia, Clara's hairdresser, answered the door. Upon seeing David, she let out a peal of surprise. "How sweet you come to see Icey!" she said. Then she frowned. "But why don't Clara bring you wid her?"

"We were supposed to meet," David lied.

The ground floor of Icey's home was made up of three large rooms with high ceilings and ornate moldings; it obviously was the parlor level. The place was filled with heavy mahogany furniture. Above the fireplace in the most formal of the three rooms was a portrait of a beautiful black man in graduation silks. Dark foliage fanned out behind him, and farther on was the sea. David wondered if this was a portrait of Icey's doomed lover, the civil servant. On the mantel below the picture was a glass bowl filled with crystal carved into fruit shapes. Alone in the room, Clara sat on a carved settee that was covered in yellow silk. She held her head in her hands, her elbows resting on her knees. Before her on the coffee table was a bottle of white rum, a glass without ice, and a sliver of lime. She seemed to have been drinking the rum straight.

"David is here," Lydia announced.

Clara looked up, bewildered, and then cried out, "You devil!" She crossed the room in several quick strides, grabbed his arm, and began yanking him toward the door. It was then that he told her about the incessant ringing of the phone, lying about voices threatening him.

"What dem say?" Clara challenged him. She shook him, malice darkening her eyes.

"They were going to 'juke me up.' " He tried to pull away from her.

"You mean to say was Jamaicans talking?"

He nodded. "Seems like it."

Clara relaxed her hold, as though this bit of information were significant to her, or at least excused David for following her to Icey's. "Probably was just children in de building see you staying wid me. Parents talk. Give dem ideas. So, devil, how you get dis address?"

David explained about tricking the operator.

"Listen na, me warning you right now. Don't start turning a detective. Walk yourself home right now, or I'll make somebody drive you."

"Please," David said, looking around. "Can't I see her?"

"Don't I tell you she's not well? This not a party we carrying on here. And anyway, she's resting."

"Let me just look in on her."

Clara clucked her tongue. "Why you insist to force yaself where you not wanted? You getting to be a bad habit of mine, like smoking."

"Or drinking," David said, indicating the bottle back inside Icey's living room.

"Don't you start monitor my excess, you understand, detective?"

They climbed a flight of steps whose middle sections were covered by a band of faded blue carpeting. As soon as they reached the second level, the mood of the house altered. The hallway was steeped in darkness; there were only yellow flickerings of candles lighting the passages. David smelled a strange odor he remembered from the last time he was in Brooklyn: the smell of burning flesh mingling with smoldering mosquito coils.

Clara led him through the dimness to the boundary of a bedroom. Outside it sat two old wizened ladies dressed identically in black skirts and red smocks tied at the waist with yellow sashes. Their heads were wound with black cotton and their faces were filigreed with wrinkles. They appeared older than anyone David had ever seen, their eyes shriveled into their heads, their mouths like cuts in bark. Their hands and arms were covered with horrible marks and burns. Two bright coils made of powdered straw were smoldering at their feet. They peered at David suspiciously as Clara led him further into the bedroom. She bade him stop at the foot of Icey's bed, which was swathed in insect netting, flower petals strewn on the covering.

Icey wore a white gown and white bedcap and lay without moving. A large sterling-silver cross had been placed between her breasts. On the night table at her bedside burned an amorphous-shaped candle. David could tell it had begun burning in the form of a man's body. In a vase of water on the other night table, there was a branch stuck with several bright enamel-headed pins.

Suddenly, David could make out stirring beneath the shroud. "Who come to me now?" he heard Icey's voice rasping. "Who bring a demon to me?" she suddenly cried out.

"Shush, is only David," Clara said, trying to silence her. Then she glared at him as though to say, "See what you cause now?"

"Shouldn't bring white into de house," said one of the old ladies by the door.

Clara turned to them. "Him is goodness," she said. "Him know Icey and well want to give her his best wish."

"But if white trying to harm her, white must not come into de house," insisted one of the crones.

Clara knelt next to David. "Honey, don't listen dem. Dem was hired to sit dere and ward away bad things. Dem is called Obeah maids. But dem full o' shit like me can't tell you."

"Come to me, child," Icey said, breaking the deadlock between Clara and the guardians.

Clara nudged David, and he approached the bed warily. Now,

through the mantle of white netting, he could more clearly see Icey's face. It looked swollen, her features quivering from fever and her forehead covered by a sheet of sweat. He was suddenly afraid of catching whatever ailed her.

"How is ya parents?" Icey asked him faintly.

He shrugged. "They're okay."

"Dem getting on all right wid their new lives?"

"I guess."

"Spending enough time wid you?" She gasped at the words and then began to cough.

David shrugged.

Icey lifted a gnarled hand and poked at him through the netting. "I worry about you, child," she said. "But you should realize . . . that woman who stand behind us love you so till. She will protect if you believe. . . . Tell me something, child." Her voice was growing even fainter. "You go to temple?"

David hesitated. "We don't anymore," he answered.

"For shame. Everybody must have their own god." Icey turned her eyes up toward the ceiling. "I know dat now." She looked at him again. "You must say a prayer for me. Go to your temple and say a prayer in your own book." She raised herself for a moment, panting for air, and David was suddenly afraid she was dying. He slowly backed up until he reached the door, and then hurried away from Icey and the suspicious stares of her Obeah maids.

As David stepped off the curb in front of Icey's house, he noticed a large woman walking hesitantly in the street. He shrank back as soon as he recognized her fur coat.

"You mustn't frighten of me." Dora spoke to him kindly. "Me not a criminal. Must be she tell you bad about me."

"She didn't tell me anything at all," David said.

Dora's flat features appeared even uglier beneath the greenish light of the streetlamp. "So you come to visit Icey?"

David nodded.

"How she looking?"

"Not so good. But I have nothing to compare her to."

"Dreadful business, dis Obeah," Dora intoned.

David started to walk on, allowing Dora room to turn into Icey's walkway. "Hold on a minute," she called after him.

David stiffened. "What do you want?"

Dora sighed. "Did Clara ever told you about Ralfie?"

"None of your business."

"I know she don't tell you."

"She *did* tell me, okay?" He began walking away again.

"She couldn't tell you de *whole* story."

David stopped and whirled around. "Why do you care?"

"Me have reasons to care." Dora's voice was anguished. "I'm quite sure she don't tell you why Ralfie's heart go to de sea; about how he shamed her; and before her, how he shamed me."

169

David suddenly found it difficult to breathe; for a moment he even wondered if he was catching the demon of Icey's disease. "What do you mean his heart go to the sea?" he finally asked.

Dora's eyes had narrowed and her face filled with hatred. "You must ask her dat. You must certainly ask her," she said, then turned away. Watching as she waddled toward Icey's front door, David wondered what Clara would do when she saw her.

As soon as he returned to Clara's hot, stuffy apartment, David opened the windows and turned the fan back on. He sat down on the love seat, thinking about his strange visit to Icey's. For some reason, he never even thought to question whether or not Dora was lying to him in order to cause trouble. He was anxious to learn things about Clara without her knowing, and realized he was thus more willing to believe anything he heard. He tried to piece the details together. Had Clara given her child some sort of a sea burial in the Caribbean? Why was Dora so anxious for him to know? If he found out, what would she possibly gain?

Clara's apartment had grown cool and soon David was shivering. He shut off the fan, watching the blades slowly ceasing to turn, their sounds of beating wings dying down. Silence, in a shudder, fell over the room. The stillness was eventually disturbed by car horns on the boulevard, by the whine of a subway hurtling along a distant trestle. A strange odor wafted up from the cemetery. David imagined it to be the putrefying smell of thousands of bodies buried below him, blending with the smells of Clara's perfume and of wax.

He lay down on the love seat. Sounds of Christmas caroling threaded their way up through the deep cold. He wondered if Clara was still at Icey's, wondered if she really believed Icey was being troubled by an Obeah man, or if this was a traditional illness for which they were finding excuses. He pictured Icey lying in bed, surrounded by friends lighting semicircles of candles, the sallow light reflecting off her rhinestone cat glasses with a mute glitter. With these thoughts swirling in his head, he fell asleep.

He was awakened by a heartrending shriek.

"Jesus Christ!" Clara was yelling. The lights were on and she was standing in the kitchen, staring down accusingly at the linoleum floor.

"Why de ras you take de plug out? Why de bumba cloth you pulling up my place?"

David leaped from the sofa, watching how in her anger Clara grabbed two spoons that were lying on the kitchen counter. She threatened him with them and then flung them to the floor. Next to the refrigerator on the floor was a dark puddle that had dripped out of the freezer down one of its white panels.

"De whole freezer melt away!" Clara exclaimed. "Ice cream nastying de floor. Put de plug back in," she ordered David.

He stepped over the spill, stooping to plug in the refrigerator, which started up with a fierce rattling of its condenser.

"Clean it up now!" Clara demanded, pointing to the sticky brown river of chocolate ice cream.

David grabbed a yellow sponge from beneath the sink and sprayed it with some Fantastik.

Clara said, "If you think you coming back wid me to Brooklyn again, you have an oddar guess coming."

"Look, I'm sorry," he told her. "I forgot to plug it back in. I had to put the fan on. You don't realize how hot it was in here. I was burning up."

"I not even so much talking of de refrigerator. But you can't just put on me fan in dead winter de way you fool wid your air-conditioner at home. Me not in enough money fe pay high electric every month de way ya parents pay. Further on, me never could understand what it is between you and cold rooms. Probably you'd be happy living in a funeral morgue."

As David was wiping up the mess, Clara found herself chuckling at the ludicrousness of the situation, and then he knew her fit of anger had passed.

"Such a strange type of a person you are," she commented. "So strange sometimes I wonder if I really do know you."

"Of course you know me," David said as he put away the sponge. "You know me better than anyone."

Clara's mood suddenly went gloomy. "Not true," she disagreed. "Never do you really know anybody well enough."

Clara came closer to David and drew two fingers along his cheek.

She shook her head. "You get to know somebody a certain way and dem change quick and fast. Even you," she said. "You are changing. Me see it in ya face, how it start to show its bones. Soon you'll be turning to a man. Won't have no use for me," she said, combing the hair away from David's eyes.

"Stop talking like this," he protested.

Clara wrinkled her nose at him.

David tried to make up for neglecting to plug in the refrigerator by folding out the convertible sofa bed himself and making it up with sheets and stuffing some towels in a pillowcase. He waited as Clara changed in the bathroom. When she emerged in a yellow nightgown, her hair plaited in pigtails, he asked her if she really believed in Obeah.

Clara frowned at him. "As much as any skeptic," she answered.

"So then you don't?"

Clara sighed, and her sigh seemed to convey an inner torment. "It's not so much I don't accept it as me know to put up wid it."

"What do you mean?"

"I seen proof in my life. I seen some people who can affect de lives of oddars, seen people who can divine de future. I myself have seen dreams—like dose in Rye—dat signify. This part of life can't explain, but must be borne. So, if somebody trying to juke up Icey from Jamaica, me must do what I can to break his juking. Though I wouldn't rely on such things from day to day—like your muddar was doing for a while."

Neither spoke for a moment.

"Does Obeah have anything to do with why you hate Dora?" David asked.

"Who tell you we hate each oddar?"

"Come on—look what happened this afternoon."

Clara walked to the window and peered out toward the Verrazano Bridge. Water was hissing through the exposed pipes that ran to an upper apartment, where someone was stomping to music. She grabbed a broom from the kitchen and knocked the ceiling with its handle. She waited until the music was turned down.

"As children, we catch a fight," she explained, leaning on the broom. "She was 'back-bench girl' like me. Happen one afternoon when we all go pestering Chinee merchant."

"Tell me how it happened," David prodded her.

Clara shook her head. "Too late for stories."

"Please, you've got to tell me," he insisted as he approached her. Clara turned away from him to fix her eyes once again upon the bridge. "Leave me alone," she pleaded. "It's not pretty."

"I realize that."

"But don't a while ago you and I agree that one can't know everything about a person?"

"This won't be everything, will it?" David asked.

She would not answer this, although she finally did agree to speak further.

While Clara was growing up in Port Antonio, a Chinese woman named Maia Quong arrived from Shanghai to open up a dry-goods store. She was the mother of twin boys the same age as Clara, who were also her schoolmates at Tichfield. Clara always found the woman to be lovely, her skin smooth and clear as an onion, her hair black as a raven night. Shortly after Maia Quong opened her business, it prospered in such a way that she was able to undersell all of her merchant competitors, quickly gaining favor with the thrifty townspeople. She logged every single transaction on her abacus, kept careful books, and was constantly seeking ways to cut costs. Port Antonio merchants, by contrast, tended to be lazy and careless.

As her business grew and prospered, the other merchants suffered. Many of the girls who sat the back bench were the daughters of her jealous competitors; and children, Clara explained to David, often act out their parents' resentments. It was Dora Cambridge's idea to have some nasty fun at the expense of the Chinese woman. After the last school bell, when she discussed her plan with the other girls—two of whom were Blanche Larkin and Icey Darden—everyone had looked to Clara for her approval, which she gave despite all sorts of personal objections. Blanche never did end up accompanying them; she made some excuse about helping her mother. She was Clara's best friend at the time and knew what was really going through her mind.

The back-bench girls found the store swept clean, its burlap sacks of flour, beans, and cane sugar arranged in neat rows and priced clearly. Eight of them stood at the counter and began to request various foods in several-pound quantities. Maia Quong carefully measured and wrapped each order, binding it into a brown paper parcel wrapped with green twine. No sooner would she finish one order than the back-bench girls would see a bottle of peppermint oil or some raspberry syrup way up on a top shelf and request it. They knew the Chinese woman would have to get out her wooden ladder and climb up carefully to retrieve the additional item. Once or twice the ladder tottered and she nearly fell. When it came Clara's turn to be helped, she politely abstained from ordering anything. She watched as Maia Quong toiled over what eventually would be wasted, going about her tasks with a look of humility.

An hour passed. Packages upon packages were piling up on the counter. The sun was falling into the sea, the moon rising early as big and pretty as pumpkin cake. Maia Quong kept processing orders; the store was pungent with the mingled smells of different coffees and coconut oil and dried fish. Clara watched shadows falling like cloaks on the knotty bins of grain, listening to the sniggers of her girlfriends. She had such nagging regrets about allowing the charade to proceed; she wanted to cry out, although she knew the damage already was done. She heard the twin boys playing in the little house annexed to the store. Their contralto voices, in the uncertain pitch of adolescence, squeaked and cracked in Chinese as they wrestled together, joked, and argued. She thought it strange that they kept so quiet in school.

Suddenly there was a shriek—Dora's signal—and all the girls cried out, "Chinee! Quaa! Pongie pong! You no good! Chinee woman!" They ran out of the shop like a brood of disturbed scavengers. Clara, however, remained to watch how the place fell still without her friends. She glanced at the scores of packages, at the Chinese woman in the midst of pouring out a half-pound of molasses from an amber earthenware jug, her face clouded with confusion. As she realized the children had deliberately tricked her, she moaned, tilting her head from side to side.

Maia Quong wept softly while Clara, on behalf of her friends, spoke a litany of apologies. She offered to unwrap everything and put it back, but the woman, feeling more profoundly cheated and used as minutes passed, bent her head upon the mound of unclaimed packages and wailed in her native Chinese. Finally she picked up her head and began shrieking at Clara, who stood there bearing the diatribe, some of which was in English: "You nasty . . . crooked . . . devils!"

Clara felt she deserved to be blamed by allowing Dora to influence her friends. She listened to the reedlike moans of the woman's anguish. She broke down and wept as merchants all over Port Antonio were closing their shops with light spirits. She told Maia Quong she'd work for her the whole next month without any pay, assuring her that "back-bench girls" were notoriously different—meaner—than the rest of the children of Port Antonio. In her mind, Clara already had resigned as "Queen of the Back Bench."

At first the woman refused her offer. But Clara insisted and finally was bade to come in the next day after school. She worked for two weeks without pay. By then Maia Quong saw she could do fine work, add sums, take inventory. She insisted Clara receive wages, and Clara worked for nearly two years after that, until the business expanded and eventually moved to Kingston.

"Was she sad to leave you?" David asked.

Clara was still leaning on her broom, staring out the window into the emptiness of the cold night. "Of course she sad. She asked if I'd come, too. I had become like a daughter to her, my own muddar pretty much a drunk."

"But you didn't go."

Clara shook her head. "Already I had met me husband. And my attraction for him was too strong to leave town. Of course now I wish I'd have gone."

"What about your fight with Dora?" David asked.

Clara turned back from the window and stared at him. "I don't get there yet. Give me berth to tell it as it must be told."

"Okay."

The night that Clara promised herself to Maia Quong for no wages, she left the store and ran through the dusty streets. She passed clusters of gossiping townsladies in their colored turbans and fishermen with grim, weathered faces whose hands were gnarled from pulling hemp lines and throwing harpoons. "Clara running like devil," she remembered people calling out, "Catch de fire before de fire catch thee." And she pursed her lips, whistling a cling-cling birdcall that back-bench girls used to summon one another. She hurried through the vegetables markets, sidestepping mangoes squashed on the cobblestones, clots of mule dung, racing past the Methodist church, where she heard the answer boomerang from the sea. Then she saw the girls perched like hawks in the gazebo of the town park. When she arrived, panting from all her running, Dora immediately began heckling her.

"What you were doing back dere all dis time?" she demanded. "Wid dat Chinee. Her store pulling down everybody business a Port Antonio—and you, you must sympathize."

"Of course me sympathize," Clara answered angrily. "Me not a cruel person. So cruel as you. But me understand why you cruel. Since ya muddar is whore and don't give you no love, and since ya father deal in kali and moonshine and never do honest day's work."

With the back-bench girls looking on, Dora ran over to Clara, caught one of her pigtails, and tried to yank her head down. Ignoring the pain searing her scalp, Clara pulled back. She felt some of the hair ripping from her head. She managed to fling Dora's arm aside and went for her neck, digging her nails into the soft flesh. Dora yelped and slammed Clara in the ear. The blow sent Clara reeling back as a high-pitched buzzing sounded in her head. And for a moment Clara looked toward the moon ascending the sky and felt herself change. A beast came out of her that stupefied the aggressive back-bench girls, who then scattered in different directions. Flailing her arms hysterically, Clara rushed at Dora. She stuck her shoulders, her eyes, and as Dora covered her wounded face with her hands, Clara threw her to the ground. By now she had no idea what she was doing and kept punching Dora's face until she finally looked down and saw her nose was broken and bits of a shattered tooth lying on a quivering bloody tongue.

"Something come over me," Clara said darkly. "Don't know what it were. So vexed was I at how them taunt dat woman, and feeling guilty dat I don't do nothing to help. I just forget myself." A tear slid down her cheek and fell on the windowsill.

As Clara stood, ruminating in silence, a large bird took off from its cold nest in the building's eaves, and David heard its wings lashing the air. The night had grown late. He was afraid Clara's capability for violence could be turned against him.

"So she never forgave you for it?" he asked meekly.

Clara was now looking beyond him, her eyes locked on the brutal memories. "She had to go to hospital. The school inquired—they learn was she started de fight. . . . I did apologize eventually; but she always do things to get me back."

"Like what?"

"Enough said for one night," Clara told David.

He watched her open the linen closet and deliberate for a moment over sheets. She had told him nothing about her son or being shamed, and he wondered what Dora could have meant. As Clara began to make up her bed, he could hear the wind whining through the cemetery, rounding out the sharp corners of the tombs. They each got into bed and bid one another goodnight, and David's sleep was filled with dreams of Chinese merchants.

On Sunday morning, Clara got up before David, put on the coffee, and took a shower. She used the kitchen as a dressing room before coming to wake him. Noticing her beige wool suit, he asked why she had gotten so dressed up, and she said they would be going to church in order to pray for Icey. She had already assumed he would be delighted to accompany her.

David remembered Icey's request that he go to synagogue and say a prayer for her. But synagogue was far away from where he lived and he had no way of getting there. Maybe if he said a Jewish prayer in Clara's church, God would hear it just the same. David hadn't brought a tie with him. He wondered if God would take him less seriously if he wasn't dressed up. He asked Clara, who said God didn't care how children were dressed in church.

She ran a comb through David's hair, wrapped a scarf around his neck, and put on her red knitted coat. They stepped outside into the cold, brisk air of that brilliant Sunday. David felt a strong pulse of Christmas spirit. On their way to the subway station, they passed a woman in a Salvation Army uniform who was manically tolling her bell for alms. He dug into his pocket and found 50¢ to give her. They went underground, huddling with what he imagined to be a subway station full of churchgoers. Soon they were on the train, rushing across Brooklyn.

Clara's church looked very old. It was built of dirt-encrusted cut stones that arched into purple and red stained-glass windows and

178

formed tall Gothic points. At the very top was a belfry, and beyond
the belfry rose a thick television antenna. Clara had often explained
to David that she belonged to a "high Episcopal order." Once they
got inside the church, David saw that the stained-glass windows de-
picted Old Testament scenes he had seen in museums and in his
parents' coffee-table art books. Lining the cold stone walls were niches
enshrining life-size porcelain saints, which were roped off from the
congregation by twists of purple silk. Hundreds of people were throng-
ing the nave, and David quickly realized he was one of only a handful
of white people. He felt conspicuous as he looked at black women in
veils and stiff, starchy hats, their faces heavily powdered and rouged,
their skin dull and silvered. Many perfumes joined together in the air,
and yet were overpowered by the scents of incense and aged wood,
the smells of religion itself.

Clara led David over to a wall where scores of candles were placed
in several rows ascending toward a scene of shepherds supplicating
the God-child, who in turn beheld them, his face glowing with beatific
kindness. The votive candles flicked wanly. David imagined them to
be the last tangible particles of dead souls. In a beautiful sweeping
motion, Clara genuflected, rising again to light a candle far away from
the cluster of those already burning. "God spare her life," she whispered over and over again, her eyes swimming in tears. David knew
she prayed for Icey. He could feel her anguish over Icey's health,
which jarred him from his wonderment at being inside a church.

Once they sat down in the pews, Clara insisted they share a prayer
book, which would enable her to point out the psalms and prod David
each time the congregation was instructed to kneel. During hymns,
her lovely alto voice rose above the rest of the congregation, flourish-
ing with its own melodious conviction. People sitting near them turned
to admire her. David crossed himself whenever she did, feeling ex-
hilarated and guilty.

Clara instructed him to wait in the row when it came time to take
communion at the altar. But he sneaked up behind her and stood
silent in the line. When she turned around and discovered him, Clara
whispered harshly, "Go sit down!"

"Please, I want to do it, too," he told her.

"But if ya parents found out"—she came closer to his ear—"they'd shit up themselves."

David looked around to see if anyone had heard what Clara had said, which now, in the midst of holiness, sounded like a desecration. "I don't care," he told her. "I still want to."

"But it's not right to do this when you're a Jew." Clara tried to reason with him. "You're telling lies when you do so."

They were holding up the line and people glared at them. "Shh," someone said, and Clara looked around wildly to find out who had dared to tell her how to act. David was momentarily distracted by the sanctified movements of a priest roaming the aisles swinging an incense censer. The bitter perfumes made him feel nauseated and faint.

He turned to Clara. "When I'm here, I feel like I'm Christian," he explained.

Her eyes condemned him. "I said go sit ya backside down in the pew!"

David refused to budge, and Clara finally turned her back on him, in an act of disassociation. He watched her kneel before the priest, murmur something, and take the wafer on her tongue. Her eyelids fluttered with feeling as she drank from her disposable cup of wine, and her throat gulped as though she had swallowed a stone. She then hurried away, and David stepped into her place, fixing his eyes on the black face hemmed in white garments. He felt the priest taking note that he was Caucasian; nevertheless whispering sibilantly in Latin, placing the wafer on his lying tongue, offering a sip from a plastic chalice. The wafer changed into a bland-tasting paste and then miraculously dissolved. Blood rushed to his temples. David was now a Christian.

Clara refused to speak to him for the rest of the mass. When it was over, she grabbed him firmly under the elbow and led him outside the church, where the sludge of darkness suddenly gave way to a cataract of winter light. The congregation was scattering like pigeons, the church bells tolling as though the entire world were on holiday.

"Boy, you really know how to get me out," Clara complained once they were strolling along the sidewalk "You know I come fe ask God to spare Icey. You think him gwan to answer me prayers when you, my charge, is mocking him right into his old face?" She clucked her tongue.

David stopped walking and banged his arms to his sides. "Clara, my taking communion has nothing to do with you," he told her. "If any rules were broken, I'll be the one who's sent to hell."

"Jews don't believe in send-to-hell," Clara snapped. "Don't know why you can't listen to me when I request. You just like your muddar."

"I am not like her!"

"Of course! When ya mind set 'pon something, you don't stop until you get what you looking for. But, David, God is not for playing wid. God is big guns!"

"Okay, I'm sorry," he said finally. "It tasted lousy anyway."

"Good you don't like it, 'cause it's not made for eating."

Out of the corner of David's eye, he thought he saw Clara smirking to herself. He knew it was best to keep quiet for a while, and so they continued to walk several blocks without talking. Just as a flock of winter sparrows came wheeling over the sky, David felt a new purpose rising within him. Swelling with hope, he squeezed Clara' hand and she squeezed his back. Could it be the communion?

Clara finally ended the silence. "Let us go cook up some rice and peas and finish off dat chicken in my fridge," she said. "Then catch de 4:10 back to Rye."

"Why don't we stay longer?" David suggested, resting his chin on her shoulder. "I only have a half-day of school tomorrow."

"Stop wid ya foolishness. Rye is ya home."

David stopped walking again and stared at Clara. His hope was now being replaced by confusion and unhappiness. "I don't want to go back there," he said.

"Ya parents don't hire me so to keep you away from dem," she scoffed, continuing to walk the few steps that remained between where they stood and the next corner.

David followed her. Waiting for the light to change, he felt the moment stretching out into several endless minutes. Clara was clutching the lapels of her coat, her beehive wig piled up on her head. Today it tilted slightly and stray tendrils of hair waved in the brisk wind.

He looked up at the sky and noticed a bank of clouds scudding into thin wisps, much like the strings of a harp.

"I want to go to Jamaica," David whispered, finding himself fighting tears. "I don't ever want to go back to Rye. Please, let's just go to Jamaica."

"You don't even know what it's like in Jamaica, let alone want to live dere," Clara objected. "Besides, I couldn't go back down right now."

"Why?"

"Not for you to know."

"I'll go alone then. I'll like living there. I know I will. Because you did."

"Jesus Father," said Clara in a ballooning exhalation of frosted breath. She looked up at the clouds David had wanted her to see. "What in heaven's name have I done this child? How could one day in Jamaica turn into such a complication, such a life? What a way." Her voice trailed off.

"But I love you, Clara." David clung to her red coat just as the light changed.

THREE

1972

Over the next year Icey's friends continued to perform their strange rituals while she made intermittent visits to the hospital for chemotherapy treatments. For a time it seemed that her leukemia had gone into remission. Clara was careful to keep to herself any news she received, so that David had to gather his information by overhearing snatches of her telephone conversations. In this way, he gleaned that the chemicals Icey was given had caused most of her hair to fall out. Blanche, luckily, had been able to procure at wholesale a high-quality wig for her, which she had spent hours styling. Icey, David remembered, had always worn a very traditional hairdo; he figured it shouldn't have been all that difficult for Blanche to make Icey look like her old self.

As the months passed, David began to notice that Clara grew more secretive. He noticed that she kept her bedroom locked whenever she was not in it. He could not understand why she was suddenly taking this precaution. On one of his daily visits to her room, he saw that Clara no longer stowed the red suitcase in the closet. When he had the chance, he searched to see where she might have stashed it. He eventually figured out that it could fit in only one place—under the bed.

One autumn afternoon he slipped behind the baby-blue shower curtain in Clara's bathtub and waited until she left her bedroom. Her footsteps trailed off, as though she were taking a few steps down the hallway to a large, walk-in closet, which was the family medicine closet, containing boxes of cotton balls, bottles of alcohol, tinctures of iodine and liniments, as well as a physician's scale. As soon as she went inside, David heard the weighing apparatus clanging. He knew Clara rarely weighed herself—oddly, she would weigh herself only after she had eaten an enormous meal—and he figured she must be hiding the key to her room in the vicinity of the scale. It didn't take him very long to discover it dangling from a small hook at the back of a shelf, hidden by the height-measuring wand.

He waited until the day his mother took Clara food shopping. Although David got home from seventh grade at 2:30, they never would leave for the grocery store much before 3:30, when the last of the soap operas finished airing. Besides shopping, they stopped at the dressmaker's and then went to the library, where Leona would take out or return books of philosophy. They never arrived home much before 5:30.

He went into the medicine closet, took the key, and for a moment stood listening outside Clara's room. Pretending to be a suspicious lover in one of her stories, he turned the handle and dramatically flung open the door. Brilliant sunlight filtered in through the open windows at a low angle, making a blistering line across the white piece of lace Clara had spread over her dresser top. The room smelled of wood shavings and cloying deodorant and more faintly of Touch of Fire. David felt compelled to inspect the contents of Clara's drawers. He fingered through her undergarments—brassieres and polyester panties. The only article of clothing he found interesting was an apricot silk nightgown—he had never once seen her wearing it—pinned with a piece of paper that said, "In case of hospital." Then he opened the night table, rummaging through the delicate skins of various aerograms until he found the suitcase key. The envelope enclosing it was weighed down by all sorts of manicuring implements, and he was careful to memorize the position of the cuticle remover, the nail file, and the nail clipper—just in case Clara had noted the exact layout of all her personal tools. Reaching into the soft pocket, he removed a shiny key that resembled a toothpick with a metal ridge. Then he bent down, dragging the suitcase out

from under the bed. When the metal clasp fastening the suitcase
flipped open, he felt a twinge of guilt. And yet, his desire to investi-
gate the contents of the suitcase ended up overpowering any regrets.

The inside was quilted with soft fabric. It reeked of old perfumes
and of humidity, a smell belonging to the tropics. Bundles of aerograms were bound in blue ribbon. Most of them had been sent to
Clara Mayfield, 376 Orchard Lane, Port Antonio. Three stacks had
been set apart from the others, each stack wrapped with a sheet of
white paper and dated: January 1968–May 1968; June 1968–
November 1968; December 1968–April 1969. April, David remembered, was the month Clara had come to America with his parents.
He decided to peruse those three stacks first, carefully untying the
ribbon holding them together and removing the white cover sheets.
He then beheld something very confusing. Each letter was addressed to Manny Mayfield, United States Naval Base, Guantanamo
Bay, Cuba, but each had been stamped "Return to Sender." And
yet, each had also been opened. Did this mean Clara had written
Manny, who refused to read her correspondence and sent it back,
only for Clara to open and reread what she had written? Feeling
short of breath, David put down the letters. He stood up and went
to her window. There was a low tide out on the Sound and moored
sailboats listed on the dregs. Wind riffled through the room, bringing in a smell of brine and mud. It flustered the letters.

David continued to look through the suitcase. He ended up finding only one letter written by Clara's husband that had actually
been mailed from Cuba. He slipped it out of the envelope and
read.

5 December 1965

Dearest Clara:

Been here two solid weeks now. Had time to think. Decided
better we don't communicate. So please, don't post me
nothing. It'll be too hard for me to continue through letters.
Just want to relax some and work hard and forget about
things. Understand? Can't say about the future, but now to

me, seems to cover pretty far forward. I'll send you little
money when I can. I must be away and in silence to try and
get over all this confusing business.

Stay well. For your own sake.

Manny.

Struck by the word *confusing business*, David's curiosity by now had
grown fevered. It was as though the rest of the world no longer existed
—only the puzzling world of Clara's past. He opened one of Clara's
returned letters.

3 January 1966

Dearest Manny:

It's cruelty that you send back my letters. At least you
could keep them, not read, not answer. But to find them in
the post box when I'm imagining you at night, sitting apart
from your fellows, reading everything I so carefully express. It
breaks all my hopes of you ever understanding. It's hard for
me to know even as I write that you might never see it.

If you only knew how difficult life is here. I should never
have left my job at Tichfield. Now I am always new person
anywhere I work, even at hotels. People just don't treat me
same way as they used to. That's the hardest thing, even
worse than knowing them call me "fallen angel." They know
how proud I am and make me suffer for pride. That's why I
pray every night that you won't neglect me too much longer,
that I'll be able to look down at them once again when you
come back to me. Until then, my darling.

Your Clara.

Fallen angel—what could that mean? Had she fatally sinned
against God? If so, perhaps that was why she attended church so
rarely and with a certain amount of skepticism. Perhaps, in some way,
God had forsaken Clara, who had been tempted by powers of evil that
would now prevent her from ever finding grace.

David was drawn to next letter because its envelope had been marked repeatedly "Contains Crucial News."

23 May 1966

Dear Manny:

The whole town knows you gone away and that my letters to you return. Of course post office was aware. Them were trying to be decent about the whole business. But now they have let go a worker who labrishes to everyone. I appeal to you, man, don't let me live out this disgrace. I'm suffering hard enough for Ralfie. How can I help what he did to us? I've done everything to reverse it, man! Even gone to church —against my better judgment. I'm the innocent party. Why you continue to punish me? To your everlasting judgment I do appeal.

Love truly,

Clara

If Clara's husband had left her over the death of Ralfie, it would make sense to David—after all, he'd always felt Edith's death had propelled his parents toward their separation. Suddenly, something provoked him to read the very last in the stack of letters that had been sent back. As it turned out, the letter was one of two written the same day. A week later, Clara had come to America with David's parents. The envelope had also been marked "Contains Crucial News."

5:30 P.M. 21 March 1969

Dear Manny:

I had hoped during last year you'd recover your heart and sympathize. But I realize now your decision comes from something not yourself. I go to the yellow villa today—owners see me, but I don't care a ras—and I look down and try to understand how compulsion can twist good people to do evil. I wonder if he was trying at last to break away from the devil, or if he was just punishing himself as you are punishing me

now. I try to divine justice of your action, justice of fate, but
it's still hard on me. I writing you a last time, hoping for just
a kind reply. I have been offered a situation in America,
which I plan to take so to leave this infernal place. I pray to
heaven you'll read this and it will not be forwarded to me up
there. I'll write with my address.

With everlasting love

Your Clara.

David knew that something terrible had happened.

He grew aware of sniffling sounds behind him. He ignored them at
first, assuming the curtains were rustling or the air duct was discharg-
ing heat. Then, out of the corner of his eye, he saw a bottle of Gelusil
had been knocked off her night table, a pink sludge bleeding into the
carpeting. A human shadow was slowly developing on the closet door.
He gasped. Clara stood behind him, tears streaming down her cheeks.
It took David a moment longer to register that she was not a hallucina-
tion, for he still was reliving the torment of this last letter she had
written to her husband.

He jumped up off the floor, glancing guiltily at the open suitcase.

"I—I didn't mean this," he said, huddling into himself, feeling
madness in his head.

"You gone too far now," she replied in a faint mocking voice.

"I didn't do this to hurt you, Clara."

"Liar!" she cried.

"You just made me curious, that night. . . ."

Clara peered blankly at David with bloodshot eyes. She seemed not
to have heard him. "How could you even consider doing this to me?"
She was trembling. "After all de trust I put into you."

"I just had to know. There's so many things. First the letters and
candles and then Icey."

"None of it your business!" she cried.

"I know it isn't. I know. But please forgive me," David pleaded.
"I hate myself. I'll do anything you say."

Clara had walked to the window. "You're a crippled child. You
make me feel dirty and ashamed."

"No!" David cried, clamping his hands over his ears.

"Worst kind of jealousy, jealousy of a person's privacy. Such a dreadful pity your life comes down to this—you act like a desperate old man, helpless in love with some young woman."

While David sobbed, Clara somehow managed to collect her own emotions. She dried her cheeks with the back of her hand and folded her arms across her chest. "Me not gwan let you live dis one down." She spoke in a rasp. "Must be ya parents gone cause this putrid selfishness. If them attended you properly, you wouldn't be up to dis devilwork. Get out my room now," she cried, grabbing the door key away from him. "I'll hide this damn key so you never find it again, even if it must be on my person. Ga scram!"

Whimpering, David trudged to the bedroom door. When he opened it, he discovered his mother standing outside. Her limpid eyes were bruised red from crying. She refused to look at him as he ran past her to the opposite end of the house.

A few hours after the disturbance in Clara's bedroom, David ventured down to the kitchen, where Leona was sitting quietly, sipping a glass of scotch.

"Where is she?" he asked quickly.

His mother looked into her cocktail and jiggled the ice. "I gave her money to see a movie—she's taking the afternoon off."

David plopped down dejectedly in one of the wooden ice-cream-parlor chairs, and now his mother looked at him in amazement.

"How could you bring yourself to do something like that?" she suddenly demanded. "I can't understand it. You've never done anything like that before—you've always respected your father's and my things."

In his heart David knew the answer; he had never felt the same way about his parents, he had never felt the same compulsion toward them that drove him to infiltrate Clara's bedroom. "You don't realize . . . " he began, wanting to say, "it has to do with Brooklyn," and that Clara acted strangely when she was away from Rye, and that there were so many things he had discovered about her that needed to be explained. But he spoke no further; he sensed Clara would be even angrier with him if he reported what he had heard and seen.

"Did she say anything to you at all?" he asked, testing his mother.

Leona shook her head. "Nothing. Absolutely nothing."

"But she must have said something!"

With fingers whose nails she no longer painted, his mother brushed frizzled bangs of uncombed auburn hair from her eyes. "You know how guarded Clara is. And you of all people should understand about her pride. You've disregarded it too many times. I assume she's going to punish you for it now."

"Can't you get her to forgive me?" David pleaded.

Leona looked at him incredulously. "How can I do that?"

"You've got to. Tell her I'm failing at school. Tell her I'm sick."

"She knows everything going on with you. Besides," Leona sighed, "I'm not so high on her list myself."

David looked down at the whorls of wooden knots in the kitchen table. "Maybe she has reasons to be angry with you," he said, suddenly glancing up at his mother.

"What are you trying to tell me, David?" she challenged him.

He shrugged and said nothing. For the moment his mother's neglect meant nothing to him.

They continued to sit at the kitchen table, where the silence of dusk was flurried by wind skidding in off the Sound; they could make out phosphorescent crowns of whitecaps long after darkness obscured the yard. They waited for Clara, held to their places by a spell of anxiety. They stared at one another, each perturbed by fears: Leona, that Clara would leave and thereby affect her relationship with Peter; David, that he would be deserted and forced to live alone in the empty world of this cavernous house.

Clara breezed in the back door with a long face close to 7:00 P.M. She greeted Leona in a soft voice, refusing, however, to acknowledge David. She climbed the stairs to her room, slammed the door shut, and watched a half-hour of news. Two women had been strangled with a length of barbed wire only a few blocks away from her apartment in Brooklyn; Clara then and there reminded herself that although David had betrayed her, she should feel lucky that she was still alive and that her life was intact. She finally went downstairs, with the intent of grilling lambchops, starting when she saw Leona and David still waiting at the table. She hummed a few notes to herself; then decided singing might act as a barometer of her mood. She wanted both of them to be anxious about the punishment in store for David.

After Clara finished the cooking, she arranged her dinner on a tray and went back upstairs to her bedroom.

"Now she's going to make me suffer for what you did," Leona complained to David when they were eating alone at the kitchen table.

David picked at his lamb chop. "She probably thinks you taught me how to be nosy."

"Not quite. I think it's more like guilt by association."

"Guilt what?"

"Nothing, just finish your dinner."

David finally went upstairs and tried to busy himself rearranging his insect mountings, but realized he was too worried about Clara even to concentrate. To console himself, he went to his closet, took out a heavy sweater, and switched on his air-conditioner. He suddenly wished his air-conditioner were a fan.

What disturbed him most was that he had no way to gauge how furious Clara actually was—whether she was angry over his intrusion, or because he had learned about things she was trying to hide. Did she actually realize how much he had learned? David's head suddenly filled with bleak images: Clara's husband standing at attention amid a fleet of American navy ships, clutching an unopened letter she had sent; Clara outside the Port Antonio post office, hanging her head over yet another letter returned. Then he pictured the yellow villa, the shrine of doom.

He tiptoed down the hall and stood outside her locked bedroom. He could hear soft murmurs of jazz music escaping Clara's clock radio. Her bridge table was creaking. He wondered if she was scribbling aerograms to Jamaica. Now she probably felt too wary of him to leave her letters unattended on the kitchen table; he imagined her keeping them carefully concealed among the leaves of an old *National Enquirer*, with the intention of bringing them to the post office herself.

The next morning, David lay in bed, hoping to hear Clara's cheerful wake-up song, "Chi chi buddo." Instead, when passing by his room, she rapped her knuckles on the doorjamb, continuing downstairs to fix breakfast. Later on, as he entered the kitchen, David tried catching her eye, but she purposely held the morning paper in front of her face, shielding herself from his scrutiny.

David tried to snag her into conversation several times while he ate his bowl of orange granola—one of the few foods Leona had added to the pantry that he actually liked—but each time he met up with the same stony silence. When he was ready to leave for school, he stood forlornly by the kitchen door, his arms laden with books, and pleaded, "Please talk to me when I get home."

Clara's response was to suck air through her lips.

"I'll do anything to get you to forgive me," he told her.

She purposely ruffled her newspaper, then put it down and took another section without letting her eyes wander.

"Thanks a whole lot." David slammed the door.

"You ras," Clara hissed after he left. "Me will learn you to trouble me personal. Me won't talk so till ya ready for Bellevue."

The reign of silence continued for a week, and by then David was deeply troubled. Whenever he detected a flicker of recognition in Clara's lusterless countenance, he threw himself upon her and begged forgiveness. But she always shrugged him off like a leper and went about her business.

By the second week, Clara's punishment had driven David to desperation. One afternoon while she was in her bedroom, he lifted up the phone in the library and dialed from one line to the other. He let it ring a long time before she picked it up.

"Hello!" She spoke gruffly, obviously annoyed about being disturbed in the middle of a television drama.

David answered Clara in the high, squeaky Jamaican voice of one of Clara's women friends, the one he was best able to imitate. "Clara, hi, is me, Blossom," he said.

"Blossie Chatelaine, wha happen? Me was longing to hear from you," Clara answered sweetly.

David pounded his chest from all his pent-up frustration and came close to slamming down the phone. "Old people here gi' me such a hard time," he said, referring to the nursing home where Blossom worked. "Dem nagging and gnaming at me. Some so feisty to ask for invitation to me house."

"Imagine a thing like dat," Clara said.

"Haven't seen you out a church lately. Where ya been?"

"You must be leave your senses," Clara said. "And you saw me up to last Sunday, telling me how you love me hat dat favor a peacock tail."

"Oh, yes, how me could forget about dat?" David's voice quavered. Dammit, as far as he knew, Clara hadn't been to church in months.

"Well, Blossom," Clara continued, "me glad you call, really. Me life up here getting from bad to worse."

"Wha happen?"

"De child get nasty. You couldn't believe. Him wait till I step out wid his muddar and den right away bust into me room and gone through me letters."

"No! A lie ya tell." David sounded shocked.

"True, as God in heaven. And to think him don't even satisfy wid dat. Him must dress up in me frock. Done his hair in me turbans and den spray his stinking self wid Touch of Fire."

"I did not!" David yelled into the phone.

"Me know it was you from de start," Clara said quickly. "Ya devil child. You must take me for a fool!" She slammed down the phone.

David wept inconsolably in the library while Clara howled with laughter up in her bedroom.

Leona was amazed that Clara was able to go for so long without speaking a single word to David. She herself would have broken down a long time ago and forgiven him. She admired Clara's tenacity, that she was able to dish out such a long-term punishment; it would certainly be the last time he disregarded her privacy. However, Leona did not realize how deeply her son had been affected by the silent treatment. Clara was punishing David by completely severing communication with him, communication that was normally fraught with complete sympathy between the two of them. As a result, David was overwhelmed.

He vented his frustration at school. When the hallways were full of students switching classes, he would hurl the vilest Jamaican insults he knew at people who jostled him accidentally. "Ga bathe, ya bumba cloth!" "Don't frig around me, ya ras!" he berated his partner on a woodworking project in shop. "Ga clear off, ya toot mum and baggai!" he snapped at anyone who even said hello to him.

Soon, David began daring his teachers to acknowledge the oddity of his speech, to punish him for his outbursts. "Wha ya cut it up fa!" he screamed in biology class when his instructor was demonstrating dissection of a frog. "Wash de crotch out, man." In French class, while practicing conversation, he tried making up French patois. *"Me na parle français, me n'écoute pas,"* he snapped at the elegant Parisian woman who was his teacher.

His instructors began to complain to the school guidance counselor, Mr. Marino, who telephoned Leona to discuss David's sudden change of behavior. To prepare for the phone conversation, he consulted the recent results of psychological tests that had been given to the entire seventh grade that previous September. Mr. Marino noted that the school's resident psychologist considered David hyperkinetic. He conveyed this to Leona and suggested she consider sending him to an outside therapist.

At first Leona thought the suggestion was preposterous. She discussed it with Peter, who was usually careful not to get himself involved in her decisions regarding what was best for David. He, however, personally knew a prominent therapist at a psychological institute in northern Westchester County that was renowned for its work with children. When she seemed interested, he called to arrange for an interview.

And so, late one morning, Leona drove thirty miles to a complex of rambling, colonial-style offices in a densely wooded area of a place called Cross River and spent two hours in conference with several psychologists. She learned that group therapy was offered to the parents of children who were in counseling. That idea, in particular, had great appeal; she immediately recognized an opportunity to show some renewed responsibility and concern for David; it was something they could do together that would be for his benefit. The next step was broaching the issue to Bill.

Leona wrote him a letter about the prospect of putting David in therapy. She also asked the institute to contact him and explain their treatment. But Bill would never take their phone calls.

"Don't you think it's a little late to start feeling guilty?" he asked when she telephoned him at his law offices, and after he had signaled his secretary to close his door and hold his calls. "You haven't been living at home regularly for nearly a year," he reminded her. "It has suddenly dawned on you that staying out so much might not be the proper thing to do when you have a kid. So now, to make up for it, you want to put David in therapy."

Leona winced at Bill's words. Her gaze flitted about the dark bedroom of Peter's book-cluttered apartment where she sat rigidly on their bed. She was alone there and felt glad that Bill was unable to visualize her surroundings. "Look," she told him, "this is not a discussion about my living arrangements, although it happens to be impossible for me to carry on this relationship any other way. I manage to see David plenty. Besides, the psychologist was not my idea. It was the school's."

Bill put his feet up on his desk. "Listen, Lee, I was hyper when I went to public school. In fact, now that I remember it, the school psychologist told my parents they should put me on tranquilizers."

"I would never put David on tranquilizers."

"I realize that. But it's just an example of the fact that school shrinks are from the bottom of the barrel."

"I took the tests up to Cross River with me," Leona said, nervously twisting the phone cord around her finger, "and the people there agreed."

Bill took his feet down and leaned forward. "Of course they agreed. They want your money!"

"They're professionals, Bill. And believe me, they've got more patients than they need. They're renowned."

Bill swiveled completely around in his chair and looked out from his highrise midtown office across the jagged skyline of the city. Far beyond, along the Hudson, he spied a barge moving northward. For a moment he wondered how long it would take until the boat traveled to a point parallel with where Leona was now on the Upper West Side. It suddenly amazed him, to the point of pain, that he and his ex-wife were both in Manhattan and would spend the night there while David was in Rye. There was something dreadfully wrong with this. It had to change. Would things be better for David if he took Leona to court and was awarded custody? But then he'd have to totally surrender his late-night, irregular bachelor life. Bill began to feel guilty, because in his heart he knew that a child's welfare easily interfered with parents whose lives were not geared to staying at home.

"Let's look at this from another angle," he told Leona. "David spends a lot of time at home, more than most kids his age. He doesn't have that many friends. Don't you think putting him in therapy is going to make him feel even more separate?"

"Then again, it might help him relate better to children his own age."

"I don't think he has trouble relating to kids his own age so much as he's just different from most of them. And also, remember, he's fascinated with Clara. He spends a lot of time with her."

"Let's not bring her into this."

"Don't get me wrong—I think Clara's great. But she's also a distraction for him. What does she think about his going to a psychologist?"

Leona hesitated. "I haven't told her yet."

Bill felt certain Clara would object. He saw his message light flashing. Business suddenly pressing in on him made it easier to conclude that the conversation had reached a point of futility. It was obvious that Leona had her mind set on putting David into therapy.

"I guess you and I are on opposite sides of the issue," he told her.

"I guess."

He covered the message light with his hand. "But of course you want me to pay for the treatment."

Leona stood up and with her free hand raised the shade and stared across the dark alleyway to the brick face of the adjacent building. For a moment she searched the neighboring apartments for a hint of light or movement, but she could see nothing. She sighed. "You're in a better position to pay than I am."

"If you look at our divorce agreement, I pay for medical bills," he told her. "What I mean is, if I'm going to pay for this, I might as well pay for a psychiatrist, someone who has a medical degree."

"I'm satisfied with these people."

"Leona, you're so easy to read. Of course you won't look into anyone else. You wouldn't dream of letting me get involved in choosing my son's therapist, and yet you want me to pay for it."

"I'll pay for it out of my alimony," she said bitterly.

"I can tell by your tone you think that's a big concession. And yet, I still have no say in David's welfare."

"I called for your approval, Bill, not your money!" Leona snapped.

"I really wish I could believe that," he said wistfully.

Clara got the news about the psychologist when she was in the kitchen dicing up new potatoes and onions and raw beef for a stew. She tried as best she could to remain calm.

"I can't believe those school people tell you to send a little child to a psychiatrist," she remarked, using her paring knife to gather translucent crescents of onion.

"A psychologist, Clara."

"Two alike in my book.

"Where is he now, anyway?" Leona asked, looking around the kitchen. "I haven't discussed it with him yet."

Clara lowered her voice appreciably. "Upstairs doing his homework. But what they will do for him—if they are for people who sick and can't manage themselves? Mrs. Hart, little children have their funny selves, bad ways that change as them get older. Believe me, I don't think you should let David start exploring what he thinking. It just makes things worse. You think after all what I'm doing him now he'll ever trouble my things again? No, sir. I control dat boy, don't you worry!"

"We have to consider more than just what he did in your bedroom. You might be able to make him behave at home, but you can't control what he does in school."

Shaking her head, Clara went to the refrigerator, returning to her cutting board with some enormous carrots Leona had bought at bulk rate from a vegetable cooperative. She began chopping them with vigor. "I know you too well, Mrs. Hart," she said. "You interest in a new mess for yaself. You just want drag this poor child into it wid you. Just the way you drag yourself to dat Gypsy. As soon as you get new idea, bam! If you want twist up your brain, that is fine. But leave the child out of it. Further on, if you only knew what I did when I was into school sitting the back bench, shrieking and bawling, you'd be shocked. Compared to what I did, this boy is a saint. And see?" Clara dropped her knife, smoothing her hands over her waist. "Me not even half crazy."

"Ssh," Leona said.

"Don't tell me ssh. I'm not your child."

"I'm sorry. Now, please don't discuss any of this with David."

Clara folded her arms. "How could I discuss when I not even speaking to de boy? As far as this discussion concerned, me have one more thing to say. In Jamaica we have expression: The higher the monkey climbs, the more he exposes. You understand what that means?"

Leona shook her head.

"The higher the monkey climbs, the more him can see and can be seen. The more knowledge people have about themselves and their own powers, the more they are vulnerable to hardness of this world. Nice thing about a child is his ignorance. Him will learn about his own brain when time is right."

Leona peered out the bay window into the backyard. Leaves were slipping rapidly from the trees, and the lawns were carpeted in mottled brilliance. She watched the pageant for a while. "Clara," she said finally, "somebody I know recommended a well-known institute north of here. It has group therapy for the parents of children who are seeing the psychologists. It'd be easier, I think, than driving him into the city. And I was lucky enough to schedule David with one of the psychologists while I'm having the group."

Leona turned to find Clara peering at her intently. "Yes, me mind told me you mixed up wid it already," Clara muttered. "Always jumping into worlds that don't concern you. But I'm telling you this now." She took her paring knife and lightly scratched an X over the counter. "I'm marking it down ten. You wasting money and time and those people are nothing but crooks. But since you so stubborn, you must go about your business. Finished off." Clara dusted her hands together noisily and fled the kitchen.

Clara finally wrote an angry letter to Jamaica accusing Pella of being unable to have any effect at all on the state of affairs in America, both in the case of Icey Darden's illness and in this latest predicament where David was about to be sent to a psychologist. Within seven days of sending her own aerogram, Clara received one addressed with spidery green handwriting. She was amazed that the sluggish period that correspondence normally took to travel back and forth between Jamaica and America had suddenly sped up.

In her letter Pella claimed to have been unwell herself for some time; but she apparently had been doing what she could since first receiving word and regretted that she had had so little effect. As far as Pella knew, no one was trying to juke up Clara; she felt the whole business of the psychologist happened on its own. Icey Darden was a different matter; the power that harmed her was too strong to be broken from afar. However, Pella enclosed the name and telephone number of a powerful Gypsy lady in Brooklyn, recommending that Clara contact her. Unfortunately, anyone Clara asked about this Gypsy woman had never heard of her.

"But what's wrong with me," cried a voice inside David's head when his mother explained to him he was to be seeing a psychologist. "What's wrong, what's wrong?" He couldn't say anything at first, he was so shocked. He thought of the pimply-faced, inward boy at school who had been going to a psychiatrist for several years but who was only getting stranger. People whispered he had been in a "psycho" ward, that he was depressed. Girls had nothing to do with him.

She had come into David's room one day after school. She was wearing a deep green cashmere turtleneck, which made her face look more angular and enhanced the loveliness of her exotic eyes. He had been sitting on the carpeting, struggling with a bonus math question: how far a car could travel at fifty miles per hour during a half-hour with two five-minute rest stops. His head muddled with calculations, David listened to his mother telling him he was unaware of the effect his father's living apart from them was having, which partly had to do with why he was unhappy at school. As she said this, he glanced at his various efforts to solve the math problem, thinking how strange that the bewilderment he had felt over homework was suddenly infecting the rest of his life.

There was nothing wrong with him, Leona kept reassuring. Psychologists, she explained, don't deal in right or wrong. David tried telling her school was okay; that he'd only gotten in trouble because he was upset about Clara; everything he had done wrong had to do with her refusal to speak to him—very little had to do with his father. His mother said the problem was much larger than just Clara, but David insisted Clara was the only problem.

"If I go to see this person, will they get her to talk to me again?" he finally asked.

"They might help you understand why you feel like disregarding her privacy," she said kindly.

"I respect Clara's privacy."

"Not really if you broke into her room."

"You don't understand," he said.

"Maybe I don't. But hopefully Dr. Stevens will."

"Stevens?" David repeated. "That's the doctor's name? Is it a man or a woman?"

"A man."

David pictured a maniac like Dr. Frankenstein. He gnashed his teeth. "Nothing will make a difference if Clara is finished with me," he unhappily told his mother.

Leona smiled. "David, she's not finished with you. Believe me, she'll come around. It's just a question of when."

She sat down next to him, enfolding him in an embrace, and said she loved him. The cashmere sweater felt gentle and silken against his face. He smelled her familiar, toasty smell, and something far within him ached. As soon as she left him alone, David ran down to the library phone and called his father's office. The receptionist said his father was talking to Brussels and put him on hold for five minutes. It was much too long to wait, and during the crackling silence David's mood swung from great hope that his father would save him to utter despair that he was doomed to be in therapy for the rest of his life.

"Sorry, pal," Bill said as he came on the line, but by then David already was sobbing.

"You don't understand," he kept telling his father, "if I go to a psychologist, they'll make fun of me at school. They'll call me a geek. I'll lose all the friends I have."

"You shouldn't worry about that, David, because nobody will find out," his father reassured him.

His father explained that he had already fought with David's mother over sending him to a psychologist, but that she insisted he go along with it, especially since she wanted to pay for the treatment out of her own alimony.

"You mean, you don't want me to go, but you can't stop her from sending me?" David asked incredulously.

"I could try, but it would cause a lot of problems."

"Like what?" David looked up into the bookshelves, which had been left empty all this time his father was gone.

"I'd have to start a proceeding against your mother," Bill explained. "People go to court over these kinds of disagreements."

David thought of "Divorce Court," which he had once watched on television. He couldn't decide what was worse: going through divorce court or going to a psychologist. "I don't want you and mom to do that," he said.

There was silence between them as David began to confront the inevitable. He thought he could hear his father's leather office chair crackling and squeaking.

"What does Clara say?" his father asked.

"Clara knows?" David asked in amazement.

"She must by now. I gather you haven't talked about it with her."

"Dad, she hasn't spoken to me in three weeks," David bitterly reminded his father, as he wondered if seeing a psychologist might be yet another measure of Clara's punishment.

"She's *still* not talking to you?"

"No," David wailed.

"She will, don't worry about that. . . . Now, for the time being, just try this psychologist. If you really hate going, then we'll discuss what to do about it. There's always the possibility your mother won't like it."

David's mouth suddenly dropped open. Clara had slipped into the library and was now standing there peering at him.

"David?" his father asked.

"I gotta go, dad."

"Everything all right?"

"Clara's waiting for me," he said.

After David put down the phone, he stood there blinking, as though a spirit had appeared before him.

"Where ya muddar?"

David was so shocked to hear her voice, he grew dizzy. "In her room," he managed to say.

"Come to me quarters," she whispered, reaching for his hand.

Ecstatic to hear Clara speaking to him again, David threw himself into her arms, joyous that she didn't try to force him away. She enveloped him in a bear hug, kissing the top of his head. "Come see de stories," she cooed, her voice soothing as a brook. " 'The Raging Tide' just finish and I'm waiting on 'The Guiding Light.' "

They left the library and walked through the living room, where limbs of high-backed chairs threw long, spindly shadows, then down the gleaming hallway and across the spotless kitchen. It was a beautiful procession; the house had never looked more lovely. David felt as though he and Clara were wandering inside the glittering chambers of a jewel. When they reached the inner sanctum of her bedroom, he rubbed his cheek against her hands, feeling that the world was once again set right. He knew he'd be able to face the sessions with the psychologist just so long as he was sure Clara still loved him.

David sat down in her comfy, tattered armchair. With great delight, he discovered that during his banishment Clara had inherited the RCA console television that used to belong in the master bedroom. It was wonderful to see her television world, once as black and white as the *New York Times,* expanded into a colorful dimension, as though she now watched *National Geographic.* On the screen a blond housewife was proffering emerald-colored dishwashing liquid. While David watched the commercial, smells of carpeting and newly pressed clothes spilled over him. The iron was steaming and ready on the ironing board, greeting him, it seemed.

Clara sat down on her bed, reaching over to clasp David's hand, making him feel giddy.

"Me want to tell you something. If dat damn doctor asks you questions you don't want to answer, you must make up the rest."

"But how?"

"Telling him stories is the best way. Lord knows you good at lying."

David looked sadly at Clara. "What's wrong with me?" he asked.

Clara shook her head. Her eyes looked glazed and worried. "David, darling, listen me." With her index finger she etched the impression of a stick figure into her bedspread. "Dis is all because your muddar don't understand you. I know it's hard for you to hear, but is only through she that you going to see this damn doctor. Now, if you love old Clara, you'll listen to what she wants to tell you. Psychologist is trouble for you. Your brain don't have no more difficulties than oddar children. Every person has their own quirks and bad points. You ever see how a tree has bumps on its bark? Well, de trunk grows round them as we all must live with our own idiosyncrasies."

"What are those?"

"Likes and dislikes, good and bad habits."

David told Clara about the conversation with his father, especially about the possibility of a "proceeding."

Clara stood up, clasping her hands behind her back, and for a moment of reflection faced her bottle-cluttered bureau. "Ya father is right. A fight wid your mother would be de worst possible thing." She turned to David again. "I will call to tell him leave everything to you and me, that we shall handle doctor in our own way. But you're not

to tell ya muddar I call him," she said, shaking her finger at David.
"Because is she brought me to dis country and if she see I get involved
so deep, might even pitch me out into de street."

"She wouldn't do that."

"If I cross her so bad? Child, you don't know what you saying."

"What if the psychologist asks me about you?"

Clara drew the air through her teeth. "Him will do it, of course.
But you mustn't tell him our private business. Because only reason
why he's listening you is your muddar paying him plenty money."

"Okay."

"Then we'll just see how it all proceed."

Each of them for a moment fell to musing. David was watching
Clara's window, where bright rashes of yellow maple leaves fell past.
"Clara," he said in a sigh, "I don't want anyone to know." He had
just vented his worst fear. "At school there's a boy who goes to one.
He's a geek. Nobody likes him."

"How you find out him goes?"

"I don't know. I guess he told people."

Clara looked startled. "Mistake, mistake." She shook her head.
"You don't tell nobody. If dem ever ask you at school, deny. And if
any of dem ask, you tell me their name. I will call they parents and
pitch a bitch. Dem couldn't come to quiz you about something so
personal. Not while I here protecting."

David walked over to Clara's bureau, regarding the portrait of
Manny that had slowly waned under a constant siege of sunlight. She
had just purchased some rose water and a new bottle of Nivea. The
large mineral oil was nearly consumed. He bit his lip and looked
dolefully at her. "Why is mom *doing* this?"

"Darling, believe you me, she intends well. She cares and loves you
true. But she trying to come back to ya life through false ways."

"I see," David said, though he didn't completely understand.

"Sounds complicated, I realize. But don't fret. You will know the
meaning of everything," Clara told him. "For soon you shall see."

Things began to happen that Clara could not explain, and for a while she and David were distracted from their concern with the psychologist. Often when they were asleep late at night, the phone would ring insistently until Clara got up and answered it; then suddenly, the line would click and go dead. David would hear her yelling "Hello, who is it? Hello? Hello?" The wind would cry through the barren trees and the moonlight would paint a rabid foam upon the restless Sound. Sometimes, after the phone had rung, they would hear the civil-defense horn wailing in downtown Rye.

Then Clara began receiving strange envelopes in the mail, letters postmarked Brooklyn without a return address. Nothing written would be inside them; enclosed were coca leaves and dried white petals of vandas. Each time Clara opened one of these envelopes, she'd have strange dreams at night. When she recounted the dreams to David, they always sounded lovely: elaborate weddings held at the summit of Blue Mountain, all the guests wearing black tie and white tulle, the ceremony dusted with fine falling snow. She dreamed of women giving birth to lovely porcelain dolls, of finding emeralds in her wanderings through the black hills of Port Antonio. Unfortunately, Clara explained, in Jamaican folklore dreams portended the opposite of their actual allegory, so that weddings meant funerals, and giving birth meant dying, and finding riches meant poverty.

Early one school morning when Leona had not stayed at home, Clara came into David's room before five A.M. and woke him. Through a haze of sleep, he saw her hurrying toward him, her yellow night-gown rippling with air. "Chi chi buddo," she sang. "Chi chi buddo. Some o' dem a holler, some a bawl, some a cling-cling, some o' dem a holler, some a bawl, some a blackbird, some o' dem a holler, some a bawl."

David frowned at her and yawned. "It's so early," he complained.

"Get up, man. We going to Brooklyn."

"Brooklyn! How can we go to Brooklyn? I've got school."

"We'll be back here by ten-thirty. You'll miss two class. Won't kill you."

"Why are we going?"

"We going to Gypsy."

David sat up in bed. "Really?" he said. "A Gypsy?"

"Yes, man. So hurry up and ready."

A taxi came to get them at a quarter to six and they drove in a drowsy silence to the train station. Heavy dew glistened on the lawns. The turning leaves, stained by early sun, were tinged with a corona of mauve. A *New York Times* truck swept through the sleeping estates, a muscled arm throwing folded papers in a high arc. Dogs were awakened and they bayed and yapped. Lights went on. Frumpy, half-asleep housewives reluctantly appeared at their front doors.

On the half-empty train, each sat preoccupied with his own thoughts. David had brought along his school things; the taxi would be dropping him off as soon as they returned. Clara was wearing one of her blue wool suits. She sat at attention, drumming her fingers on a patent-leather purse Leona had recently handed down to her.

"There's something about movement dat makes you feel at ease," she said, turning to David. "I suppose it's because there's some sort of reason dat always make you leave one place and travel to de oddar. One place keeps you until an oddar one call, but between two o' dem you not really yaself. When me travel dis train, sometimes me feel to have so much resolve, but as soon as I come off at Flatbush or even in Rye, me don't feel so resolve again. Seems like I made best decisions when the wheels were going 'bam bam, bam bam,' like heartbeat of an oddar life. Sometimes when I have all sorts of worries, me take de subway. Me love to ride it out Coney Island. A far trip not so many people ride as it go along. And I always feel fine because me know at de end is de sea."

"Are you worried now?" David asked her as he gathered his school books closer to him.

She nodded, then she pointed to her solar plexus. "I'm churning up in here."

"Why are you churning?"

"A lot of things gone sour. Icey, first of all, not really getting better. Then ya muddar taking you to head doctor. And now all dese letters and dried herb."

"But what do they mean?"

"Could be somebody trying to push me not to trouble."

"But who could be sending them?"

Clara turned from the dirty train window to peer at David. "Who you think?"

He shrugged. "Dora?"

Clara raised her eyebrows. "Only party I know would trouble me so till."

"But she's Icey's friend. Why would she want her to be harmed?"

Clara paused for a moment. "Yes, a true dat. Though would be I suppose like killing my sister—Icey sort of play dat role. My only sister dead when I was small."

David brushed the hair out of his eyes. "You never told me that."

She turned to peer at him scornfully. "Good I don't tell you since now we both know what you capable of doing. A lot me will never tell you now."

Though he wanted to speak up, David purposely remained silent. They had never yet discussed what he had read in the letters; though he knew Clara realized he understood a lot more about her than she had actually let on. He looked around the train. It was not quite 6:30 and there were only a few commuters in business suits. The majority of the passengers seemed to be people coming off night jobs: stocky black women in white hospital uniforms and grizzled men wearing coveralls.

They got off the number 4 train at the same stop in Brooklyn they usually got off at to go to Clara's apartment. However, they walked in an altogether different direction down unfamiliar streets. Clara

seemed to instinctively know her way around. She mused under her
breath as they passed familiar delicatessens, shops, and houses. At
one point she turned to David. "Mr. Chatterbox, Blossie Chatelaine
live dere," she said, pointing to a seedy four-floor brick walk-up.
"Since you two so familiar." They finally stopped at a commercial
building a half a block down from Blossom's apartment. Clara peered
at the number above the door and bunched up her lips. "This a dry
cleaner. She don't live in no dry cleaner."

"Maybe she lives upstairs," David suggested.

"But me na see no steps."

David went to the opposite side of the store, where he had noticed
a door. He cupped his hands against the dusty glass to ward off the
sun's early-morning glare. In the dimness he could make out a steep
flight of narrow stairs. "Here we go," he said.

As they climbed up to the fifth floor, behind several apartment
doors they heard what David imagined to be hungry children crying.
Each time they reached a landing, a door would crack open until it
pulled against the chain lock, and a suspicious black face would peer
out at them. "Ginal," somebody even muttered.

"Jamaicans," David remarked to Clara.

"Seems so," she agreed.

When they finally arrived at the appropriate apartment, Clara was
panting from the climb. "Wouldn't surprise me if people coming wid
Obeah trouble dead on de way," she rasped. "Problem solved. Mission accomplished."

She knocked and they heard several minutes of shuffling around
inside before someone came to the door. David noticed that the woman
who answered didn't check first to see who it was.

He was disappointed by what he saw, having imagined a wild-
haired woman with frenzied eyes who painted her dark cheeks with
gold triangles and wore dresses made of torn paisley bedspreads.
Orgena—that was her name—actually looked like any middle-aged
Jamaican woman David had met at Blanche's Beauty; the style of her
hair was the only thing that set her apart. She wore it straightened
and oiled, quite long, and separated into twenty braided locks, each
of them fastened to gold beads.

As Orgena introduced herself to Clara, they walked inside the two-room apartment cluttered with thrift-store furniture. The whole apartment reeked of Martinizing. David noticed a red fester on Orgena's right cheek: a knife wound, perhaps, that would not heal. Flies that had managed to evade the cold buzzed around the dingy rooms and kept alighting on her sore.

Orgena kept staring relentlessly, which made David uncomfortable. She had exotic eyes. "Sit down here in de living room," she instructed him in a low treble voice. "On de sofa." She pointed to an old captain's bed.

The dirt-encrusted windows in the living room were glazed over with steam rising from the dry cleaner's downstairs. Every so often the floorboards would rumble from the motion in the metal vats below, which David imagined to be constantly spinning with delicate silks and wools being washed by special dry-cleaning chemicals. He began noticing wooden objects all over the apartment, some of them mahogany figures with deep gashes for eyes and long, meticulously crafted handles that held together hundreds of thin rushes, which collectively resembled some sort of weapon.

Clara had brought with her the weird letters she had received. She opened her patent-leather handbag and showed them to Orgena, who glanced at the coca leaves and the vanda blossoms and told her, "Dis rubbish. You have nothing to worry. Somebody just trying to frighten you. This not Obeah."

"Good cigar," Clara said, relieved. She took a few deep breaths and then went on to explain about Icey's illness, which, though stable, would eventually kill her.

Swatting a fly away from her wound, Orgena asked if by chance Clara knew the name of the Obeah man working against Icey from Jamaica. Clara shook her head and said she would try to find out.

"Would help me if you could get dat, though I don't insist. I have ways to interrupt him. Though more powerful, him can't compete with my closeness. But better you arrange to bring this friend of yours to me."

Clara said that would be impossible; and then Orgena offered to go and see Icey. Clara thanked her for such a kindness. Finally, Orgena clapped her hands and got up from where they were sitting and led

Clara over to a bureau, on top of which were a dozen ivory figurines, naked men and women, pierced with pins at vital places. The pinheads were large colored baubles: red, turquoise, and black. "Only have two woman left," she explained. "Me sent to Jamaica for more. Now, you must do exactly as I tell you." Orgena beckoned Clara to follow her into the bedroom.

A few minutes later, Clara emerged from her private conference in Orgena's bedroom. She beckoned David. "Time for you."

David instinctively shrank into himself, now overcome by the fumes of dry cleaning, which to him smelled like a mixture of talc and gasoline.

"Come on now, child," Clara insisted. He finally got up off the sofa and followed her into the bedroom.

The light was dimmer there than in the living room. He sat next to Orgena on a sagging bed whose springs complained. Orgena reached toward him. "Come let me look at your hand."

David stuck out his arm rigidly, eyes closed, and felt her scratchy fingers tracing the lines along his palm. "Yes," she said in her low, husky voice. "Just as I suspect."

"What?" David asked, opening his eyes.

"Two o' you knowed each oddar from a past life."

"Really, we did?" David was terribly excited.

"From where?" Clara asked, surprising him with a tone of skepticism, as though she felt Orgena had gone a bit too far.

"In Bavaria it was," Orgena said loftily, which sent Clara into peals of laughter.

"What de devil wrong wid you?" Orgena asked her.

"You mean to say that I was snow maiden and him was me consort?"

"I see plenty of such things in hands," Orgena insisted.

"All right, what you see?"

Orgena paused significantly, peering even closer. "Your worries about his muddar—perfectly right. But if you do what I say, you will prevail. Unfortunately, I see something later on. I see years of torment."

"Which torment?" Clara had turned serious.

"Not sure," Orgena said, shaking her head. "You must remember dat love always give way to sad. Use this, though; then it won't be so hard," she said, reaching to a drawer in a small, worn, wooden night table next to her bed. She took out an amber-colored bottle of oil and a small, frond-shaped candle and gave them to Clara.

Every Thursday afternoon at 4:30, Leona and David climbed into Leona's Oldsmobile and drove north on the Saw Mill River Parkway to the Cross River Institute. Since they usually didn't get back to the house until close to nine in the evening, Clara would dutifully pack David's dinner in a Tupperware bowl: chops—pork, veal, or lamb— on a bed of iceberg lettuce saturated with oil and vinegar. David would eat his meal in the car before they arrived at the Cross River Institute. More often than not, the salad dressing dribbled on his pants. After the first two mishaps, Leona took to carrying a Baggie full of baking soda in her purse and made him dust the powder on his stains.

They would finally leave the Saw Mill River Parkway and drive several miles along a lonely dirt road that eventually brought them to a whitewashed rustic building that reminded David of a day-camp office. They went inside and walked down a creaky hallway to a bank of cramped offices. On the first visit, out of one of them emerged Dr. Stevens, who introduced himself to David. Dr. Stevens was short and pudgy with a round face and pommaded jet-black hair that grayed dramatically at the temples. He gave a limp handshake; his fingers were pale and stubby and there were lots of dark hairs on the crowns of his hands.

As it turned out, David did not have his therapy at the Cross River Institute, which was where his mother's group therapy was held. He would now drive with Dr. Stevens five miles up the road to his private

215

office, which was in the basement of his own home. After the session, David would take a taxi back to the institute.

David was angry that his mother purposely had not explained to him all these logistics. Perhaps she'd thought he might refuse point-blank to drive with a stranger, although this man *was* supposed to be his psychologist. During that first car ride together, Dr. Stevens tried to make David feel comfortable. "Has your mother discussed with you why you're coming to see me?" Dr. Stevens had a habit of clicking his gold wedding band against the steering wheel.

"She basically told me. We didn't really discuss it all that much," David answered in a small voice.

They were driving through a long stretch of road where there were no houses; piles of rotting leaves stood at the side of the road. Dark was thick around them and David felt nervous. He suddenly heard a sucking sound and then saw a flame. Dr. Stevens was lighting a pipe.

"Do you have to smoke in the car?"

"Oh, sorry. Smoke bother you?"

"Neither of my parents smokes. I'm not used to it."

"Just a minute then," Dr. Stevens said patiently, and put down his window. Scarves of cool air blew in, entangling the smoke and pulling it outside.

"Anyway, as I was saying, do you understand why you're coming to see me?"

"I've got problems," David said self-importantly.

"You say that as though someone else told you to say it."

"Well, *that*'s true. Mom told me I was coming here on account of some test at school. My grades are okay. So I don't get it." David purposely tried to sound thickheaded.

Dr. Stevens laughed. "Some test at school," he echoed. Then he turned to David confidentially. "Can I tell you something?"

"What?" David pressed against the window, repelled by the feeling of intimacy Dr. Stevens appeared to be forcing on him.

"I saw that test. It was a load of garbage."

"It was?" David asked happily.

"Are you kidding? Tell you another thing. Your results were just fine, as far as I could tell. And I see these kinds of tests every day.

So let's start with this idea, David, and that is you're perfectly okay. You don't have any more problems than other children your age. You just have more things standing in your way. But if you and I can talk about these obstacles together and you try and let me know what you feel, we'll have a successful visit together."

"How long do I have to keep coming?" David asked.

"That all depends."

"But I don't even know you," David said, his heart brimming with dread.

"Exactly," Dr. Stevens said. "We have to get to know each other. And that's going to take time. So, at least for now, we can just chat about anything you want."

"Can I eat as we talk?" David asked.

Dr. Stevens shrugged. "Didn't you have dinner?"

"In the car."

"Actually, I'm glad you mentioned eating, because when we get to my house I'm going to have to have dinner with my family. Just for twenty minutes. But I have a wonderful office and playroom downstairs. You can read *Highlights* or look at the encyclopedias until I come down."

"That's swell," David said, rolling his eyes.

Dr. Stevens lived in a refurbished two-level colonial house on five wooded acres. The front and back doors were painted hunter green. Mrs. Stevens greeted them at the back door. She had a bony face and permed red hair. Dr. Stevens ushered David through a passageway that led to an office annex. As they walked down it, David heard a terrific barking and stopped, stiffening.

"What's that?" he asked Dr. Stevens.

"Our German shepherds," he said proudly.

"Do they bite?"

"Heavens, no. They're just good watchdogs."

They walked past a door with a window through which David could see into the main house. He saw huge dogs circling and sniffing the air. Beyond them, huddled over an erector set, were two towheaded boys, who turned to gawk at him.

"Are they your sons?" he asked.

"Yes, indeed."

Before Dr. Stevens left David in his office, he showed him where the playroom was in case he felt inclined to use it. The office reeked of pipe tobacco and its walls were lined with books. David sat down in a leather chair next to Dr. Stevens's antique desk and riffled through his collection of sterling-silver pens and pencils and a gallery of studio portraits of his wife and children that were taken against a sky-blue backdrop. He wondered if the doctor's family would feel pity for him, his problems being such that he had to be driven thirty-five miles to see their father. In a way, David felt insulted that Dr. Stevens's personal life was given priority. Couldn't Mrs. Stevens keep her husband's dinner warm until after David had his session? Then David realized it was probably good for him to have a few moments alone. After all, Clara said he was supposed to be clamming up during sessions or making up stories, and that was like going on stage. Which required composure.

When Dr. Stevens finished dinner, he came back to the office and from his desk took out a leather-bound book of inkblots. He asked David to look at each of the blue smears and tell him what they reminded him of. David said they all resembled either butterflies or praying mantises. He knew his interpretations were crucial and hoped these were the answers normal children would give. After he put away the inkblots, Dr. Stevens asked David what he and his father did on Saturdays. David described how he had been going to the city for quiet dinners, how during the summer they would play their games of golf and then eat a late lunch at Burger King. Dr. Stevens asked if he had more fun with his father than with his mother; and David, thinking Dr. Stevens was leading up to something, said, "I love my parents both the same."

Next, Dr. Stevens tried to get David to talk about school—which classes he liked the best, what he thought of his teachers, and how his teachers made him feel. In the middle of everything, David said, "And you think this is like friends talking?"

Dr. Stevens frowned. "You tell me."

"I don't discuss this stuff with friends. I don't even discuss this stuff with myself."

"I see. What do you discuss with yourself?"

"I just like to get school over with and go home. School is just school. Sometimes it's fun. Sometimes it's not."

"You'd rather be home after school."

"I have fun at home."

"How do you have fun?"

David paused. "Well, Clara—that's the lady who takes care of me, she's from Jamaica—she and I write to the soap operas and tell them what we think should happen in the stories."

"So you like to watch soap operas?"

"We watch them every day. When we don't like what we see—well, we've already kicked in two televisions."

"Isn't that a little wasteful?" Dr. Stevens asked skeptically, as though he didn't believe David.

"Not really," David said, "because one of the TVs we kicked in was a really old black-and-white that didn't work very well. Although we did kick in a new one. But Clara won that from a contest she entered in the *National Enquirer.*"

Dr. Stevens raised his eyebrows. David knew he was more convinced now. "What else do you and Clara do?"

David sighed as he cast inwardly for something else to say. "We throw darts at pictures of my father."

Dr. Stevens shifted uneasily in his chair. "Really?"

"After my parents split up, mom boxed a whole bunch of dad's photographs. Clara and I tack them up on the back of my bedroom door. We throw darts and bet against each other."

"What do you bet?"

"If I lose, I clean my room. If I win, she bakes totos."

Dr. Stevens lowered his head and belched. "Toto is something Jamaican?" he asked.

"Pronounced 'tawe-tawe,'" David said.

"And what else do you do?" Dr. Stevens asked.

David sighed, feeling like a Yo-Yo. Then he had an idea. "In the afternoons, Clara doesn't ask me a lot of questions like the way you're doing. So I'm not used to this."

Dr. Stevens glanced at his watch. He smiled. "It's time to conclude for tonight anyway."

He went upstairs and called a taxi for David, who remained downstairs in the office waiting for it to arrive. He was minding his own business, flipping through a *Highlights* magazine, when he heard the clicking of toenails on the polished wood floors. He looked up and saw two ferocious faces: The German shepherds had managed to get loose. War dogs, was David's first thought. He bristled and his movement worried the dogs, who sat down on flexed, muscular haunches and commenced barking at him. David climbed up on his chair and started shrieking, "Get away from me! Leave me alone!"

Dr. Stevens came running in and herded the dogs out of the room. "David, I'm awfully sorry about this," he boomed nervously. "It's never happened before. Somebody must have left one of the doors open. Come down off the chair. There's nothing to be afraid of. They don't bite."

"Do you realize how big those dogs are?" David asked angrily. "They're big enough to scare the shit out of anybody."

Dr. Stevens smiled uneasily. "I told you, they're just watchdogs."

"Tell that to the coroner."

David's taxi arrived a few minutes later, and as he left the office, he noticed the youngest of Dr. Stevens's children staring out into the passageway. He narrowed his eyes and wagged his finger accusingly at the boy, who stuck his tongue out at him. After he got back to the Cross River Institute, he had to wait another fifteen minutes until his mother's session ended.

When they got home that evening, David hurried into the house while Leona jockeyed the Oldsmobile into the garage. Clara was sitting in the kitchen, wearing pantaloon pajamas, reading the evening paper.

"Wha gwan?" she asked him.

"Dem ras up dere, you know."

"Don't you speak such nasty words. Especially round your muddar. Don't vex me tonight."

"You won't believe what happened."

Clara made a harlequin face and lifted her finger to her lips. "Ssh. Wait till she gone to her bed, then come to me room and labrish."

"Eh-heh," David said.

"Go look in the fridge now. Something waiting on you."

David yanked open the refrigerator door, causing the bottles inside
to clang against one another. "Gizzarda!" he cried gleefully.

"Mind you break the whole damn fridge tonight," Clara scolded
him.

Leona came into the house to find David stuffing himself with the
banana-shaped bakery cookies Clara had brought from Brooklyn. "He
shouldn't have both totos in the afternoon and these at night," she
complained to Clara. "You're going to make him into a tub."

"Is all right," Clara said coldly. "Him need something sweet when
he comes home. After dat mess," she said under her breath.

"What did you say?" Leona asked.

"Nothing, darling," Clara said. "You mistake heavy breathing for
words."

"Goodnight, Clara," Leona said in an exasperated tone, and walked
to the staircase.

"You know, love," Clara called after her, "you really do look tired.
I don't think night driving agrees with you. Perhaps you should
reconsider this whole thing."

Leona shook her head and kept walking.

After David got into his pajamas, he hurried to Clara's room. He
found her sitting upright in bed, her face blued by television. She was
alternating between reading a paperback copy of *Rosemary's Baby* and
watching a Rockettes special. On her bureau two human-shaped candles were flickering. They had a sweet yet sickly smell, like burning honey. Their flames looked weak and irregular, and David felt
skeptical of any changes they could effect in the scheme of his
own world.

"So, wha happen tonight?" Clara asked, splaying the book against
her belly, glancing for a moment at her candles.

First David told her about the dogs.

"You mean to say him come to ask you why you get afraid?"

David then told Clara that Dr. Stevens had said the school tests his
mother had made so much of meant nothing at all.

"Ya too lie!" She was shocked.

"Yes, man, I telling you," David said, and then explained how he
had to be driven from the institute to Dr. Stevens's house, where he

was gawked at by Dr. Stevens's family, and how he had to wait while they all had dinner.

Clara screwed up her face and slapped her hands upon her cheeks. "God in heaven, dis worse den I ever imagine."

"It's not that bad," David said.

She looked at him shrewdly. "You don't find it peculiar?"

"How am I supposed to know? I never been to a psychologist before."

"All right, so what you told dat crook in dere?" Clara asked.

When David explained about mashing up the televisions, she giggled, but when he told her about throwing darts at the photographs of his father, Clara got upset.

"Dat is de wrong thing to said to him!" she cried out. "Don't you dare put me up 'gainst ya father, even if it be in joking."

"But you told me to lie!" David exclaimed.

"Not in reference to Mr. Hart." Clara took the book off her stomach, leaned forward, and grabbed David's arm. "You father is not to fool wid. Understand what I say. Me tell him not to fret, that you and I would juke up de doctor. So me can't have you telling de doctor I disrespect *him.*"

"Okay, okay, I'll be more careful," David said.

"Mark you, me not angry," Clara said more softly. "You just get me excited." She shrugged. "Must always be room for mistake when you playing such a game." She reached to the night table for her Timex. It was ten o'clock. "Okay, child, night getting late," she said. "Come kiss me and go to ya bed."

David put his arms around Clara's neck. "I'll be more careful next time," he promised her.

"Good cigar," she said, kissing him on the cheek.

The next time David was waiting in the office for Dr. Stevens to finish dinner, he was drawn to the vast bookcases, whose top shelves were too high for him to reach. The more inaccessible they were, the more interesting he imagined they'd be. He dragged an antique spindle chair across the cable-knit rug and stood on it, making a survey of the titles. The books, advertising all sorts of psychological behavior, were wedged tightly together and seemed not to have been read in a very long time.

David yanked down the volumes from their dusty haven, thumbing through them to see if there were any pictures of naked people. His fingers had an oily residue left from Clara's salad dressing and made marks on the pages. Eventually, he discovered a five-volume set called *Sexual Behavior*. He dislodged the books and sat in the chair. Thrilled, he began flipping through the first one, stopping whenever he got to drawings or photographs. He saw the human body in different stages of growth; women's breasts; pubises that formed bushy triangles; and pages of men and women in sexual positions. He began to feel a tingling in his groin he had never felt before. His palms got sweaty. He grew breathless as he read and reread descriptions of the vagina and ovulation and menstruation. Finally, he found the chapters on abnormal sexual behavior.

All during his perusal, David had been keeping his ears cocked for Dr. Stevens's arrival. When he finally heard the door to the passageway open, he stood up quickly, replaced the books, dragged the chair back next to the desk, and sat down. Frightened that Dr. Stevens might discover his erection, David covered his crotch with his jacket. He tried to picture gory scenes on hospital operating tables or fatal car accidents to calm himself down.

"Tell me about some of the things you and your parents did before they got divorced," Dr. Stevens said, taking out his pipe, filling it with tobacco, and tamping it down.

David shrugged. "Not very much. My father usually went off by himself."

"Surely the three of you did things together sometimes."

"He was at the golf course all weekend. And in the winter he played squash. And at night, he and mom locked themselves in their bedroom."

"How did that make you feel?"

"I didn't want to be around them."

"Why?"

" 'Cause they were acting weird."

"What do you mean by weird?"

David groaned. "You really want to hear this?"

Dr. Stevens grinned. "Of course I do."

"Well, you see, when he got home from work, he and mom would get dressed up."

"How do you mean?" Dr. Stevens put his pipe down in a ceramic ashtray and began stroking his clean-shaven chin. David wondered if he would look more like an authentic psychiatrist if he grew a beard.

"She dressed up like him and he dressed up like her." David paused, waiting to see how Dr. Stevens reacted.

"Could you be a little more specific?"

"Well, she got into his golfing clothes, and he put on her mink and stockings. Then he started acting like her. He waved his hands and served her a drink."

"How would you know this, David, unless you saw it?" Dr. Stevens asked.

"I've never seen them. I've just figured it out. There were clues. Over a long period of time. And then Clara saw them once by accident. It was a Saturday morning and I was at a friend's house. They thought she had gone to Brooklyn the night before, but she hadn't left yet. They did it with their door open."

"Clara told you she saw?"

"No." David knew it would be wrong for Clara to tell him this. "But I overheard a telephone conversation she had with her friend Icey."

"I see."

"After that, on weeknights when my parents used to do it, Clara would deliberately keep me with her in her bedroom, which is on the other side of the house. 'Cause you could hear the noises."

"Hold on a second," Dr. Stevens said. "Did you sleep with Clara those nights?"

"No way," David said, knowing that sleeping with Clara would prompt a whole barrage of other questions.

"Now, what noises?" Dr. Stevens asked.

"Dad talked real girlish and mom lowered her voice and boomed like a man."

"David," Dr. Stevens asked sternly, "are you being truthful with me?"

"Why would I lie?" David asked him.

Sitting in the taxi on the way back to the Cross River Institute, David realized he was still aroused. He kept thinking of the close-up depictions of the vagina and the descriptions of foreplay. When he arrived at the institute, he went into the children's playroom, closed the door, and lay on the linoleum floor. He thought more about the pictures in Dr. Stevens's books and began touching himself through his pants. As he rubbed harder and harder, the room began to pulsate and then to spin. It was as though there were an itching inside his penis, which needed to be scratched, except the itching would not go away, grew deeper and deeper, and soon exploded in a strange shudder of immense relief. David had never had this experience before and suddenly felt terribly guilty about giving himself such pleasure.

He dozed for a few minutes and then got up. Hunching over his softening erection, he tiptoed to the conference room, where Leona's group therapy was in its final moments. He listened outside the door.

"Well, your sister-in-law sounds screwed up to me," a man was saying.

"I was trying to tell you that," a woman answered him. "She

smothered her kid and he never had a chance to make friends. That's overprotection."

"Well, I have exactly the opposite problem." David heard his mother speak up, which made his heart jump. "I don't smother David. If anything, I pay him less attention than I should, and he still won't make friends."

"Yeah, but that's because he spends so much time with that housekeeper you have," the first woman said. "She's probably the one who's overprotective. She's probably the one who smothers him."

"It's not like that at all," his mother said emphatically. "If anything, he smothers *her*. It all started with him speaking her Caribbean patois. Now he can do it so perfectly he can even fool her friends over the phone if he wants to."

"Sounds obsessive," someone said, which annoyed David.

"You said you're never home very much," another man went on. "So I can understand why he might get obsessed with her."

"What about children of working mothers who are taken care of by nannies?" Leona said. "They don't necessarily develop obsessions."

"Okay, we're out of time," someone else said. David heard chairs scraping against the floor.

He was upset and embarrassed that his mother was discussing him with strangers and that the strangers gave opinions about him without even knowing who he was. He felt shamed that she had spoken about his "obsession" with Clara to the other members of her therapy group. David ran back to the children's room and slammed the door so as not to be seen by anyone.

"Mom, what do you talk about in your sessions?" he asked her innocently on the homeward drive.

"Mostly marriage problems."

"Not about me?"

She shifted uneasily behind the steering wheel. "Oh, sure, sometimes."

"You don't say anything bad, do you?"

"Why would I do that?"

"Aren't you supposed to say what you feel? Aren't there things about me that bother you?"

Leona turned and peered strangely at David in the darkness, repeatedly broken by the light of highway lamps, which rotated through the car like blades. He sensed she suspected he had eavesdropped. But she didn't say anything. Maybe she felt it was wrong to show such distrust.

"If I talk about you, it's only as a reference for how you make me feel about something. I don't discuss you in detail, if that's what you're asking."

Liar, thought David. "Does everybody talk about sex?" He asked the question that nagged at him the most.

"Yes."

"About things like impotence and frigidity?" He used new words he had learned in the book on sexual behavior.

"Who the hell told you about that?" Leona asked.

"Dr. Stevens."

"Jesus." She inflected heavily on the first syllable.

"Mom, do people take their clothes off in the conference room?"

She turned to him, her face lit jaggedly. "If you don't stop this ridiculousness, I'm going to slug you."

"Sorry," David told her.

"I'm sure you don't tell de doctor how you fart up me room nights," Clara told David when he came to see her later that evening.

"Why would I want to tell him that?"

"Because if you supposed to chat everything, might as well chat dat, too."

"I don't want to tell him about that."

"Then just remember to tell him where to get off at when him ask you too personal."

"Me tell him some things make him shit up himself," David boasted.

"Wha ya tell him?" Clara sounded delighted.

"Me tell him say me parents lock up in they room. That me father dress a woman and me muddar dress a man."

"Ya too lie! Hiiiii," Clara laughed. "What else you said?"

"That she talk like man and him talk like woman."

"Good cigar. But where you get such cleverness?"

"I found books in his office." David spoke normally again.

Clara looked shocked. "Shame on you, man! I thought I learn you not to trouble oddar people's things."

David turned and smiled at her. "Only people I care about."

Clara reflected for a moment. "Well, I don't suppose it will harm any of us; after all, it gives you something amusing for to tell him."

"Him couldn't believe."

"Listen na, me have something to add," Clara said as she leaped off her bed and began prancing around the room. Her eyes shone with wickedness. "Next time you go there, tell doctor ya parents forced me to serve them their dinner without me clothes. Them made me come in wid all sorts of food and sweetie. Tell doctor I pitched a bitch first time but I'm far away from me country and can't manage myself without this job. I take off me clothes and bore my breasts when it was the last living thing I ever wanted to do."

David was dumbfounded. "You really want me to say that?"

"Yes, bebe. Tell him. And listen na," she added. "When the whole thing finished off, I'll gi' you something for to feed his ras dogs, make them shit up his house like duck!"

"Why do you find Clara so interesting?" Dr. Stevens asked David at the beginning of their next session.

"It's not that I find her interesting as much as that I spend a lot of time with her."

"Why do you spend so much time with her?"

"Because no one else is around."

"Don't you ever see friends after school?"

"Sometimes. Not that much."

"How come?"

"Because I don't like any sports but swimming, and everybody else always plays basketball or baseball. And also because I guess I like to talk to myself."

"In patois?"

David shrugged.

"Why don't you describe patois to me a little more."

David clammed up, thinking if he talked about patois, it would in some way compromise Clara. "It's nothing really, just English with a funny accent."

"And you speak it to Clara?" Dr. Stevens asked.

"Only sometimes," David said, beginning to peel his thumbnail.

"But when your school called, they told me you were speaking patois incessantly in class. That you've used it like a secret language."

"I only did that when I was frustrated. When Clara was angry with me."

"About what?"

"I went into her room and read through some of her letters."

"Tell me more," Dr. Stevens suggested.

"She was acting so mysterious when it came to them. She kept them in her suitcase and read them late at night and always made a big deal about locking them up."

"All the more reason for you to be curious," Dr. Stevens sympathized. "What did you find in the letters?"

David suddenly realized he had carried the conversation too far into a subject he knew Clara would heartily object to. It was time to retreat. "I didn't have a chance to read much. Her friends' handwriting was pretty illegible. I only looked at the letters, you see, because I love to talk to Clara, especially listen to patois and even see her Jamaican friends. It bothered me she was keeping any of it from me."

"Sounds like patois is important to you," Dr. Stevens pointed out.

"Well, it's just part of Clara."

"Do me a favor then, just speak a little for me."

David shook his head.

"What's there to lose?" Dr. Stevens asked. "You spoke it at school to your teachers, why not speak to me?"

David looked at him directly. "I said no and I mean it."

Dr. Stevens flushed, and David felt sure he was angry.

"So you told him how I served ya parents stark raving or not?" Clara asked when David arrived home from school the following afternoon.

They were in her bedroom and she was sending a package of Leona's unwanted clothing to a needy family in Jamaica.

"We didn't get a chance last night," David said, "though he did want to talk about you."

"So him start on *me*," Clara muttered as she carefully fitted several blouses and a pair of hose into a cardboard liquor box. She reached for a ball of green twine that was in her apron pocket and began winding it around the box. "So what you tell him?"

"I spoke patois for him."

Clara dropped the ball of twine. "No, you don't. Ya not so stupid to tell him something private you and I share."

David picked up the ball of twine and gave it back to Clara. "Oh, I just sang him a song and got it out of the way."

"What you sang him, you professional fool?" Clara asked angrily.

"I just sang him 'Donkey City,'" David said, trying desperately to keep a serious face.

There was an angry silence. "But you don't sing him de part I taught you—'Me gone down to Donkey City to circumcise my kitty' —do you?"

"But that's the best part," David said, bursting into giggles.

Clara was still glowering at him. "You running a joke wid me, right?" she asked.

David nodded, continuing to laugh.

Clara drew the air through her teeth. Then she grabbed a pair of house scissors off the ironing board and began shearing the air before David's face. "Dis stuff not for ramping. Me don't want him know me tell you nothing 'bout no circumcising kitties. For den him will twist it 'round and tell ya muddar I talking to you 'bout such things. And den ya muddar would cut me right out her life for double-crossing her."

"She would not."

"A true, man," Clara said, working the scissors again. "As God is in heaven."

"She'd never fire you."

"If she knew me have you making up lies—what you saying?" Clara replaced the scissors on the ironing board and sat on her bed. "Come here to me for a minute," she told David.

David went and squeezed next to Clara, tilting his head on her shoulder while she snaked a plump arm around him.

"It's not my pleasure to cross ya muddar, but I must do it for I believe this psychiatrist—"

"Psychologist," David corrected her.

"Don't interrupt me."

"I'm not going to a psychiatrist!"

"Two of dem de same."

"They are not."

"You listening me or not?" Clara fumed.

"All right, go ahead," David said with exasperation.

"I must trouble dis business for I feel it will hurt you if it get out of hand."

David nodded. "Don't worry, Clara. I understand."

When they finished their dinner that evening, Clara confessed to a hankering for ice cream. She was about to call a taxi to go to Baskin-Robbins when she remembered that lately Leona had been using Peter's stick-shift Volvo (which got much better gas mileage than the Oldsmobile) to drive back and forth between Manhattan and Rye.

"Me would drive us quick and fast, but me don't have America license," she told David. "Besides, don't see good at nights."

David shrugged. "So what do you want me to do?"

"Don't your father used to take you out driving before him get dis new car him have?"

David looked at her timidly. "But I haven't driven in a long time."

"But you can do it," Clara coaxed him. "We don't have to go far. "I'll coach you. Ya muddar keys upstairs."

David frowned. He was afraid. "What if a policeman stops us?"

Clara peered out the window into the darkness. "How dem gwan see who driving at night? Long as we don't do crazy things? If you sure you can drive properly. Anyway, if police stops us, I will control," she boasted. Since me get to know some o' dem already . . . " Clara reflected for a moment. "Could always said on de way to hospital, dat me get heart attack or burst appendix."

David reluctantly left the kitchen table and went into the living room to get an embroidered pillow off the sofa in order to prop himself up in the driver's seat. Clara waited for him in the kitchen. By the time he returned, she had put on her knitted coat, rubbed some rouge into her cheeks, and covered her head with a paisley scarf. They went out to the garage and climbed into the Oldsmobile. Petrified, David started the engine. He managed to place the car in gear and back carefully out of the garage. Once they pulled out of the driveway, he began to relax somewhat as he accepted the irrevocability of his driving Clara into the town of Rye. David realized she actually inspired daring in him.

Darkened properties flew by them in a precise sweep of their angular hedges. "Better not run dis car so slow." Clara back-seat drove. "Police surely will notice if you drive so. Probably dem will think we two drunks weaving back from a bar."

David squeezed the gas pedal and the speedometer inched up to forty-five.

"Too fast now, David . . . mind dat car, boy!" Clara depressed an imaginary brake in front of her in reaction to a Mercedes that was shooting out of a driveway fifty feet ahead. "Imagine, dem didn't even look!"

"You're making me nervous," David complained.

"Den you must concentrate 'pon de road," Clara said, tilting back her head and expiring a long sigh.

They made it safely into the town of Rye, pulling up in front of Baskin-Robbins. A crowd of patrons were milling in and out of the ice-cream store, which, painted pink and outrageously bright, stuck out in utter tastelessness in the midst of the otherwise sedate wood frontage of the more quaint-looking businesses adjacent to it. Just as they were looking for a parking space, they heard the revving of what sounded like a formula engine. A yellow GTO convertible was double-parked half a block away. Although the weather was in the forties, the top was down and a red-haired girl sat on the crown of the back seat, darting her tongue at an ice-cream cone. Two sturdily built Italian-American boys were in the front. They wore their shirt sleeves tightly rolled up and had their arms cocked on the window jamb, inadvertently flexing their biceps. Their hair was oiled and slicked back.

"Look at David Hart!" the girl hollered when she caught sight of David driving.

David automatically slumped down in the seat.

"Pansy!" shouted the driver. "What the hell are you doing? We'll call the cops on you!"

"How dem know you?" Clara demanded.

"They hang around the school parking lot. She's in tenth. They're in eleventh. Let's go to another ice-cream store."

"Me don't want no oddar ice cream," Clara insisted. "Me heart set 'pon Mandarin Chocolate Sherbet. And if me don't get what I looking for, you will see how I vex."

"But they're looking for trouble," David insisted.

Clara had unwound her scarf and now was retying it carefully, checking herself in the visor mirror on the passenger side. "Dem better not be looking trouble from me," she said, patting the scarf. "For I certainly will gi' it to dem."

A car several spaces ahead of them started up. An elderly gentleman jockeyed his sputtering Plymouth Valiant out into the thoroughfare.

"Take dat space," Clara ordered.

"I haven't really parallel-parked before," David tried to explain.

"Just try." Clara was getting anxious.

By now, David regretted having ventured out in the first place.

He pulled ahead, well forward of the vacant space, and then threw the car into reverse and drove tentatively backward. "Start cutting de wheel," Clara ordered, but the car veered into the space way too sharply. Out of the corner of his eye, David saw the GTO backing up until it pulled alongside them in a double-parked position.

"You better quit while you're ahead," said the kid on the passenger side. His nose was large and crooked, as though it had been broken. "You don't know how to park. You're going to get in trouble. Let us have the space."

Clara clucked her tongue. "Dem have an oddar guess coming. Pull ahead and try again," she said, her voice smoking with anger.

"But they're blocking me," David protested.

"Dem will move."

With great reluctance, David put the car into drive and began to creep forward. His heart was racing.

"Watch out," the other driver cried. "What the fuck are you doing?"

"Keep it coming," Clara said. By now, the back of David's shirt was drenched with sweat.

They had brushed up to within a few inches of the GTO, which finally veered out of their way. By some miracle of Providence, this time David made all the right moves and the Oldsmobile backed perfectly into the space. His head was spinning.

Clara clapped him on the shoulder. "Good cigar."

David turned to her, afraid to get out of the car. "There's another Baskin-Robbins in Portchester," he said hoarsely.

"Dem don't have Mandarin Chocolate Sherbet."

"How do you know?"

"Me friend Eula working over dere. We discuss it and she say dem don't have such flavor."

David sighed. "You're not being truthful."

Clara snorted. "You right, I bullshit you. Because nobody scares me off. Dem is just children. Dem couldn't do me one thing. You should only see people who try to cross me in Jamaica."

"But these kids are townies—greasers," David explained. "They beat up people at school. *I* could be dead tomorrow."

"Doubt it," Clara said, staring out at the GTO, which was idling only a few feet ahead of them, silver smoke curling up from its rattling tailpipe.

They finally got out of the car. The cold made David's sweaty back feel clammy.

As they were walking toward the ice-cream store, one of the kids taunted, "Look at Hart and his dumpy maid." David thought he heard one of them spit. Clara whirled around, clenching her fists. "Dem don't know what dem is doing," she snarled.

"Let's just get the ice cream," David begged, managing to nudge her into the store.

Clara was immediately able to shrug off her angry mood, her face brightening when she saw the long list of ice-cream flavors. "I think

I will have two scoops of Mandarin. But I feel you should try Baseball Nut. I well want to taste dat."

When they left the store, holding their ice-cream cones, David noticed the GTO had backed up and was once again boxing in the Oldsmobile. He began to tremble. Meanwhile, Clara refused to acknowledge the predicament; instead, she turned her attention to a fabric store that they were passing. "Look at dese lovely cloth." She pointed to the window display of bright tartans and ginghams. "Me really should buy dem up and send to Jamaica."

David wanted to get into the car on Clara's side, to avoid having to step near the GTO. He was just about to climb in when one of the kids said, "Look at that fright wig she's wearing, the nigger bitch!"

"You get ethnic wid de wrong person!" Clara shouted venomously. "Two of you a couple of rain slugs. And she's ya whore." She pointed to the girl in the back seat. "Parrot shit is higher in God's order den you in your banana car and your stinking woman!"

For a moment, the teenagers were surprised by Clara's aggressiveness. Then the driver shouted back, "And you're a fucking monkey nigger!"

Clara, holding her half-eaten ice-cream cone, moved slowly toward their car until she stood next to it. David was now so scared he felt numb all over.

"Fuck off," said the girl, puckering up to spit. But before she could do so, Clara smoothly jammed her ice-cream cone into her face. David heard the cone crunching and watched the ice cream mushing all over the girl's cheeks. She yelped in pain, her eyes opened wide in shock, and she began to sob. Then the kid on the passenger side jumped out of the car.

Clara didn't flinch. She calmly reached into the apron pocket beneath her coat and wielded the house scissors. Her eyes blazed with rage, her teeth clenched, grinding over themselves. "Yes, come on," she said in a coaxing voice. "Come right to me and see what I will do you."

The kid froze, wondering what to do. He glanced back at his friend, the driver, who was looking at Clara in horror. David realized they were scared.

"Me na scared o' you." Clara spoke even softer, her voice almost seductive. "Come to me an see how I will cut you to ya balls."

"Get over here, Vito," the driver finally yelled out. "Leave her alone. She's nuts."

A moment later the GTO was screeching away, nearly colliding with another car at the intersection. In both cars, dazed passengers got hurled forward.

David felt too shaken to drive and for a while he and Clara sat in the car, recoiling from the incident in their own whirling silences.

After a long time he said, "You're not somebody to fool with, are you?" once again afraid that such power might be turned against him if he ever did something to make Clara angry.

She seemed to divine his thoughts. "Yes, a' true," she said gravely. "Sometimes I don't know myself. But dat only happens if love not involve. If love exists, anger binds my hands. It only bores inside me."

David started the car, and they slowly drove home in oppressive gloom. They no longer worried about being caught by the police or causing an accident. Puzzled by the whole incident, he kept glancing over at Clara, as though to reassure himself that what had just happened was more than something purely imaginary. By now Clara had lost her own self-possession and had grown extremely agitated. Her fingers dithered on her lap, her lips seemed to form all sorts of unspoken words she wanted to let forth. And as they drove through the protective wings of the quiet estates, David found himself comparing their descent into Rye with those trips to Brooklyn, Clara's other life striking him more and more as filled with violent secrecy.

On David's next visit to Cross River, he brought along Clara's house scissors. While Dr. Stevens was having supper with his family, he took down the volumes on sexual behavior. Selecting the juiciest photographs he could find, he carefully snipped them from each book: couples fornicating in acrobatic positions, some close-up spread shots of a vagina. When he was done clipping, he folded the pictures carefully and put them in his coat pocket. As soon as he got home that evening, he slipped the photos into an empty pink photo album, which his mother at one time had planned to use for Edith's baby pictures, and then hid the album underneath his bed.

One afternoon a few days after he stole the photos, David stopped in to see Clara, who was engrossed in an exciting segment of "The Guiding Light."

"Don't trouble me now," she said, waving him away. "Have you done cleaning ya room like I ask you?"

David shook his head.

"But it's wanted cleaning from long ago. Favors a foul roust in dere. Go about it now!"

David was about to leave when Clara called after him, "Take de blasted vacuum cleaner, lazy child!"

He obediently went into the storage closet down the hallway from Clara's bedroom and took out the new Electrolux, a log-shaped machine painted a metallic turquoise. But when he lugged it back to his room, he was unable to muster enough energy to vacuum. Instead, he took the pink album out from under his bed, lazily flipping through the portfolio of pictures until he found his favorite: a photograph of a couple fornicating dog-style. He began to feel that excited breathlessness he had discovered up in Cross River and then the itching sensation in his groin. He flipped on the vacuum-cleaner switch. He was titillated by the cool, prickly sensation the steel nozzle made when it sucked up the flesh on his palm. He ran the attachment along one side of his cheek. The hose drew part of his mouth inside it and with his tongue David felt the indentation. Then he began to run the vacuum all over his arms and thighs, and then finally tried it between his legs. His heart pounded; the feeling he got with the vacuum cleaner was more intense than he had ever imagined. The suction quickly brought him to a quick, spectacular orgasm. He fell back on the floor, exhausted, and never got around to cleaning his room.

Two days later, when Clara invited him into her bedroom to watch a documentary on Eskimos, he matter-of-factly suggested it might be a wise idea if he vacuumed his room again.

"Good boy," Clara said. "Finally you getting some responsible."

"Uh-huh," David said to himself while lugging the vacuum cleaner out of the medicine closet en route to his bedroom. He turned it on, waiting a few minutes to make it seem that enough time had elapsed for him to vacuum his entire room—in case Clara was listening. Then he took out the pink album, focusing on a picture of a woman straddling her partner, and guided himself into the vacuum-cleaner hose.

The unfortunate thing about using the vacuum cleaner was that due to the powerful noise it made, Clara would hear every time David used it. This meant he had to wait at least another few days so his activity would not seem overly suspicious. The next time he went to the medicine closet, however, the vacuum cleaner was not in the usual place. He hurried into Clara's room.

"Where's the machine?"

"What you talking?"

"Where's the vacuum?"

For a moment, Clara looked puzzled. "Oh, sorry, darling, me leave it downstairs all de way in de library."

David hurried to fetch the machine. After he had carried it back to his room, he was so anxious to masturbate he forgot to wait the few minutes he figured would make Clara assume he was actually getting vacuuming done.

When he brought the machine back to the medicine closet, he noticed Clara had vanished from her bedroom. "The Raging Tide" was airing on television and Jocelyn Martin was listening in on one of her husband's telephone calls. It puzzled David that Clara could have left her favorite drama before a commercial. Suddenly feeling hungry, he thumped down the wooden steps to the kitchen and fixed himself a peanut-butter sandwich. When he came back upstairs, she was sitting on her bed, her attention once again focused on television. She waited until the credits were rolling before addressing him.

"So, you get ya room cleaned?"

"Uh-huh," David said, the peanut-butter sandwich sticking to the roof of his mouth.

Clara stared at him incredulously for a moment. "God in heaven, for such a young boy, you do have a big bamboo!"

David's mouth flopped open. "What are you talking about?"

"Wait, you must be take me for fool!" Clara exclaimed. "Vacuuming ya room practically twice a week!" She folded her arms across her chest. "And the thing is, you too lazy to bother cleaning your place after finishing wid yaself."

David was mortified. Tears welled in his eyes.

"Me was in dere today watching de whole thing," Clara told him. "From start to finish."

Squeezing his eyes closed, David let out a howl.

"Yes, sir, right dere in ya closet. Me want tell you something. In Jamaica we have belief: If too much of a man drop 'pon the floor, a devil can grow from it. Further on, ya thing might come right off if you continue to stuff de Electrolux. And if ya thing don't break, de machine certainly will." Clara suppressed an urge to laugh.

David managed to swallow his mouthful of food. Then he turned away, hiding the tears of shame rolling down his cheeks. Clara had no right to hide in his room; he felt cheated and duped. He looked back at her, his face quivering. "I promise, Clara, I'll never do it again. Please, just don't tell anyone about it."

"So, who to tell?" Clara asked quickly. "Ya muddar?"

"I don't know—anybody."

Clara grunted. "Ya muddar would certainly vex. Keep you at psychiatrist for de rest of your life. You stupid to think me'd tell ya muddar. Don't we share plenty things she don't know?"

David shrugged. "I guess."

"Certainly don't want ya parents think you crazy."

"Do you think I'm crazy?" he asked her in sudden earnest.

"Of course I don't think you crazy," she said, hunching her shoulders. "Me know dat boys get urge that must relieve some way or oddar. I even knowed somebody in Jamaica who kept himself a goat, like you keep ya vacuum cleaner."

During the very next session, when Dr. Stevens returned to the subject of his parents' sexual life, David quite innocently explained what Clara told him about how they forced her to remove all her clothing and serve them dinner. Dr. Stevens asked how he knew all of this.

"How do you think? Clara told me, of course."

Dr. Stevens swallowed hard. "David, this is serious, what you're telling me. I hope you're being as truthful as you can about it."

"Why would I lie?" David asked. "You mean other parents don't do this, too?" He wanted Dr. Stevens to think he was innocently describing what went on without assuming anything was wrong with it.

"I'm not saying that."

"Although my parents probably wouldn't admit to doing it if somebody asked them." As soon as David said this, however, he realized that it probably made his lying more obvious. He was afraid he had gone too far.

This was confirmed the moment they arrived at the Cross River Institute for the following session, when they found Dr. Stevens waiting for them. He motioned to Leona, and they disappeared into one of the offices. David began pacing the children's playroom. He plunged his fingers into a vat of clay, then wrote his name on the blackboard in several different colors of chalk. He thought of the night he had lain on the floor and masturbated. Fifteen interminable minutes passed, and finally his mother emerged from the office. Dr. Stevens stood behind her. His eyes met David's for a moment, and David quickly glanced away, ashamed.

"Let's go!" Leona said, grabbing him by the ear.

"Ouch! Lay off!"

"You son of a bitch. Start walking. We're leaving."

"But we just got here."

"Shut up and get in the car."

Leona quickly started the engine and soon they were flying down the dirt road toward the parkway at an incredible speed. There was urgent silence in the car and David was afraid to ask his mother what was wrong.

"Why did you tell him all that crap?" she finally asked.

"Because I couldn't talk to him! Because I hated going!" he cried out.

"You should've discussed it with me, then."

David shook his head. "You wouldn't listen to me."

"All those lies about your father and me."

"I'm sorry, okay?"

"Where did you get all that smut?"

"I made it up."

"Like hell."

"Don't believe me."

Neither spoke until they reached the Saw Mill River Parkway and the car was rattling along at sixty miles an hour.

"You know, David," Leona said, "Dr. Stevens didn't call me in to verify what you told him. We never would've gotten on that subject at all if something else hadn't happened. He called me in because he found several of his books destroyed. They were missing some pictures that seemed to have been cut out. Sexual pictures."

David froze, his eyes popping out. "I don't know what you're talking about," he said, slinking down in his seat. "Besides, why should he think I did it? Plenty of other people could have."

"Stop lying already!" Leona snapped. "You can't get out of this one. First of all, you were the only patient of his who waited inside his office when he wasn't there."

Lucky me, thought David.

"And anyway," she went on, "his children spied on you the last time."

"Those punks!" David cried.

Leona caught him off-guard; while steering the car, she was able to elbow him and then sweep her right hand at his face. He ducked quickly and she only managed to graze his chin. Finally she grabbed his arm and squeezed. "You nosy brat! Violating people's privacy was one of the reasons why I sent you to him in the first place!"

David fought off the urge to weep, and as he did so, he was struck with an answer to his mother. "If you hadn't sent me, I never would've read his books and then I couldn't have made up those stories about you and dad."

Leona suddenly grew quiet. David glanced over and saw that her shoulders were shaking. Suddenly, a smile rippled across her face. And then she burst into laughter. She laughed until she started crying. She had to pull over to the shoulder of the highway in order to compose herself.

Leona held her head in her hands, shaking it as though she would be eternally dumbfounded. "How did I ever end up with a kid like you?" she implored David. "Telling him all that garbage. I just realized I don't even give a damn what you told him. Let's just go home." She eased the car back onto the highway.

They arrived at the house a half-hour later. "Get ready for bed," Leona ordered David once they got inside.

Clara was sitting at the kitchen table, and as David passed by, he rolled his eyes to let her know something was up. She stared fixedly at him, though she didn't react.

"Gypsy candles worked," he managed to whisper.

"Get going!" Leona yelled, waiting until she heard David climbing the staircase. Then she turned to Clara. "I'd like to speak to you upstairs in your room."

"Yes, mu dear." Clara slowly got up from the table, walked across the kitchen, and began climbing her wooden steps. When she and Leona got inside her room, the door slammed. David, meanwhile, slipped quietly down the hall and placed a burning ear against Clara's cold door.

"You're not going to believe this. Or maybe you will," his mother was saying.

"What, darling?" Clara said.

"Dr. Stevens told me to fire you."

There was a dreadful pause. "Him should go suck his balls," Clara snapped. "So what you told him back?"

"That I'd send him a check for what we owed him. That neither David nor I was coming back."

"Good. And what about ya group talk?"

"It was a pain in the ass. The people were really dreary. And I admit, the driving *was* getting to me. David gets impossible when he's cooped up in the car. Question after question after question."

"Well, him is intelligent child."

"Too smart for his own good," Leona said, going on to explain about David's lies and how he had torn sexually graphic pictures from Dr. Stevens's books.

Clara gasped. "No, Mrs. Hart. I don't believe! Don't say no more or you'll get me too upset."

God, Clara was hamming it up, David thought.

"But I knew it was all over when he suggested I should let you go. That scared me. I told him he had no right to tell me how to run my life."

"Good," Clara said. "Such people need somebody to show dem where to get off at."

"The unfortunate thing about all this is that David ended up getting an advanced sex education. He's not even thirteen and now he probably knows more about sex than I do."

Silence endured for a long time following Leona's remark.

"God judge me, Mrs. Hart," Clara suddenly exploded. "You didn't listen me when I talking to you first time."

"What? What are you saying?" Leona asked, alarmed.

"I saying as I said before: You let dat boy climb up, and now you'll see him can't climb down again."

FOUR

1973

One warm morning in June, Clara danced into David's bedroom and awoke him singing "Chi chi buddo." She was wearing a nightgown with a pattern of tiny red hearts. As she raised the shades and warm sunlight flooded in, she gleefully announced that Icey Darden had nearly recovered from her illness. "Must be our Gypsy a Brooklyn," she remarked as she sat down next to David on his bed. "Certainly juked off de bad ways." She went on to explain that Icey's cancer symptoms had disappeared so significantly that even her doctors were perplexed. Icey was now able to get out more, and her hair had come back to the point where she could stop wearing the wig. Blanche had styled the hair that had grown back into a short, severe bob, which Clara claimed made Icey look a lot younger.

"So." Clara wiped the sleep from David's eyes and stroked his sandy hair. "Everything should be happy. This could be a lucky summer. Right?"

"Hopefully," David said as he yawned. He was thinking that there were only two weeks until swim practice began.

"But there's something dat don't make sense," Clara said as she gazed distantly out his window.

"What?" David asked.

She dipped her chin to the collar of her nightgown and shut her eyes. "I having lovely dreams," she explained. "Dreams of reunions, and of people ice-skating wid joined hands, dreams of old ladies forgiving they children. And though I might wake up into me bed

247

with feelings afresh, I frighten is something dark they portend."

A moment later David saw the wisping train of Clara's nightgown as she left him to go downstairs and fix breakfast.

That afternoon, David and his father were on the Hutchinson River Parkway, driving to a golfing range in Scarsdale where he would be taking a lesson. The sky was riddled with moist tufts of clouds and there was a distant threat of rain. David leaned back in his seat, cocking his arms behind his head, turning his face to the warm, fragrant wind coming in through the sunroof. For the past few minutes of silence, he had noticed that his father kept turning toward him with an anxious smile.

"You seem nervous about something, dad," he finally said.

Bill pushed himself back in the seat until his tanned, muscular arms were locked straight against the steering wheel. "What would you think of going to private school?" he asked David, keeping his eyes on the road.

David shrugged. He pushed up the short sleeves of his knitted polo shirt and stared curiously at the hair that had begun to darken on his arms. "The kids I know in private school have to study a lot more than I do," he said. "Plus, they have to wear jackets and ties."

"The school I would want you to consider allows you to dress any way you want," Bill said as he put on his directional signal to exit the parkway.

"Where is it?" David asked.

"In Manhattan."

"I'd probably have to get up real early to get there, wouldn't I? Although they have car pools, don't they?"

"Yeah, for those people who live in the suburbs."

A jittery quiet suspended itself over the car as Bill took the turnoff. David suddenly felt there were miles of leather seats separating him from his father. "I live in the suburbs," he murmured. "Remember?"

"I remember," Bill chuckled. "But you might not always live in the suburbs."

"Of course I will."

"Don't be ridiculous—what about when you go to college?"

"When I say always, I guess I mean through high school," David amended.

"You mean you'd never, ever want to live in the city?" his father asked.

They were driving beneath a lush canopy of maple trees. The driving range with its yellow and blue pavilions was just ahead. There was a long row of automatic golf-ball feeders, a mown green field of a fairway staked out with metal bull's-eyes that marked 100, 200, and 300 yards. A constant swinging of golfing irons kept catching the sun.

David turned to his father. "What's going on, dad?"

"What's going on is . . . " Bill drew a deep breath. "I'd like you to come and live with me."

David turned sideways in his seat and faced his father slack-jawed. "Are you joking?" he said.

Bill shook his head. "I haven't been happy with the way your mother has been raising you since she and I separated. I don't like the way she's gone overnight all the time. And to be honest, ever since all that business happened with Dr. Stevens, I've spent a lot of time thinking about having you come live with me."

"If you objected so much to my seeing Dr. Stevens, you should have stopped her from taking me!" David snapped as he turned away.

They were pulling into the driving range. Behind the yellow and blue buildings, he noticed a shivering vault of aquamarine. They had put in a swimming pool!

"I should have," his father answered. "But instead I listened to Clara. And you got shunted all around Westchester County. You learned about sex—from doctors' books," he said disdainfully. "I didn't even get a chance to talk to my own son about sex. I realize it's partly my fault, that I just should have tried harder to stop your mother from sending you to a shrink."

"But it's all over with!" David exclaimed. "Nothing really bad happened. I'm still here. I'm still alive."

"You're still alive," Bill echoed him. "But it's a pretty strange life you're living: your mother never around and your world revolving around a housekeeper."

"I like the life."

"Well, I don't and I'm your father. And I'd like to take responsibility for you on a day-to-day basis if your mother isn't going to do it."

David sat there, stupefied, as his father drove through a row of occupied parking spaces, looking for an empty spot. The sunlight was glinting harshly off chrome fenders. Would the injustices in his life now continue with his having to give up Rye and move to Manhattan? He always seemed to be holding his breath, waiting for something terrible to happen.

He looked meaningfully at his father. "You'd have me live in the city even if I didn't want to?"

Bill looked stricken as he pumped on the brakes. Both he and David got jerked forward. They had stopped in the middle of the parking lot and David's heart raced; for a moment he was afraid of being slapped. But then he watched his father's large chest heave and was confused at what might be passing through his mind.

"I would never force you to live with me, okay?" Bill said finally. "But listen to me, David, your mother eventually has to sell the house."

David looked doubtfully at his father. "Why would she sell the house?"

"It's a proper house for a large family. It's impractical for her because it's so costly to keep up. You know, David, she only gets a certain amount of money every month, out of which she has to pay maintenance. So it gets a little extravagant to keep the place going just for you and Clara."

"But Clara . . . " David was sputtering now. "You said when you first got separated that I needed her."

"At the time you did. But you're thirteen now."

"So?"

Bill shook his head. "You can't expect a housekeeper to stay with you for the rest of your life."

"But she loves me."

Bill looked miserable. A lock of limp hair had stumbled over his gray eyes and with his large, weathered hand he swept it out of his face, unsuccessfully trying to plaster it back down on his head. He suddenly spotted an empty parking space and raced the car around the corner. "Her love must have its limits," he said as he jockeyed the car in between the white parallel lines.

"You're wrong," David told him. "You don't understand her love at all."

The car glided to a halt. In the midst of his anxiety, David looked toward the golfing pavilions. He saw Anthony, the fat Italian golf pro who had been giving him lessons periodically ever since he could remember.

Bill turned off the ignition. "I'm sure Clara doesn't expect to be burdened with you for the rest of her life," he said as he got out of the car.

David sat there rigidly. The sun was beaming through the tinted windshield, roasting the leather seats. The car smelled strongly of hide. He had never even considered the idea that he might be a burden to Clara.

The trunk opened. He heard a clunking and rattle of clubs as his father began to unload their golf bags. Suddenly, despite the car's claustrophobic warmth, David's armpits and shoulders were prickled with cold. He hated the fact that his father always was able to manipulate their conversations to his benefit. This had to cease. The act of leaving the car precisely when their talk had become the most hurtful gave his father's words a rhetorical finish, protecting them from being refuted.

As David got out of the car, Anthony came over to chat with his father. Anthony's belly swelled a little more each year, bulging farther out over his canary-yellow golf pants. He always wore alpaca cardigans buttoned at the bottom so that his gut had room. He was short and stocky with thick silvery hair and dark bushy eyebrows that knitted together above his small, tired eyes. In appearance he seemed an awkward, unathletic sort. Until he swung the golf club and the ball went rocketing off, rising straight, leveling off to perfection.

Bill normally would leave David with Anthony to go hit buckets of balls. Today, however, he lurked off to one side, watching the progress of the lesson. From all the tension in the car, David's mouth had gone dry, his stomach rumbling in cold fear. He wanted to get something to drink, but somehow imagined that today his father was crazed with impatience and would object to any such digression. Normally, after disagreements or uncomfortable moments, Bill would try to smooth things over with a smile or a kind word. Today, however, he seemed removed and sullen, and David knew what they had talked about in the car was extremely important to him. David was afraid that his father already had decided what he wanted and would not allow himself to be swayed.

Anthony carried over two large buckets of balls, most of them sporting the driving range's characteristic red stripe. David needed time to warm up, so his first few shots were ill-timed. The balls took off in low bursts, either plunging a hundred yards off the tee or immediately coiling to the left or right. But eventually, with Anthony coaxing, "Keep your head down, kid, and follow through," David began to drive long and straight. Prior to a correct, clean shot, he always got a sense that everything was synchronized, feeling great relief to watch the ball acting properly. Today, however, before each fine shot, his heart seemed to fail. Learning the right golfing technique was like learning the final touches of how to be his father's son. And that, suddenly, was something David did not want to be.

Even Anthony noticed his father's mood. Normally gentle with David, his patience grew short a few times, as though he felt monitored and judged by Bill's scrutiny.

"Gee, Bill, you going to hit some balls or wha?" Anthony finally asked.

"I like watching," Bill said in a dreamy voice.

"But you're making the kid nervous," Anthony told him.

"How could I make my own kid nervous?"

Anthony turned up his palms, sharply shrugging his shoulders, and threw his beady eyes up to the sky. Monstrous purple clouds were scudding in from the Sound. *"Dio mio,"* he murmured in Italian.

David, meanwhile, had stopped his practice swinging and turned to his father. "It's true, dad, you're making me nervous."

"Just concentrate on what you're doing," Bill ordered him.

Using seven and nine irons, Anthony and David began practicing the chipping shot. It was David's favorite stroke. The ball was supposed to travel a short distance while taking the highest flight. Chip-

ping was somewhat like shooting an arrow into the sky. His first few
were flawlessly executed, but then the ball began to spit forward,
taking a low rise before lurching down.

Anthony stood there frowning as he ran his stubby fingers through
his grizzled hair. For a moment he seemed perplexed as to what David
was doing wrong. Then he made the mistake of glancing over at Bill,
who took it to mean he was soliciting an opinion.

"Jesus, Anthony, don't you see what he's doing? He's picking up
too soon. His head always gets in the way."

The statement seemed to define more than just David's ability to
play golf. His eyes brimmed with tears and the bright fairway before
him blurred. Then he looked up; Anthony's face had turned scarlet.
"What do you want from me, eh?" Anthony roared at his father. "You
don't like the way I give lessons, take the kid somewhere else! I don't
know why you bother me year after year. For Christ's sake, it's
obvious he hates to play golf. Why the hell do you force it on him?
So you can come here and give me your fucking attitude, you *stroonz?*"

The outburst, in all its truth, somehow—at least momentarily—
unburdened David of his father. For a moment Bill stared furiously
at the ground. Then he stalked away. Silently watching his procession
of anger, Anthony managed to smile apologetically at David. "It's
okay, kid," he assured him calmly. "Your old man's got some bug up
his ass today. Take him home and put him to bed. I'll see you next
time," he said.

Peter's Volvo was parked in the driveway, which alerted David's father to drop him off at the entrance to the property. When David entered the house, he noticed that his mother and Peter had opened up the kitchen doors and windows, and flies were freely buzzing in and out. Although it was hot outside, Peter was dressed in a black cotton turtleneck shirt; Leona was wearing a white gauze top and a pair of cutoff shorts. They were busy preparing a lunch platter of bread and cheese and cut-up vegetables, which they planned to bring up to the bedroom.

Leona immediately noticed the look of bewilderment on David's face and stopped slicing the cheese. When she asked him what was wrong, he began to explain what his father had said and then what had gone on at the driving range.

Peter, who had abruptly ceased peeling carrots when David began speaking, turned to Leona. "Why don't we take David into the living room and talk about this?"

David chose to sit in one of the soft armchairs; his mother and Peter sat together on the sofa. For a moment he looked around the living room, a place where he rarely spent any time. Next to the sofa on an antique mahogany stand was a blue porcelain Chinese lamp. One of the living-room walls was paneled in a wormy chestnut recessed with niches that housed small bronzed statues of athletes; his father had bought them before the marriage but had not taken them with him to his new apartment.

Peter spoke first. It was the first time he had ever gotten involved in family matters, but David was glad; he knew Peter would explain things more clearly than his mother. Peter seemed to give each of his ideas careful consideration so it was easier for David to understand them. As he nervously fluffed his fingers through his thick white hair, Peter explained that Bill had been sending Leona letters that charged her with neglecting David and blamed her for what had gone on while he was in therapy with Dr. Stevens. In his letters Bill had urged Leona to remand custody of David to him.

David glanced over at his mother, who peered anxiously back at him. Her knees were chattering up and down and he noticed how pale her legs were; it had now been four summers since she had sunbathed. Peter explained that they had chosen not to tell David what was going on simply because in order to get custody of him, his father would have to take his mother to trial.

"But dad said he wouldn't force me to live with him," David said.

Leona answered, "He's just trying to be reasonable."

"But then he said something about you selling the house."

Leona glanced meaningfully at Peter and then turned to David. "Well, besides being enormous, this house is very costly for me to run."

"Wait a second, honey," Peter interrupted her. "We've got to be completely clear and forthright about this." Clasping his bony hands together, Peter said to David, "First of all, you've got to understand that selling the house would be inevitable one way or another. It's a waste of money to live in a place as big as this when you use so little of the space."

"So you could get a smaller house closer to town."

Leona glanced at Peter. "We could," she said.

"And that would include Clara, wouldn't it?" David asked.

"It would if we decided to do that," she said.

David stood up. "So then there's no problem."

"Sit down," Leona said. "We haven't finished yet."

"Why?" David said.

Leona took a deep breath and in so doing took Peter's hand. "Well," she said, "we want to move to California and we'd like you to come with us."

David suddenly felt flushed and dizzy and slumped back into his

chair. For a moment he was perplexed; it was too much to take in.
Soon, the anger began to rise. He gripped each side of the armchair
until his fingers blanched, and then bolted upright. "Move to California?" he shouted. "What are you trying to do? You don't want to take
me with you."

"Yes, we do," Leona insisted quietly. But her eyes were fearful, her
lips drawn back as though something were lodged in her throat. "We
want you to come with us, David," she said.

"Why should I believe that?" David asked.

"Because it's the truth," Peter said.

David turned to him. "Maybe she's saying she wants me to come
because she knows she's supposed to want me, that she's expected to
want me."

"Your mother loves you very much, David," Peter told him.

"Maybe she loves me, but she doesn't need to be around me."

Leona gave Peter a glance that seemed to say she had expected this
reaction.

"This is where it gets difficult to understand," Peter warned David.

Leona stood abruptly. "Listen to me, David," she said as she began
pacing in front of him. Her head was bowed, and as a tendril of auburn
hair strayed from her loose bun, with a finger she looped it back over
her ear. "I couldn't bring Peter to live here with me, so I had to choose
whether or not I would stay with him. In the end I had to choose for
my own happiness; your father didn't have to—he could do what he
wanted ultimately because he saw you only on weekends. As far as
you're concerned, I'm selfish because in the end I chose myself over
you. And you're right to feel that way. Right now I don't expect you
to understand what I did. But I'm hoping one day . . . " She broke
off.

But David did understand; he just distrusted her sentiments. He
was afraid his mother was *too* selfish to be capable of having the
conflicts she described.

"Does dad know you want to move to California?" he asked her.
Leona nodded.

So his father knew about their plans, which undoubtedly was why
he suddenly made his bid for custody. However, his father obviously

wanted to see if David would choose to live with him before David realized his mother was bound for California.

"But, mom, why do you want to move so far away?" he unhappily asked.

Leona sat down again and squeezed Peter's hand even tighter than before. She said that her life in the suburbs had ended when her marriage ended. She wanted to live a different life now with this different person she had found. They had a chance to buy a 100-acre avocado ranch; producing avocados was one of the thriving agricultural businesses in the state of California. The ranch was located in a small town thirty miles east of Santa Barbara. She wanted to live on a large, quiet tract of land and invest her money in it; she wanted to live on the West Coast.

David's head now filled up with so many dueling images of the future, he didn't know what to think. Then one nagging issue made itself known. "If I wanted to go to California, wouldn't dad fight it?" he asked his mother.

Leona came and stood before him so that her knees were practically touching his. But when she tried to put her hands on his shoulders, he stiffened so that she backed away. "Your father and I have been fighting about this since February," she said. "We finally decided we don't want to subject you to a custody battle. It wouldn't be fair for you to watch us fight, for you to learn what we each have against the other. It would be too hurtful. So we decided the only fair thing is to let you decide for yourself."

A silence ensued. David found himself looking at the bronze sculptures of the athletes, suddenly wondering if his father had lost out on them when he and Leona were dividing their possessions during the divorce, or if he had just plain abandoned them. He turned to his mother and Peter. "But I don't know what I want to do," he said, although secretly he wished to live with Clara at her apartment.

His mother and Peter both looked glum. Had they hoped he would immediately decide to accompany them?

David continued. "Look, even though I might not want to live with dad, maybe Clara could live in the city with me."

"But there's no room in your father's apartment," Leona said.

Peter spoke up. "Let me ask you this, David, and this is important. Would your choice to live with your father hinge on whether or not Clara remained with you?"

"Yes," David said quickly.

"Well then, maybe you should talk to your father and see if he'd commit to it," Leona advised.

"You also should consider whether Clara would agree to live and take care of you in Manhattan," Peter told David.

David was silent for a moment. "Would Clara move to California?" he asked them.

"She'd certainly be welcome," Peter said, "though I doubt she'd come."

"How do you know?"

Peter reflected a moment. "I believe she needs to have contact with her friends. I think it'd be too lonely for her out there."

"But she'd have *me*," David said.

"She loves you very much," Peter agreed softly, then paused, his eyes lighted with compassion. "But if you assume that she could be happy just being with you, and even with us, I think you underestimate her need. You give her great comfort, but she needs Jamaicans, too. And she wouldn't have them in California. Especially where your mother and I want to go."

David suddenly understood exactly what Peter had been suggesting: that his relationship with Clara might not flourish elsewhere; it might be too delicate to be transplanted unless he moved in with her in Brooklyn, which he knew his parents would never allow. Something, he was afraid, was going to get in the way. She would refuse to live in his father's apartment, or his father would deny her.

Then Peter said he had grown quite fond of David, and since he did not have any children of his own, in a way he felt he could eventually be like a father. And David, although he loved his father deeply, and although he did not love Peter, wondered if Peter could actually come a lot closer to being like a father.

"Talk to Clara," Peter said. "See what she wants to do. And think about it for a while."

But David didn't want to think about it for too long. The indecision was hurting him. He was ready to choose, although he made it seem as though he needed time to decide.

Clara kept her head bent over the ironing board. She dipped her fingers into a Tupperware bowl filled with distilled water and sprinkled the blue oxford shirt of David's she was ironing. Leona watched her combating an inner fury while continuing to press the sleeves and collar, remembering how she had once said what a miracle it was that a man could be born from a woman's body.

Clara looked up at her. "But Mr. Hart na interest to take care de child. Him is frigging out every night wid dis one or dat. What de child would do living under such a life?"

"He thinks that would be better than being home irregularly, his claim about me."

Clara was shaking her head. "To tell de truth, Leona, you ask for too much last year or so. One night, maybe two nights a week at most, you could stay out. But when it comes down to four, it just make you look bad."

"But, Clara, David always had you. Even before I got divorced, he only really listened to you. And then when I was making plans in my mind to live with Peter, I kept figuring I'd see David a lot, but that he'd always be able to rely on you—I mean, sometimes he even seemed glad that I was gone."

Clara set the iron on its end. "Well, okay, you right about de first part. Was different because of special way David and I are together. And so to you and me it don't seem so neglect. Though it was. And don't matter how David act, him cares for you. Children hide disappointment most times. Bury deep in their hearts. But I saw de way him gone into ya room, especially when you didn't come around for days. I told him to clear off, but him loved to regard your things like dog lost its master. I know you think him now loves me more than you. Not true." Clara paused, shaking her head wistfully, and then continued in a tremoring voice. "You used his love for me to justify going off wid your friend."

"That's not true," Leona said flatly.

Clara disregarded her. She left the ironing board for a moment and

went to the window, where she peered out into the bursting of early
summer. The Chicano gardener was below them, watering the flower
beds, sculpting the hedges that now only she appreciated. All along,
Clara had kept insisting they maintain the property, ordering bulbs
and shrubs when Leona would have let the grounds run fallow and
be overrun with weeds.

She turned to Leona. "How do you know you can count on him,
dis man you involve wid?" Clara lowered her gaze. "My experience
wid mens is dem can't control dem goosie leg. Must always find oddar
women. Must always betray."

"Peter isn't like dat."

"Oh, yes," Clara said as she went and took up her ironing again.
"Probably once upon a time you think dat about Mr. Hart."

"I never did."

"So where you will go, if you sell dis place?"

Leona hesitated. Outside she could hear water beating against the
metal flange of the garden hose. She felt a strain in her throat where
the words lay waiting. "We want to go to California," she finally told
Clara.

There was a brief electric silence, and then Clara recoiled. At first,
in an incredulous chuckle, "California? Dat what I heard you said,
California?"

"Yes, California," Leona said nervously.

In sudden fury, Clara clapped her hands together. "Mrs. Hart, is
your extreme dat most vex me! Can't satisfy enough to gone off wid
you man, can't be sensible and stay near where de child grow up?
Hold on." She waved her dark hands in front of her face, as though
erasing the last few moments of conversation, expecting their talk to
begin all over again. "You mean . . ." She now spoke in a wavering
voice. "You mean you'd go so far to risk losing de child forever to
his father?"

"I want David to come with me."

"But him won't go!"

"You can't be sure."

Clara wrung her hands. "Don't matter. You shouldn't go there right
now. You must wait at least till he's older. It's selfish. You must see

danger. You can't predict you'll always have happiness wid dis Peter. A child is de only real thing you have, Mrs. Hart." She was pleading now. "A child is constant. Whereas love wid a lover is a most strange thing. Some days you so sure it's dere and then tomorrow it suddenly gone like sandpiper."

Leona fell silent. "I guess I'll have to take that chance," she said finally. "I think it's worth taking."

Shaking her head, Clara walked to her bureau. "Headache coming now. You make me pressure raise. Need some aspirin." She fumbled nervously among the cluster of drugstore lotions until she found an amber bottle of Anacin. "Americans always seem to be looking for a change," she said, putting two pills in her mouth and throwing her head back to swallow them. "Car is old after two years, a dress no longer the style, so you pitch them away. Same thing wid house, work, family, and love."

"But, Clara," Leona objected, "I was floundering until I met Peter and I saw he could save me. And I knew all along that David would be set with you, that he'd be protected, that he'd be loved."

"Mrs. Hart, wait, don't you think I know?" Clara asked, smiling. "You just don't realize how often I told myself to left here, to force you come back. But I also knew you thought this man was your last chance to be happy. And as much as I don't want, I understood what dat feeling was like." Clara shook her head resignedly. Her eyes now came to rest on the sun-faded cameo of her husband. She shut them for a moment, rolling her head back and forth. "We're certainly different people, you and me," she remarked. "You depend on others to cure you. Me, I only trust myself wid me own worries and keep dem close to heart." Clara reached among her lotions and screwed the cap tighter on the Anacin bottle, as though hoping to clamp a lid on the pain of the past. "Sometimes I wish I could tell you so much," she said softly. "Wish in a few seconds you could look over me whole life. Then you'd know why you must hold on to your child, that children are de only thing you really have."

Reflecting five years back to that vacation in Port Antonio, Leona wanted to say that she understood a lot more than Clara realized, but she couldn't bring herself to.

"So strange, you don't even grab hold of him," Clara went on sadly. "Tell de truth, why you don't feel such love for him? He's a lovable person. So lovable that sometimes I even wish . . . " She hesitated.

"What?" Leona asked quickly.

Silent, Clara stared out at the waterline on the Sound where her eyes had found a slow-moving schooner.

"That he was your own son?"

Clara still would not answer.

Leona felt jealous of that unspoken yet obvious desire. She was suddenly afraid this might be one of their very last conversations. She glanced around the bedroom: at the night table covered with manicuring tools; the bureau with its fortification of lotions and pills; the foldout bridge table where Clara had been writing letters earlier in the day, strewn with floral leaves of stationery and onionskin envelopes. As she turned to walk out, Leona smelled a faint scent of jasmine coming from somewhere.

The beauty-parlor girls wanted to give Icey Darden a surprise "recovery party." The problem was that even if they pooled their money, they would not have enough capital to rent a dance hall. Clara came up with the idea of using Icey's brownstone—since in summers past Icey had been in the habit of giving large outdoor parties—and making all the arrangements secretly. It was agreed that on July Fourth, Clara would take Icey out for the day, and by the time she brought her home, the party would have been set up with all her friends waiting. Clara decided to use David as part of her ploy to get Icey out of the house. Since he had never been to Coney Island, Clara thought she would take him and invite Icey to come along.

Unfortunately, the weekend of the party had its darker side; it was the weekend David finally had to decide whom he wanted to live with. His father already had consented to hire Clara in Manhattan—however, not as a live-in. But this consent was more like a concession. He was willing to pay her a weekly salary only to ensure that David chose to stay in New York.

The first night David and Clara discussed the future together in her bedroom, he held one of her dark hands and stared at the pink hierogylphic scar on her wrist, a reminder of her other life. She had put a pillow behind her back and was propped up against the headboard of her bed, and he had squeezed in alongside her. He told Clara their life was nearly perfect as it stood; she told him he felt this way because now he knew that this life was finite.

"But I don't want us to be separated," he said.

"Neither I."

"So then I'll stay in New York."

Clara smiled painfully and squeezed his hand. "Listen me, child. Listen me good," she whispered. "Much as I want you to stay, I feel you should consider before you said anything to ya parents. Once you speak up and tell de duhty lawyers, dem won't allow a change of heart." She paused for a moment. "Just don't know if you'd be happy wid your father. Two o' you so different and him don't have steady woman and is out all de time. Could be lonely for you."

David edged even closer to her. "But you could come work for us," he said. "And then we would be together."

Clara shook her head. "David, much as I love you, me can't manage dat. Here in Rye me have a purpose. I control dis house. In Manhattan dere would be nothing for me to do. Further on, I don't trust fathers. Funny, though ya muddar vex me plenty, I know she'd never cross me."

David told Clara he would get through those weeks with his father, knowing he could see her on weekends, that his real life would take place then. But as soon as he spoke those words, he was afraid of the feelings behind them.

"You still must talk more to your muddar," Clara told him. "Since dem going to buy a lovely ranch."

"But it's so far away from here," David complained.

"Yes, a true you talking," Clara said, looking away. "But you'd get used to it. Might even enjoy living dere. Certainly would be more like family."

David took a deep breath and asked if Clara would consider coming along if he decided to go out to California. But she in turn compared the idea of her living in California to a porpoise trying to survive on an island. "Nothing for me out dere," she said as she stroked his head. "Dem people wouldn't trouble me—probably would be only black in dat small town."

There was a thunderous silence all around them as David wished he could reverse time.

Clara tucked her legs up under her and tightly folded her arms across her chest. "Child, you must promise me not to decide just now. Allow things to play in ya mind for a time."

"But I know what I want," he told her. "I want to stay near you."

"I'm glad to hear dat. But still you must wait," Clara insisted.

Icey was waiting for them outside her brownstone. Clara already had warned David, "Don't startle when you see her, because she favor deep dread." However, he still didn't expect to find Icey looking so emaciated and weak. Normally a frail woman, she had wasted away until now she appeared to be a victim of near-starvation. Her eyes had large yellowed hollows beneath them; her arms resembled sticks with sagging flesh like bags of fluid; her skin had a grayish pallor. But she still acted imperious, standing there in the street with her head held high.

"So how ya keeping?" Clara asked her.

"Feeling much better today," Icey said, swiveling her bony shoulders as though she wanted to seem energetic. Her rhinestone cat glasses sat crookedly on her face. Without asking permission, Clara leaned forward and took them off. She bent in one of the temples and then put them back on Icey again, this time making sure they looked straight.

"Now you looking better," Clara remarked, although David wondered how Icey could have looked any worse.

A few moments later a Chevrolet station wagon pulled up. Behind the steering wheel sat a big lumbering fellow named Gonder, a friend of Clara's from Port Antonio who had offered to drive them to Coney Island. He had a hauling business and his customers were mostly Jamaicans who lived in and around Brooklyn. On several occasions he had even driven up to Rye to pick up clothing barrels Clara sent to needy families in Port Antonio. David recalled Clara arguing over the phone with Gonder, who at first had refused to drive so far from the familiarity of his borough. Somehow, though, Clara had been able to persuade him to help her. The first time Gonder came to Rye, David noticed immediately that this large, fleshy man held Clara in a sort of fearful awe. Despite his own misgivings, Gonder seemed wary of denying her what she wanted.

David would always remember that July Fourth as one of the most sweltering days of his life. They were calling it a "scorcher" on the radio; the weatherman claimed the air was saturated with humidity. They drove with all the windows down and the wind that rushed into the car felt as though it blasted out from a furnace. Clara sat with Gonder in the front seat, chattering away about how so many Jamaicans had been unable to make ends meet in America and were being forced to return to the island. She kept turning around to check whether or not Icey was comfortable, whether she felt overheated or faint, as she traded gossip of marriages in Kingston, people given promotions, and honors won at Tichfield School by children of their friends.

Icey, meanwhile, sat silent in the back with David, dabbing herself with a lace handkerchief. She kept her head turned to the window, eyeing the streets that were packed with droves of beachgoers lugging Styrofoam coolers along with bright bath towels and transistor radios. Icey seemed to look at them as a reaffirmation that there was, indeed, life in the world and that she would continue to participate in it.

"I'm glad you're feeling better," David said, trying to draw her into conversation.

Icey nodded. He could see a flaky gray scalp through her short, downy bob of a hairdo. It was quite obvious to him that her hair was styled this way from lack of choice. "Used to count each day as a blessing," she said finally, "wondering how many de Lord would grant until I was into de ground."

"Well, you can relax now," David tried to assure her. "You're doing great."

Icey shrugged, her shoulders protruding from her sleeveless violet-print housedress. Ironically, they were just then beginning to pass a large cemetery, perhaps even larger than the one outside Clara's window. The monuments spread out all the way to the horizon. David could see scores of bouquets decorating the graves as well as miniature flags placed in the ground in honor of the holiday. They drove by a fish warehouse, which Clara explained had recently been converted to an ice-skating rink, and then an outdoor market. In the distance, finally, he could make out the brightly painted configurations of rides at Coney Island.

As Gonder pulled into a crowded public parking lot, Clara turned around to the back seat. "Don't suppose you'd want to come wid David and me 'pon de Cyclone?" she asked Icey gleefully.

"I don't know if *I'm* going on that with you," David said.

"What you talking? Of course you'll be going! You think I arrange to drag you all about and not go on a Cyclone?"

"Go by yourself," David told her.

"She need somebody to hold on to," Icey said. "So you will go wid her," she ordered.

David said nothing, afraid of displeasing Icey.

Clara didn't want Icey to walk around the amusement park too much and asked Gonder to bring along a folding bridge chair so that Icey could sit down and rest as much as possible. They went first to an arcade of air riflery and throwing games. Adjacent to the row of booths was a large shady overhang where Icey sat down in her chair. Before Clara bought David a shooting round, she took one of the air guns and showed him where to place the butt between his armpit and shoulder. She told him to aim the lollypop sight at the row of revolving yellow ducks, take a breath, let out half of it, and then squeeze the trigger.

"How do you know so much about guns?" David asked suspiciously.

Clara put down the rifle and looked at him shrewdly. "You didn't know me was wanted for murder in Jamaica," she said darkly. "Dat is me secret. Dat is why me come up here. Dat is why me can't go back."

David's face paled. He could see striped plumes of umbrellas on the beach beyond the arcade, where the light seemed so bright it was blinding. He could smell sweet cotton candy being spun in an adjacent booth and heard the screams of passengers riding the Cyclone. Suddenly, Clara threw back her head and laughed a toothy, greedy laugh.

He turned away in anger. He tried aiming his rifle, but each time he pulled the trigger, he could hit nothing. Then Clara stepped into his place, casually aimed, and shot three ducks—almost like an afterthought. The barker gave her an enormous stuffed monkey, but she threw it back at him and demanded a panda.

"Look so you two well amusing," Icey remarked when Clara and

David walked back over to her. Gonder was digging in his pocket for some money. "Me getting some snow cones," he told Clara. "You want it?"

"Yes, get four o' dem," Clara said. "Cherry."

"I don't want cherry," David said.

"Cherry is de best flavor. De oddars taste nasty," Clara told him.

"You're really bossy today," he remarked.

She peered at him with widened eyes. "Me have lots of things to do today. Worries on me mind. You know what I saying?"

David shrugged, assuming Clara was referring to Icey's surprise party.

After playing a few more arcade games, they eventually made their way over to the Cyclone. Next to the ticket seller's window was a small painted billboard of a boy with a cowlick. A sign said, "You must be as tall as me to ride." When David saw the top of the boy's head only came up to his shoulders, he felt embarrassed about being afraid. But then he lost his appetite. Clara already had finished her snow cone and he asked her if she wanted the rest of his. She grabbed the ball of cherry ice and squeezed it into her mouth. Her cheeks hollowed and sucked until it melted.

Clara took a place on line and David reluctantly joined her. They watched as each group of anxious customers piled into the roller coaster. Then the concatenation of cars would inch its way to the top of the first and steepest rise. David's heart leaped each time he saw the roller coaster race steeply toward the bottom of the first loop. Every time the passengers shrieked, he was filled with dread.

"I really don't want to go on this," he finally told Clara.

She drew the air through her teeth and turned to him. He spied something in her eyes he did not like. "Listen na, child," she said. "It really not so bad. Sure, when you first gone up to de top, you sort of feel you 'bout to fall into hell, but it's much more fun den that."

"That's exactly the way I feel right now," David told her. But that feeling only worsened when it finally came their turn to ride the roller coaster. Clara wanted to sit in the very first car. David drew back instinctively and looked at her in horror. Clara laughed as her eyes darted over him mischievously. "Come climb in and you'll see

how fun it is," she reassured him. "It's fun to frighten a little."
"No it isn't."

She tugged his arm. "Yes," she insisted. "Because you know de
fear of it can never last."

Confused by the meaning of Clara's words, David noticed the rest
of the customers in their group already were avoiding the first car. He
grew winded as he faced the inevitability of having to do what Clara
wanted. As they climbed into the first car, his whole being seemed to
rest heavily in the pit of his stomach. But he told himself that he would
ride in the most fearful position to prove his love to a woman who did
not seem to be afraid of anything. And if he ever did decide to go to
California, which in his heart he felt he could not do, he would know
his love for Clara was more powerful than any fear.

The attendant made certain all the safety bars were locked into
place before pulling a lever that hooked the cars into a pulley. As they
were winding up the steep incline to the top of the first rise, David
got so petrified he came close to fainting. During the moment before
the roller coaster began its plunge, he could see up and down Surf
Avenue, the endless boardwalk subsumed in people, who vanished
into a glaze of heat toward the horizon. The amusement park was a
serpentine of rides jerking and whirring, beyond it the tall, mush-
rooming spindles of the extinct Parachute Jump and the Steeplechase.
Suddenly, David stood up in his seat; he wanted to jump out! But Clara
grabbed him and shoved him back down as the world went topsy-
turvy. The roller coaster pitched convulsively into a bottomless flue,
and then rushed along tilted sideways. While Clara howled with
laughter, David began vomiting over his side of the car. Something
deep inside him was chilled.

At Icey's house, gas lanterns had been strung up and long white banquet tables laid with cornucopias of peaches, plums, and grapes. The entire trellis of her brick patio was festooned with camellias imported from Jamaica. There were ceramic vases brimming with hibiscus, marigolds, and trumpeting datura.

The moment David, Clara, and Icey walked into the living room, a crowd of dark, perfumed people dressed in bright colors yelled "Surprise!" in unison. Icey puckered up her lips and threw Clara a look of devilish accusation. Then she turned back to the laughing guests and placed her frail hands over her wasted cheeks. Her eyes spilled over with tears.

"Come get her a chair," Clara ordered a young man dressed in a tight nylon tank top. "It's too hot in here. Let's bring her outside." While he went to fetch a high-backed chair from the living room, two middle-aged ladies dressed in sarongs and paisley headscarves helped walk Icey out to the brick patio, where the majority of guests were lingering. There was a shiny metal garbage can full of ice chilling bottles of beer and white wine. Guests kept scooping their hands inside it and pulling out clear cubes, which they rubbed on their arms and foreheads to keep cool in the extreme heat. At the far corner of the garden on a small wooden platform, a West Indian band had set up their steel drums and guitars.

Suddenly, David felt Clara stiffening next to him. She nudged him with her elbow, and instinct told him what was bothering her: Dora was standing among the crowd of guests. She was wearing a royal-blue

gown that was too tight and revealing for her squat figure. "Me tell
Blanche not to invite her," Clara complained. "I tell dem straight me
na want her mucking around here. But dem don't listen."

"Maybe they were forced to invite her."

Clara scowled at him. "What you mean force? Who was calling
people all week wid de arrangements?"

Dora noticed Clara glowering at her and purposely turned away to
speak to a middle-aged woman in a white dress.

"Perfectly right," Clara said. "Now she know she not wanted."

At that moment, two men wearing Hawaiian shirts purposely jostled
Clara. As soon as she saw them, her mood swung completely around
and she let out a belly laugh. "Wait. Lord 'a'mercy, when de you two
brothers Farley get up here?"

"A month ago," one said.

Clara cocked her hands on her hips. "So why not you come and see
me?"

"Too busy looking a job," he answered.

"You lucky," Clara remarked. She began fanning herself. "Hot
enough up here fe you?"

"You kidding?" said the other one. "Hotter here in summer den
Jamaica."

"No trade wind, darling," Clara told him.

The fellow then frowned at David and asked, "Clara, who dis boy?"

But before she could answer, Blanche, wearing a tiered sequined
dress, her eyelids painted bright blue, suddenly came over and
grabbed David's arm. "Come wid me. Me well want you to talk patois
to some girls I know."

"Gwan over," Clara told him with a gentle smile. "And let me go
change into a cooler dress."

As Blanche led David across the room, he wondered how Clara was
explaining their relationship.

"Hello, David." He turned his head and saw that Dora had spoken
to him. She was standing alone now, quite obviously drunk. Her eyes
were bloodshot and she was listing slightly to the left. David nodded
to her, although he said nothing. "Come and talk to me later," Dora
told him.

"Don't trouble Dora tonight," Blanche warned him with a nervous flutter of her hands. "Me don't like de devil mood she into. She can well become troublesome when she want, though she really *not* a bad person. Now come and talk patois." Blanche addressed a group of young women standing together. "Girls, him now will talk to you his favorite language. All right, David," she cooed, "let us hear something deep bad."

But before David could begin, he realized sadly that this was actually the very first time a Jamaican had asked him to speak patois. As he began to sing "Me go down to Donkey City to circumcise my kitty," Doris Williams joined the group. "On the way I met wid a mule . . . "—the ladies began to giggle—"and de mule said to de donkey, saddler boy, na saddle him b'hind me." They were roaring by now. "Donkey, hi, na kick up na dust b'hind me, I tell you."

Everyone applauded. "Come sing 'One Chinee Man' fe us," Doris Williams coaxed David as she did a trot in place.

He frowned at her. "Me not a display, ya know," he snorted. "Me not a poppy show." There were more shrieks.

"Come do Chatelaine," Blanche egged him on. "Come do Blossie 'fore we dead from laughing."

David guiltily hunched his shoulders and glanced around him to see if Blossom was standing nearby.

"Is all right, she not coming," Blanche reassured him. "She had somewhere to go tonight."

But just as David opened his mouth to imitate the high voice of Blossom Chatelaine, he saw two women standing motionless, separated by a patio full of constantly moving festive people. Clara had changed into her lovely black and white polka-dot sleeveless silk dress and she and Dora were glaring at one another. He saw venom in their eyes and knew there was something to that hatred he did not understand. He shut his own eyes and opened his mouth once again and became a Jamaican.

An hour into the party, one of the brothers in the Hawaiian shirts lighted a rose-colored sparkler and stuck it on the bandstand. He cupped his hands around his mouth and cried, "Come, clear de patio and dance away!" Tables and chairs were taken inside as the band

began to strike up popular Jamaican tunes. They performed histori-
cally for the benefit of all the generations of people who were present
at the party. Starting somewhere around the limbo, they played up
through the rock-steady and finished with the current reggae dances,
jerking sexual steps where people ground against one another in
provocative entwines. Clara periodically approached David to try and
teach him the movements of a particular dance; but when he tried
copying her, he only trod on her feet. He ended up finding an incon-
spicuous corner for himself.

He was struck by the physical effect of the music. The sound of sand
blocks reminded him of crickets; the plaint of the steel guitars made
him feel a strange longing, especially when he heard lyrics such as
"Hail to Jamaica . . . who lies in white waters at rest, like a maiden
quite close to her true mother's breast. . . ." He noticed that the exotic
music exerted an influence over the way people moved. They didn't
walk around the party, they glided, swaying back and forth while they
spoke and laughed with one another. He remembered the people who
used to come to his parents' garden parties; Clara's countrymen
seemed merrier, so much less inhibited, they seemed to love and
appreciate one another so much more. For a moment, David felt
wistful that he was not allowed to choose Brooklyn and such people
for his future.

· From time to time he found himself watching Clara closely. It
seemed she purposely kept busy, afraid to relax. She kept careful
supervision over the waiters, would hurry to the kitchen and conjure
up more plantain fritters and fish cakes and johnnycakes and chocho.
She refilled the silver punch bowl and served new rounds of drinks
in Icey's prized crystal glasses. She flitted from crowd to crowd,
interjecting one-liners that sent her countrymen into fits of laughter.
The deference shown to her by friends and acquaintances, which
David had observed on a small scale when she had had visitors in Rye
or when she went to the beauty shop, was more telling in the midst
of all these people. Everyone acted cordially to Clara; indeed, some
seemed almost to revere her. Yet he sensed an element of reserve, a
discomfort among the guests, who shifted from foot to foot and fluttered like grounded birds whenever she swooped by. They turned

their attention to Clara out of a certain wonder, but also, David thought, out of a fearful respect. And although he tried to reassure himself there could be nothing but love for her in their hearts, he felt they were condemning her in some way, not because they wished to, but because they had to, as though she had violated some principle that lived in all of them. For no matter how saintly Clara appeared to him, David knew she had an inescapable history, that for some reason she was the "fallen angel."

"David." Blanche had come up behind and tapped him on the shoulder. Running her fingers nervously through her Afro, she said, "Some of dem young girls you amusing well want to ask you for a date. But you better come by de Beauty so me can show you first how dating is done," she joked. "'Cause if dem get ahold of it, you might not get it back." She laughed, showing her tobacco-stained teeth. "Oh, Lord, look a' dat." She pointed toward the center of the patio where the guests had suddenly cleared away.

Clara was dancing by herself. Her full lips puckering, braceleted arms beckoning the stars, her legs pumped out convoluted steps that spun her in double turns and hops. The guests cheered after each of her variations, but David was shocked. He'd never known Clara had this talent. Finally, upon popular request, she did a rhythmic, bawdy dance called "Lift-up." As she moved diagonally across the patio, her bottom, as though completely disconnected from the rest of her torso, wagged in a circle. Every eighth beat, she thrust her pelvis forward and yelled "Bam!" There were catcalls: "Gwan, Clara, gwan, girl! Lift it up and around." She pointed her finger up to the heavens, crying "Wait for me, Jesus, wait for me!" Her dance finally ended with a splash of applause.

In a daze, David turned to go inside to the bathroom. As he wove his way among the dark, fragrant bodies of the guests, someone bumped into him and he found himself looking up. He saw a filament of blue light streaking across the sky. No firecracker; David knew it came from far beyond the earth, that it was a shooting star. No one else had seen the arc of light, no one else had even noticed him standing there thrilled and musing. He grew convinced that Clara's dance ended precisely when the star had fallen.

He was waiting his turn for the bathroom when someone grabbed his arm. Dora was standing next to him. "You having yaself a good time?" she asked flatly as she glanced out at the patio. A line of sweat ran between the fleshy folds of her large, hard breasts. "She certainly can dance, ya momma can."

"She's not my momma," David told her.

Dora raised her plucked and stenciled eyebrows. "Den what she be, child, ya lover?"

David shuddered. "Get away from me, will you!"

"I well want to tell you something first," she said, grabbing David tighter. Her breath was laced with alchohol.

"Let go of me," he ordered Dora, trying to wrench himself away. But she would not let go. Meanwhile, outside, someone had just given Clara a Catherine Wheel, which she was placing in the middle of the patio. "She doesn't want you to talk to me," David said, feeling his heart pumping in his throat.

"Me na 'fraid of she."

"I don't believe you," David told her, momentarily abandoning his struggle. Clara ceremoniously struck a match. The Catherine Wheel caught in silver fire, whistling as its tiny flaming jets reeled in a circle.

"Me want to tell you about dat shame," Dora said darkly, trying to press David to her. "About de dirty shame her son Ralfie do. How him was foul and how him hurt us."

"Clear off, you bloodcloth!" David snapped as he once again tried to pull free.

"Dem ugly words, dose words you talking. You know what dey mean?"

"Let go of me!"

"Den don't you dare insult me," Dora scolded him.

Suddenly, someone grabbed Dora's shoulder and spun her around, nearly knocking her off-balance. It was Clara. "Wha ya troubling him fa?" she demanded, boldly placing her hands on her hips. "You have no right to involve in me business," she snarled. "Just clear off my boy!"

A hush veiled the room. Dora's hardness had melted away and she was staring blankly at Clara. "Don't you call him your boy," Dora rebuked her softly. "You don't have no boy. Ya boy is dead."

A collective gasp was uttered by the listening crowd.

"That him dead is my business," Clara said, trying to contain her fury. "And so is dis child. You not to involve wid either."

Dora was trembling all over. "Den you must tell him."

"I said, not your business!"

"Tell him why your boy don't deserve to live."

Clara shut her eyes tightly and her purple lips quivered. She was losing hold of her last measure of composure. "Get outta here 'fore I pitch you into a sleep you'll never wake from."

Dora tried to grab David again. "I kill you if you touch him!" shrieked Clara. With a speed that was shocking, she leaped between them and punched Dora in the face. Dora pounced back at Clara and tried to scratch her, but Clara only punched her again, this time knocking her to the floor. "Masse me God!" David heard people yell. "Lord have mercy!" Several men converged around Clara and pulled her away.

"Don't you desecrate, don't you desecrate my son!" Clara cried as she struggled against her captors.

Dora continued to lie quietly on the floor. Her eyelids were fluttering and her bright lipstick was smeared. She pressed a hand to her bloodied lips. "Desecrate?" she cried back in disbelief as she peered at her blood-smirched fingers, "Desecrate?"

Icey Darden was weeping hysterically, Blanche trying to comfort her. "You must tell him," Dora cried out again. "Tell him what de truth. You know him has a right to know what de cliff boy do!"

The party had been unable to recover its mood of festivity, and shortly after the fight, guests began to depart. Gonder offered to drive Clara and David the short distance back to her apartment, and in silence the car sped through the hot, crowded streets. In the distance, fireworks began to go off. When they stopped for a red light, a cherry bomb exploded nearby and startled them.

As soon as Clara and David got upstairs, she pulled out a flask of Jamaican white rum from her red suitcase and took a huge swig. In the semidarkness, the clear, potent fluid dribbled down her dark lips, shining like a streak of silver. She caught David looking fearfully at her.

"Why you staring at me?" Clara challenged him.

"You know."

She looked away. "Dora had no right to start up wid me in such a way, to ruin Icey lovely party."

"Then why did she?"

"Me as confused about it as you," Clara said with disgust. "She was talking stupid drunken foolishness."

"I don't think so," David said.

"Den you must go to ask her what she mean," Clara flared up.

"I don't know how to find her."

"Don't matter. Since you needn't know things that don't concern you!"

"But I *want* to know," David insisted. "You've said things to your friends I've overheard. And don't forget what I found out . . . "—he hesitated—"in your bedroom."

Clara walked slowly to her window, where the world outside was coming even more alive, the booming of fireworks increasing. The heat was fierce and humid and the sky had gathered unnatural light and turned the color of topaz. "I reread all dem ras letters," she muttered. "Nothing in there you could've found out."

"So then there *is* something to find out?"

"Only my privacy."

"Something more than privacy. Why does Dora call him the cliff boy?"

Clara shrugged. David could see she was sweating at an alarming rate.

"Dora once said his heart was in the sea."

Clara started violently. "Dat bitch, she!"

"Did he jump off a cliff?"

"Not important what him do," Clara said as she went to get a fresh towel from her linen closet to dab herself down. "Me keep certain things from you because in most case you not old enough to understand."

"I *am* old enough," David disagreed.

Clara held each end of the towel in her hands. "You already get more knowledge den is good for you. I don't want responsible to learn you what pains people most in life. And shame is about de worst pain of mind. Why should you learn dat from me?"

David's expression was full of accusation. "You *have* to tell me what happened. Even if he jumped off a cliff, why does Dora care? Why is his death so important to *her?*"

Clara drew her hands apart until the towel pulled tightly between them, but she did not speak.

"You can't not answer," David agonized. "Not after what just happened."

"Course I can."

"I won't let you. I demand you tell me."

Clara looking meaningfully at David. "When you get older, you'll realize knowing de full truth sometimes a curse. Plenty things you'll find out about people make you wish you were kept a fool."

"Let me decide that."

She threw the towel on the sofa and went into the kitchen, where she had left the flask of rum. She took another long draft, shutting her eyes for a moment, and convulsed from the bitter swallow. "You don't understand," she muttered. "Ralfie was always excitable."

David looked at her strangely. "What do you mean?"

"I mean dat as a child him had a nervous stomach. Every little thing disturb it, even bad news in de paper." Clara paused as she put the bottle back down on the counter. "Once when his father get into car wreck up Aracabesa, Ralfie was into bed fe two weeks wid attack of nerves. When him get to be fifteen, some days him couldn't stop from sleeping. Don't eat. Things were troubling him dat couldn't explain."

"You never found out what they were?"

Clara shrugged. She took the bottle of rum and walked out into the living room. "We made him go to church confession. Took him to Pella. Took him to doctor, who said something chemical not right, to gi' him lots of goat milk, and don't gi' him no worries.

"Den, when him was twenty-one, him fell in love wid a Kingston girl. She named Thunbergia. A beautiful Kingston girl. But Thunbergia decide last minute she want to be a nurse in England. Left Ralfie high and dry." Clara was now looking through David. "Him wound his head with black bandanna, take a scythe, and go up high 'pon de cliffs to shred bamboo grass."

David looked at her, bewildered.

"I'm telling you how him eventually did bring himself to his death!" Clara cried out.

Neither spoke for a few moments. "But that's not what Dora was talking about," David said.

"You don't understand," Clara insisted softly, now looking out the window. "In Jamaica when a child dies in such a way, means a terrible shame."

David clapped his fists at his side. "No! No!" he cried. "You're not telling me. I know he did something. What is it?"

"Dat is all it is. I telling you!"

"Did he hurt somebody? Did he *kill* somebody?"

"No!"

"Did he try to kill Dora?"

Clara suddenly threw the bottle of rum against the wall. The crashing sound was even more deafening than the fireworks. David could make out the wet splatter, which in the darkness resembled bloodstains. And then the distant booms began again, now with a boding sound. Clara threw herself down in a huddle on the love seat, digging her elbows into her sides, rocking and rocking.

"What did he do, Clara?" David asked softly.

Clara peered down at the floor. "Him don't kill nobody."

"Then what?"

"Him raped her," Clara whispered.

A cold tendril of dread rushed through David's veins.

"Dat is it—what you looking for—all dis time." Clara spoke as she shivered. "Dat is de past me was trying to contain."

The sky above the Verrazano Bridge was suddenly filled with a display of gold hoops, from which sprang indigo bullets, from which sprang scarlet pastilles. Stung with awe, David left Clara sitting on the sofa and retreated toward the kitchen.

"You know de rest," she told him. "Me husband couldn't take it.

So him left me. And then I was shamed. People don't come to see me again. I take job after job until I come up here to you."

Then Clara began to weep freely and David sat down next to her and tried to comfort her. They held one another for quite some time. As he pressed his face to her soft neck, feeling the cords of her muscles straining from her sobs, he wondered if, indeed, she had finally told him everything. He watched a fire rocket whistle up to the heavens, level off in a wide arc, and then, overcome by the pull of gravity, fall into a doomed spiral, fizzling into lavender ash.

For many months afterward, David would have dreams from which he would awake gasping. He would be standing on the brink of high cliffs, contemplating the clear swirl of a sea below him. Suddenly, a man would come up from behind him and try to shove him off. They both struggled for their lives, but the man always won out. And as David slowly plunged toward the rocks, he felt unafraid; he knew what came next was irrevocable, and the lack of choice calmed him. Embraced by a column of warm tropical air that smelled like Clara's suitcases, he felt no pain at all when the impact finally came.

On the following Monday, his father was scheduled to call at the house at seven in the morning and his mother was supposed to drop by at eight, each of them expecting to hear David's decision as to which one of them he had chosen to live with. Coincidentally, Monday also happened to be the date of Jocelyn Martin's death on "The Raging Tide." David hadn't watched the show for several weeks, but Clara had precognition of what was to occur. A half-hour before her story was due to go on, she told David, "You must watch today, something exciting," as she had said so many times during the five years she had been taking care of him.

Jocelyn Martin went to a dark local tavern to threaten a woman she suspected to be having an affair with her husband. For a while she sat alone at the bar, ruminating over her miserable life while she slugged down two vodka martinis. Finally, a woman came in. Jocelyn Martin got up and went over to accuse her of being the mistress of her husband. When Jocelyn Martin finally left the bar and entered the dark, rainy street, she was shot by an unidentifiable attacker and fell screaming into the gutter.

As the scene faded from the color television, a lighthearted commercial for Downyflake waffles replacing it, Clara and David looked at one another significantly, each recalling their meeting with the woman on the train.

"Cheap script if I ever see one," Clara complained. "Her murder don't even grow out de story. Dem transplant it to shake her off de show."

"I completely agree," David said.

"Imagine a thing like dat," Clara mused. "Dem kill her off after all dis time."

The phone rang just then and David glanced at Clara. "Watch how everybody will call me now," she said as she trotted over to answer it.

It was Blanche on the line. The beauticians, who watched the stories in the salon, were in an uproar. Parrotlike screeches were filtering through the receiver.

"Tell dem relax," Clara urged Blanche. "Jocelyn Martin put off de show because she get too much hate mail. Tell dem write channel two a letter and get everybody to sign. Plenty people will be cross wid such foolishness. Tell dem we want her back, don't care if she must raise from the dead."

Clara finally hung up the phone. She looked at David with raised eyebrows and sighed. "Well," she said, "everybody vexed."

"God, Clara, it's only a soap opera."

"Don't matter if it's not real, it's how *we* entertain." She scowled. "What I must do lock up here widout a good story?"

"I never knew you thought it was such a prison here," David said.

"You know what I saying." Clara looked at him intently. "Let me ask you one question. What you'd do if dem knife me down just like Jocelyn Martin? What you'd do if dem killed dese old bones?"

"Why are you asking me this now?"

"What you mean? Dem kill already two people near to where me live a Brooklyn."

David was agitated by Clara's conversation, and to reassure himself, he reached for her hand. But she drew away from him in order to prompt an answer.

"I don't know why you're making me worry about this," he said, looking out her window where shafts of sunlight cascaded through tall maples, fracturing through a trellis of Sterling roses at the far corner of the patio. The garden seemed so abundant with flowers, and everything there was completely calm.

"Me just want to know if you feel your life could exist widout me," she said. "Because of course I'm concerned you'd finish properly, to begin to get ya own friends and activities."

David turned to her. "But you know that when I'm with you, I don't need friends or activities."

"Don't be foolish. What about when you gone to college? I won't be dere. You'll be forced to rely on friends."

"Maybe I won't even go to college. Not everybody goes to college. Maybe I'll study art. Maybe we'll go to Jamaica," David said, noticing a sleek new sailboat setting out from the neighbor's dock, its white sheet held in close haul.

Throwing up her hands, Clara rearranged herself on her bed. "Boy-oh-boy, I was looking for a spark in you. Don't you know why I bring up dis now?"

"Because of my decision?"

"Of course."

"But I'm going to live in New York. And see you as much as I can."

"Come to me here, David," Clara said, outstretching her dark arms. David was getting annoyed with her and decided to hold his ground.

"You going to live wid your father just so to see me?" she asked.

"What's wrong with that?"

She shook her head. "I'm afraid for you."

"Why?"

"Because so much as I love you, I believe children bound to dere mother. It's instinct dat goes beyond friendship, I'm afraid."

"But not ours," David said. "Because you're more than a friend."

"Yes, but hol' on. When she sell dis house, I won't have a job. Wha happen if me can't find work and must go home to Jamaica?"

"I'll face that when the time comes."

"You'll be stuck wid—him," she said.

"But you love me, Clara," David agonized. "You're supposed to want me to stay near you."

"But you not listening me. I talking necessity now. What happen if me find five-day job makes me work weekends?"

"I'll come to you after school."

Clara shook her head. "Somehow Manhattan seems a world farther from Brooklyn even den Rye," she said wistfully.

"Then I'll stay with you sometimes."

"Don't you see? It's changing!" Clara's voice broke. "Me don't want the change, but we must face it. You have to go school. I to find oddar work."

David's throat was like an empty shell. He noticed the sailboat had just raised a blue and white spinnaker; the wrinkled sheet quickly inflating with wind. His heart felt just like that. "You're getting to be just like mom," he said with horror. He'd never thought Clara would ever forsake him. Part of his acceptance of his mother's flight was his firm belief in Clara's constancy. But now even that was shattering. "You're going to back off when things don't suit you." He allowed the words to roll off his tongue and felt such an emptiness afterward.

"Me?" Clara pointed to her chest. "You can't compare me wid her. She's blood. I'm just an old black housekeeper who loves you."

"You're a liar!" David cried. "You *don't* love me! You're trying to abandon me." He pounded his fists on her bureau, disturbing the talcum powder, the Touch of Fire, the portrait of her husband.

"Don't you trouble me things!" Clara jumped off the bed and ran to protect them.

"You just loved me 'cause you were desperate. 'Cause you had no one else. And all the rest of it was selfishness. You had a free place to live—and money. Now you want to get rid of me!" he cried, sweeping everything off the bureau top. Bottles bounced, powder dusted the carpeting, and the picture of her husband was cracked.

"You nasty, duhty child to call *me* desperate, to call *me* selfish." Clara got down on her hands and knees to salvage the photograph. "You de one too selfish to see me have your interest at heart. . . . Look what you do to me only picture of Manny. You mean son of a selfish bitch."

"That's right, I'm a son of a bitch. But you should've left me alone when I asked you to go back to Jamaica that first day you came here. You made me love you. And now you're backing off 'cause it got to be too much for you. You just want to forget about me now. You'll get another job and never see me again. You'll just—you'll just be like a *nigger* in the end!"

Silence fell like a boulder. Clara was blinking perplexedly at David and soon let out an awful groan. She dropped the bottles, the shards of picture glass she held in her hands, and fled from the room out into the hallway. Regrets rending his heart, David chased after her. But she ran into the medicine closet and slammed the door. He went and put his ear against the wood. He could hear violent sobbing, each of Clara's heaves of misery exploding needles into his soul. Remorse crashed upon him.

"Don't you see?" he cried out to her. "You make me so angry. You make me scared. I didn't mean to say it," he said. "I'm sorry." But Clara kept weeping in the darkness of that closet.

David was shaking with fear. He dimly remembered that Clara sometimes drank Galliano to calm her nerves. He ran downstairs to the liquor cabinet, took the bottle, and went to the kitchen for some orange juice. After opening the refrigerator, he stared for several moments at the cooled series of metal grids that supported the food Clara and he had bought together at Shopwell earlier in the day. She had arranged everything neatly and orderly inside. Breakstone's sweet butter, fresh cartons of ranch eggs, and a white globe of mozzarella cheese. This chilled little world, in comparison to his, seemed so beautifully defined, so full of a specific purpose, so complete. He mixed the Galliano with the orange juice and ice cubes, but could drink only half a glass before he began to feel nauseous.

With his head in his hands, David sat slumped at the kitchen table. How could he have spoken so evilly? He had never thought to say such a thing before. But then, why did she have to deny the power of their love?

Daylight was flooding the kitchen, and Clara's favorite pots on the stove were glowing with dull brilliance. They were to be neglected that evening, for the first of many evenings, the blue pilots never to make flames.

The phone rang as he was climbing the stairs to his bedroom, and he went back down to answer it.

"Hello, David." It was his father.

"Hi, dad."

"You sound preoccupied."

David shook his head and sighed. "Dad, you were supposed to call at seven, remember?"

"You mean to tell me you still haven't decided?" Bill asked incredulously.

"I didn't say that," David said irritably.

There was an uncomfortable silence.

"Dad," he garbled, "I'm a little . . . are you calling for a reason?"

His father could hear the shaking in his voice. "What's wrong, pal?"

"We had a fight."

"Who had a fight?"

"Clara and me."

Bill didn't even register this. "Look, I know I'm calling you a little early, but I just heard some great news and I'm really excited about it."

"What news?"

"I just got a commitment for a really fine private school for the fall," Bill said. "The only thing is, I have to give them a deposit within a couple of days or else you'll lose your spot."

His father's ill-timed insistence made David furious. "Look, I'll decide!" he snapped. "But I won't decide now." He suddenly realized he was in control of the situation, and that surprised him.

"Jesus, don't take it out on *me*," Bill said.

"You should know when not to put pressure on me," David told him, slamming down the phone.

It rang. He lifted the receiver and quietly replaced it. It rang once again, but finally it stopped.

A little drunk from the Galliano, David stumbled up to his room, managing to turn on his radio tuner before collapsing on his bed. He sobbed until he fell asleep.

The sultry voice of Allison Steele on WNEW woke him up at seven-thirty. He had a terrible racking feeling in his chest, and for a split second couldn't actually pinpoint what tormented him so. Then an image of Clara's tortured face rose before him, a vein pulsating above her eyebrows. He doubled over and groaned. Suddenly remembering that dinner would force contact between them, he sniffed the air, dimly hoping to smell cooking odors. But he smelled nothing. A while later, through his stupor, he heard the electric garage door opening. How could he face Peter and his mother?

David heard Clara hurrying down her wooden steps, and chairs scraping against the linoleum floor. There was low conversation. He knew she was telling them what had happened. A while later he heard his mother and Peter climbing the stairs to the master bedroom. They were being unnaturally quiet. They would not disturb him—unlike his father, they probably knew better than to demand any decision from him just now.

Feeling dizzy, David managed to climb out of his bed and tiptoe downstairs. Clara, unfortunately, had by now returned to her bedroom. He looked through the bay window into the waning light and on impulse crept outside to the garden. Shadows were blanketing the shrubs and there was an insistent humming of cicadas. It seemed to have rained while he was sleeping; many of the blooms, weighed down with droplets, bowed their brilliant heads to their leaves like birds huddling to wings. A few pink rhododendron flowers lay on the flagstones. As David reached for one, he peered up to Clara's window. Caressing the webs of petals that felt as soft as membranes, he rubbed them vigorously until they turned to a bitter-smelling pulp. Feeling so afraid, he went back inside and plodded up the front staircase. He gobbled four aspirins before lying down once again on his bed.

Was it late at night? David didn't know what time it was. All he knew was that Clara was standing at his door, looking like an apparition. "You better wake up now," she said. "For me have something to tell you."

David felt feverish; he supposed it was the effects of alcohol. He propped himself up on his elbows, his heart beating frantically. He feared the worst.

"I'm leaving here tomorrow morning," she told him.

He was so stunned, he could barely speak. "You can't," he managed to whimper.

"What you saying—I can't?"

"Please, you have to forgive me. I know I'm the most miserable person in the world. But you scared me. You upset me. I was afraid you were going to do—what you're doing now."

She vehemently shook her head. "You must just accept this as fate, David. Don't help to apologize. Too late for apology. Too many risks you run wid me after all," she said.

David wished he could see her face, to know how serious she was being, or if she was bluffing; but the hallway light cast her in a dark silhouette so that he was unable to tell.

"The things I said were so terrible." He began to cry. "They were so awful, such a mistake. You have to understand. . . ."

Clara groaned. "Boy, you'll never in ya life know how dat last word cut me. It really do. Never expect from you. Never dreamed . . . " She paused for a moment of reflection. "But you see, I sort of expect what happen to happen. Dat's why I try to hide my life from you. I knew you'd wonder about me, would doubt truth of me feelings when you heard about me son. And what worse is you almost right to doubt me."

"Don't double-talk me, Clara."

"Me? Me de last soul in de world to double-talk. But what you said tonight cannot be reversed. Words can't be eaten once dem come out. You deny us. Ya reasons were so wrong."

Clara crossed the room, peering out the window into the blue of night. She could somehow see that the evening paper was lying halfway in the rhododendrons. "Him miss again," she said under her breath.

"What are you talking about?" David got up off the bed.

"Paper boy," she said wistfully. "Well, I won't have to worry meself over him no more. Him was wretched to deal wid. Never get de moneys straight."

She turned from the window and came a little closer to David, who could smell a hint of bay rum.

"You've been using your compresses, haven't you?" he asked.

She nodded.

"Has it been your pressure or just a headache?"

She looked down at her bedroom slippers. "Both o' dem." Then, oddly, a smile curled her lips.

"What are you thinking, Clara?" he asked.

"Just dat you care. Despite everything you said. Me know dat caring goes deep."

"Then why do you want to go?" he moaned.

Suddenly, she crossed her arm over David's and their skin touched. Hers was so dark and smooth and his so pale and sickly with its ugly network of blue veins.

"We really not de same blood, nor even de same race," Clara said in wonderment, as though realizing it for the very first time. "Like when me was looking at dose bad, insulting children at de ice-cream place, me was thinking, Dese are white people insulting you, a black woman. But you, David . . . were different." Her face clouded over and she whirled away from him, pressing her fists to her temples. "I don't know, man, so strange, but I really believe a force was in dis world dat bind us. A long, lovely moment you and I had, like a wave coming from de sea and curved so perfect round us and connect us even closer dan blood." She shrugged. "Suppose it couldn't ride forever, it have to break."

And as David had done as a child, he knelt and hugged her legs and wept.

"Stay a few more months," he begged her. "At least until the house is sold?"

"Never happens so neat. And anyway, it would only be pain."

"Then I'll come see you. I'll come visit as much as possible."

Clara shut her eyes tightly. "Don't want you to come see me—for a while."

"But why?"

"Better dat way. Probably soon I'll go back to Jamaica and try again to live dere."

She took his hands and made him stand and face her. "Only one more thing I want to tell you, David," she said. And he peered into her eyes, knowing his own face looked distorted and grotesque from weeping. She touched her chest with her fist and said, "Only you is in dere, David. Only you in my heart."

He lay awake the entire night, watching the heavy darkness rolling into gray and then blue. A yellow square of light finally appeared on the carpeting, shadowed with the cross sections of the windowpane. He heard doors slamming, a car pulling into the driveway, the gravel rumbling under a tread of wheels. He went to the window and looked down on a Rye taxi, whose headlamps charged the mist that hung over the yard. There was whispering downstairs.

Hurrying down the hallway, he was hoping to find Clara still in her bedroom. Her door was wide open, the bed carefully made, the evening paper folded up on the night table. No one was there. A warm breeze dribbled through a window, stirring the leaves of newsprint. The room smelled of mustiness and camphor. He quickly cracked all her bureau drawers, finding them empty. He flung open the closet door, but the inside was barren. Then he heard rustling in the kitchen and rushed to the top of Clara's wooden steps.

"Goodbye, Clara," he heard his mother saying.

"Goodbye, Mrs. Hart," Clara told her.

As much as David wanted to run down the stairs, he held back, not wanting his mother to intrude upon him bidding Clara goodbye. He assumed Clara would come upstairs to him before leaving, and thereby returned to his room. He got into bed, swathing himself in covers.

Seconds passed at an alarmingly slow rate, and the sheets grew hot and itchy and bothersome. He finally kicked them off and ran to the window. The driver was fitting her red suitcase inside the trunk. Clara was standing outside, wearing the same knitted coat she wore the first day they ever met. Strange that she had it on during summer. She was really leaving. But when was she going to come say goodbye?

She gazed up at David's room, and as she did so, he made his decision. She murmured to herself, a prayer perhaps, touched her breast with two fingers, and then, kissing them with her purple lips, blessed the house and his window. She hurried to the taxi before he could cry out, "Clara!" and was driven away, leaving a spray of gravel in her wake.

FIVE

1973

It was a many-leveled Victorian house flanked by hundred-year-old oaks. Six steps led up to a wide front porch, where enormous beveled windows rose on either side of a door with a brass knocker shaped like a strong arm. David had twice climbed up and down those six steps, hesitating because he was afraid of being turned away, afraid that Clara had changed.

So he stayed for a while in the street, collecting himself.

It was September. The summer had passed and the next day he was moving to California with his mother and Peter. He had not seen Clara in two months and she had not answered his letters. Since she left him, he had dropped a good deal of weight. The weight loss first began with a lack of appetite, which was brought on by his depression at losing her, but after a few miserable weeks, David realized he somehow needed to leave himself in order to find relief.

He discovered a way to do this, a way to get through the rest of the summer, and that was taking long swims along the shoreline of the Sound. He eventually quit organized practice and began to swim solely in salt water. First he went in for an hour, swimming part of the way from Rye to Mamaroneck harbor, zigzagging from boat mooring to boat mooring. When his mother and Peter discovered him doing this, they insisted he either stop swimming by himself or get somebody to accompany him. But David insisted he needed to swim alone. He warned that if they kept bothering him, he would swim at night while they were asleep. By the end of August, he was spending up to three hours a day in the Sound. He would come out with fingers and toes shriveled by prolonged exposure to the salt water, and his hair got bleached many shades lighter. He lost more weight, and as he did so, his torso grew firm and hard.

He had been able to get through to Clara only on weekends; he never got her on the phone during the week. It seemed that she had almost immediately found another job. Whenever David did get through, Clara always spoke warmly to him, but cut short their conversation at the five-minute mark. The brevity of their talks helped her elude his inquiries about where she was working. And whenever he asked her when they might see one another again, she always said, "More time must pass, darling." It was as though that morning she left Rye, Clara had set an inner timer that was now monitoring the proper term of their separation. At first David thought it would only be a matter of days until he saw her, and then he was afraid it would be months, and then he wondered if it might even be years. He imagined that she was employed by another family; his worst fear being that she had taken another boy under her wing and in so doing had canceled him out of her life—the way his mother had canceled out his father.

David had actually started the day by taking a train from Rye into Manhattan in order to say goodbye to his father. He was walking through Grand Central Station when he began to notice familiar signs and staircases leading to the Brooklyn subways and was suddenly overcome by a powerful desire. He stopped in the middle of the crowded terminal and looked up at the gilded domed ceilings. He shut his eyes and struggled against the longings that were welling up inside him. Then he heard something familiar, yet strange. Patois. He opened his eyes and saw two middle-aged Jamaican ladies carrying shopping bags and umbrellas. They were gossiping intently as they hurried past him, obviously having someplace to get to. And without a moment's further hesitation, David followed behind them until he was riding a train out to Brooklyn.

He went first to Blanche's Beauty. When he entered the shop, the beauticians stared insolently at him as though they did not know him. He wondered if Clara could have told them what he had called her.

But then Blanche came running over to him, her mouth agape, and he reminded himself that Clara would never tell anyone why they had been pulled apart.

"For gracious sake," Blanche said, shocked. "You get so small I don't recognize you. What happen, devil living inside you?" In a moment, Lydia, Doris Williams, and Felicia had crowded around David.

"Jesus Father, who would know you?" Doris Williams remarked. "You looking lovely now. So trim and strong."

"Who color ya hair?" Felicia asked suspiciously.

"It's the salt water," David explained.

"Lord, you looking handsome," Lydia cooed as she sidled up to him.

David blushed as he followed Blanche over to her hairdressing station. While he watched her set the hair of a client, he explained that he was leaving the next day for the West Coast, where he would live with his mother and Peter on the avocado ranch they had bought. He then made small talk for another few minutes, hoping Blanche would mention Clara. But Blanche would not bring her up.

"How is Clara?" he finally asked.

"She doing quite nicely," Blanche said through a mouthful of metal hairclips. "Come into de shop all de while."

"She ever talk about me?"

Blanche resolutely shook her head. "Don't discuss you again." She looked at David intently. "But dat don't mean you not in her mind." She grinned. "No, sir. Because sometimes when I see her sitting 'pon dat dryer chair, a smile come cross her face and I know she thinking of you."

"Give me her address." David had trouble hiding the desperation in his voice. "Let me surprise her."

Blanche looked at him peevishly. "Not fair to ask me where she working. What happen if she vex I gi' it to you?"

Perhaps patois would do better to convince Blanche. "She won't vex, she don't know herself," David assured her. "She'd happy to see me."

"You know dat not de issue," Blanche said.

"Me will tell her Icey gi' it to me."

"Cha, man, Icey tight as drum," Blanche said. "Icey na chat."

"How about Dora?" David said, looking around the shop.

Blanche sighed. "Dora went down Jamaica for a time."

David wondered if that fight with Clara had anything to do with Dora's departure. As he watched Blanche continue to set her customer's hair, he racked his brain for someone else to ask for Clara's work address. Suddenly, he heard Blanche cluck her tongue. She had put down her teasing comb and was reaching into a marbleized drawer for her address book. "Since you going away tomorrow, I don't see why I should keep you from saying goodbye to Clara," Blanche said. "Just don't pin it 'pon me." She flipped through the pages until she found Clara's work address, which she wrote on a piece of beauty-parlor stationery and handed to David.

"I'll try not to," he said as she escorted him to the door.

From there, David said goodbye to all the beauticians and then turned to give Blanche a farewell kiss. As he leaned toward her, she grabbed a strand of his bleached-out hair. "Needs a trim, boy."

"No thanks," David said, remembering what she had done to him the last time she "cane-rowed" his hair.

"Why don't you come and sit down in me special chair?" Blanche offered. "I'll cut it for nothing. I'll do it for Clara's heart."

Hearing the very last words Clara had spoken to him in Rye, David touched his hair, feeling the residue left by Blanche's Dippity-Do fingers. The pink light in the salon was suddenly blinding and his pupils turned to pinpoints. The sadness he had been trying to repress, which had its low and high moments much like a tide, now swelled into every bit of his body.

"I can't," David told her. "It'd make me too unhappy."

Blanche cocked her hands on her hips and smiled forlornly at him. She seemed to understand. "All right," she said. "Good luck in California." Then she shook an admonishing finger. "But keep in touch wid us. Don't be a stranger."

David once again climbed the stairs of the Victorian house, and this time built up the nerve to knock on the door. He heard shuffling and mutters of complaint before a dumpy, middle-aged white woman answered the door. She wore a leopard-print polyester housedress and was clutching a cigarette in her wrinkled fingers.

"What is it?" she asked him imperiously, rubbing away a fleck of face powder from a lower eyelid.

"I'm David Hart," David stammered. "I would like to see Clara Mayfield."

A look of genuine surprise molded the already exaggerated features of the woman's face. Her watery gray eyes looked sarcastic. "You the kid she used to work for?" she asked, taking a deep, nervous drag on her cigarette. Her voice sounded weary and resentful of the unexpected intrusion.

"Yes," David said.

"Hold on a minute, then. Clara!" she yelled up a wide, spiraling staircase.

David looked way up to bands of sunlight bursting through the picture windows in the upper reaches of the house. Motes of dust were swirling. He saw a figure whose white uniform made her look darker than she actually was. His heart thumped frantically, waiting for her reaction. Then he heard a low groan, like the one she had made that night when he had denied her. She rushed down the staircase and stopped a few steps above him. "Must be you lost twenty pounds!" she exclaimed. Then she continued down to where David stood and embraced him. But he felt so strange and removed from her.

"Son of a hoot," she chuckled in his ear. "Knew I couldn't live here too long without you finding me."

"You mean, you don't mind that I came?" he asked.

"Cha, man, somehow I did expect it."

She bit his ear jokingly, and her warm breath made his spine tingle. She disentangled herself to stare once again at his thinner body. Her brow furrowed and she touched a place between his eyes. "How you get so small?"

David wanted to tell her it was from missing her and from so many yearnings he did not understand, but he ended up saying, "From lack of toto."

Clara laughed. "Toto is bad influence. Better you don't have it. Just don't grow up before ya ready."

"I won't," he said.

"Promise me to take you sweet time?"

And David was charmed again, just like that, and the intermittent pain of separation he'd felt for those two months was overwhelmed by the gratitude he felt just to be listening to her inimitable voice. Then, without warning, his vision telescoped the way it once did when he had been ill with the flu and his fever broke and hovering over his sickbed was Clara's loving face. In a few moments, however, he was able to look carefully at her again, although he was perplexed by the temporary lapse. Her face looked drawn.

"So who did tell you I was working here?" Clara asked.

"I heard it through the grapevine."

"Which grape?"

"Come on. Aren't you glad I came?"

She smiled as she took David's hand and they began to climb the stairs. As they wound their way higher, the whole interior scheme of the house fell into place. The living room, off to the left, had imitation Chippendale chairs and charcoal sketches of Paris and the Eiffel Tower on its walls. In the dining room, the stirring crystals of an elaborate chandelier made trembling rainbows on the wooden floor. When they reached the second level, Clara pointed down a long hallway to a room filled with sunlight. David could see curtains billowing slowly, the fringe of a hospital bed, and the outline of a motionless body.

"Dat's de crone," Clara explained.

"The who?"

"The old lady I hired to take care of."

"An old lady?" David asked. "I had no idea. You mean . . . there's no little boy living here?"

Clara frowned at him. "A boy? You think I'd break me backside to care a little boy again?"

David squeezed her arm; he felt relieved. "And you've been here the whole time?"

"Start here just a few days after Rye," Clara said.

The transition between Rye and this house suddenly seemed too easy, and David momentarily felt betrayed by it.

They continued climbing to the next level, where Clara had her bedroom. On an old, eroded bureau, among lotions and medicines, was her shrine of family pictures; the one David had broken of her husband had been repaired. The double bed was piled high with nightgowns and long-line brassieres. David approached the rolled-glass windows, whose imperfections blurred the view of the scraggly, untended backyard and the upper branches of the oak trees.

"Is guava season in Jamaica." Clara would say anything to break the uncomfortable silence. She was squinting at David, searching his face as though something present there two months before had since been worn away. "Yes, it frightens me how older you looking in so short a time," she remarked. "Must be loss of weight does it. Ya face has more strength to it. Ya jaw getting bold."

"You look different, too," David told her.

"Of course. Look especially 'pon me eyes."

There were faint dots of yellow on her dark irises, and the whites were laced with red. "Don't sleep so good most nights," she said.

"How's your pressure?"

"Sometimes gets me terrible. Like today even, me na feeling me best." Clara massaged her forehead with her thumb and middle finger. The bangles on her arms pinged. "Like me gone to doctor all de while and him don't do a thing but charge me plenty money fe a couple of pills make me feel worse. . . . Anyway, me must stop from chatting. Time to feed de old sow."

And so the requirements of Clara's job thrust their way between them. David followed her down the stairs to the kitchen. The middle-aged lady was nowhere to be seen. He watched Clara set about the task of preparing the old woman's lunch. First, she opened the refrigerator, taking out a plate of cooked flank steak from which, with a paring knife, she trimmed away the congealed fat. She grabbed two tins of vegetables from a cupboard and dumped them into an Osterizer. She diced up the meat, adding it to the vegetables, and then dumped in a cup of tomato paste. She flicked a switch and they watched everything blending into an olive concoction. She poured some pineapple juice into a small plastic tumbler and then put the liquefied meal into an orange bowl.

Having arranged everything neatly on a tray, Clara led the way up

to the next level. The old woman's room had bare white walls and a
large bookshelf filled with *Reader's Digest* condensed novels. There
was a small portable record player on a night table that abutted the
hospital bed. A dusty, scratched record sat on the turntable, an album
called *Getting Ready for Death* fanned out next to it. David turned to
look at a spindly old woman with vacant blue eyes who lay quietly in
bed. Her hair was swept inside a plastic shower cap. "Hello," she said
in a slurred, low-pitched voice.

"Mrs. Thomsky, this me friend David." Clara enunciated her words
as though the woman were terribly hard-of-hearing. She then put the
lunch on a metal tray with two prongs on one end that plugged into
a corresponding place in the hospital bed. She propped Mrs. Thomsky
up, pushing the tray in until it stopped an inch from her rib cage. Then
Clara took a plastic spoon and straw out of the pocket of her uniform.

"Thank you, missy," said the old woman, taking her eating uten-
sils. She wore a silly smile as she stared adoringly at Clara, and her
eyes were filmy with cataracts. She drank a long draft of juice and then
bent over the blended mixture, slowly spooning it into her mouth. She
burped loudly, then shrugged, as though to say that having little
control of her body functions was a humiliation she lived with but had
never quite gotten used to. David was suddenly afraid such a thing
might happen to Clara and inwardly made a vow to take care of her
if it did.

"At least she can feed herself," he whispered.

"Not always," Clara said. "Lots of time she just don't have
strength."

"What's wrong with her, anyway?"

"Half paralyzed from a stroke."

Suddenly, Mrs. Thomsky dropped her spoon, lifting up both her
hands to scratch her head in an enfeebled fury.

"Darling, please stop from that now," Clara gently scolded her.
"She gets heebie-jeebies," she explained to David. Then she turned
back to the woman. "Come now, Alexa, stop from scratching ya
head."

David noticed a faint patch of blue on Mrs. Thomsky's withered
forearm. At first he thought it was a bed bruise, but then recognized
the brand of a concentration camp.

Eventually Alexa overcame her fit and continued to eat her lunch. At one point she looked up at David. "Who are you?" She spoke in a scratchy, wavering voice.

"I told you, this is me boy, David," Clara explained in a loud, clear voice. "I used to work for his family."

Mrs. Thomsky's head began bobbing. She was looking at Clara sadly. "You care for me more than my daughter." Her crinkled body shook and tears began to flow.

"Come on, Thomsky." Clara stroked her head. "Why you start in wid ya crying today?"

The woman continued to sob.

"But what is troubling you?" Clara demanded.

"Oh, oh . . ." The woman wept for a while. Then she glared at David, her lips twitching with the urge to speak more quickly. "Is he going to take you away?"

"Don't be stupid!"

"I won't do that," David reassured her.

A drool of blended food wandered out of the invalid's mouth, slowly spilling down her front. David shrank back, horrified, while Clara jumped into action, clapping Mrs. Thomsky on her back. "Stop it now or you'll choke!" she scolded.

Mrs. Thomsky lurched at David, clutching his arm frantically as though she were being engulfed by darkness and he was the only light. "Don't," she pleaded. "Don't."

Clara hugged Mrs. Thomsky while glancing wearily at him. "I get caught up again, same way," she muttered as they left the room and began climbing the stairs.

Her remark disturbed David, who stopped climbing. "What do you mean by that?"

Clara shook her head. "Oh, Lord a mercy, you take it de wrong way. It's not how I mean."

"Maybe it *is* true," David wondered aloud. "Maybe you were too caught up with me."

"No, sir," Clara said, turning around and grabbing both his arms. From the chandelier downstairs came the sounds of kissing glass. The house suddenly seemed as enormous and imposing as the church they had gone to that Sunday a year ago, the moment even holier than then.

"I meant more myself, how I feel toward people," Clara whispered. I should leave dis job and find easier work. Me must lift her all de time and change de sheets and bedpan. But me feel so bad that she can't manage herself. I pity her so."

"And did you pity me?" David asked.

Clara looked stricken by the question. "First time I did," she admitted. "But not when I get to know you. Because in you I see so much . . . promise."

They went back upstairs to Clara's room, where she pushed aside piles of blouses and undergarments and brassieres on her bed so they could have room to sit.

"Do you still watch the stories?" David said.

Clara smiled, then began to chuckle, and he asked her what was so amusing.

"I guess you don't know what happen 'pon dem," she said.

"I haven't watched since . . . that afternoon."

"Jocelyn Martin appear on de 'Search for Light' Clara explained.

"You mean as Jocelyn Martin?"

"No, de actress. Her name now Lydia King—she's a rich benefactress—though me and de girls still call her Jocelyn Martin."

"They must've lost a lot of viewers from the other show," David remarked.

Clara nodded. "Every time she come on, me think of de old Jocelyn, which reminds me I'm watching a story instead of watching life."

"Maybe it's better that way."

Clara shook her head in disagreement. "Used to be dat 'Raging Tide' in de afternoons let me forget who I was."

A long silence unraveled between them. Clara glanced at the electric clock on her bureau. "Well, only a couple more hours till I gone home for me little weekend." Then she sighed. "You know, David, sometimes I tell meself, 'Stop dis foolishness and pride and just go back to Jamaica.' "

"Nothing is stopping you," David forced himself to say.

"Maybe some o' dem would have forgotten me by now."

"Maybe."

She looked at him imploringly, her eyes moistened. "But can I ever really go back?"

"Are you afraid?"

She looked away. "Yes . . . still afraid to return to de old shame."

"But what happened was in no way your fault," David insisted.

"Child, you not old enough to understand."

"What do you mean? You always tell me that."

"Because it's de truth."

David drew in his breath. "There's something you haven't told me, isn't there?" he said.

She nodded her head resolutely, focusing her sad eyes on the blurred oak trees out her window. "We need more time, darling, you and I. We not finish yet," she whispered. "You must listen to me now, child. You must go now. Go wid you muddar. Go and grow into a man, and when you're a man I will send you a sign to come and hear the most hurtful part."

David was silent for a moment. "What kind of sign?" he asked.

Clara had bowed her head and was staring down at her knees. "You will know," she said. David could see the roots of her hair, which were graying. And he felt as though he were looking at some rare, nearly doomed bird he had found through a sort of miracle.

But David had been unable to wait for Clara's sign. And so that night he had gone unbidden back to her apartment in Brooklyn and stayed up talking with her until the light grew pale. The boxing program had been replaced by a late-night thriller, and then for many hours the television had broadcast a blue cottony fuzz. Now the sun was shining and Clara got up from the kitchen table to raise the yellowed shades. Birds were wheeling over the building and she watched them for a moment before sitting down again. Her hands trembled and she kept swallowing.

David knew her pressure was troubling her. "Don't be so upset," he told her. "Don't be afraid."

But for her the moment had more significance than he realized; she had every right to be nervous. David watched her carefully as she got up again and walked to the boundary of the small kitchen. Darkness still overtook the rest of the apartment, which seemed as vast as a forest. Then she began to hack.

Afraid the tension was making Clara ill, David went over and held her in an effort to calm her down. As soon as he came near, she grabbed on to him, squeezing with all her might. Then she shook her head. "Still hard to speak even after all de time I live wid dis."

"I can understand that."

"Me quite sure you know by now dat I don't tell you for good reason. Lying is good if it protect people."

David looked at her strangely. "Then how can you ever trust anyone?"

Clara muttered, "Child, such question you asking de wrong woman. No one me ever know could me trust. Not me husband. Not me son."

In the bedroom now, there was an early-morning church program airing on television. David could hear the preacher's voice inveighing against greed. A background choir, accompanied by a trilling organ, sang "Amen" at each appropriate pause. For a moment Clara also listened. But upon hearing the preacher's singsong proselytizing, she wrinkled up her face, reminding David that she distrusted the power of God.

He looked at her keenly. "So, what is it, Clara?" he asked. "What really happened?"

Clara nodded her head. By the rapt look in her eyes, David could tell she already was slipping into her living dream. "Don't make sense to me, dis life," she complained to him. "Dat afternoon . . . certainly don't make sense."

"Let's go sit down again," he suggested, leading her back to the kitchen table.

She explained that talk of shame began in the black hills of Port Antonio, in the shantytown of back-country people who still believed in idolatry. The shantytown was known as the "abscess of Port Antonio," because water used for cooking and bathing was often impure and spawned malaria. But rarely did the back-country people bring their sick to hospitals; they relied upon the remedies of Obeah men.

Shanty husbands would work either as port laborers or in the fields; their wives were often alone from early morning until late at night. Crimes in the abscess were not taken very seriously, often committed by one shanty person against the other. And so when the news spread that a man had raped a peasant woman, people just assumed it was one of the working husbands gone mad; who else would take the time to make that difficult climb up steep cinder paths, through jungles of Spanish moss, allowing himself to be preyed upon by copperheads and swarms of flying red ants? The raped peasant woman reportedly heard a word repeated by her attacker. She told the shanty folks, who told the people in Port Antonio, and by the time the word reached Clara, it had turned into a phrase of Gypsy.

That same week Clara began dreaming of having white babies: twins and triplets, the loveliest, whitest babies she had ever seen.

Later on Pella would tell her the dreams meant giving birth to the darkest, evilest babies, giving birth to vermin. As Clara kept having her dreams, the shame stole into Port Antonio. A single shriek of a woman was heard at dusk. Someone had crept into her house, blind-folded her, and bound her hands with hemp before he raped her. The victim told the police the man kept whispering over and over again a single word. It was *Thunbergia*, the beautiful orange ivy flower.

David interrupted. "But as soon as you heard the name, didn't you make the connection—with that girl, the one Ralfie loved?"

"Wait na! I telling you how it goes," Clara insisted. "For no matter how touched him ever was, still I couldn't presume him would go to so bad." She paused, sadly shaking her head, then continued. "It was hard to accept, though I might have clues. . . . About dat time him really did start behaving more strange. Used to go up a back country to be alone. I believe was up dere must be him caught malaria from a wild grass him suck that was growing near a duhty stream."

"What does malaria have to do with it?"

Clara would not answer at first, rocking backward and forward several times in her chair. "Me getting to it, David," she said. "So listen me now."

An alarm spread as soon as the town got wind of that name. Thinking it might beckon the devil, people growing Thunbergia laced their gardens with kerosine and there were mass burnings. Armed with vessels of holy water, clergymen came from the churches to bear witness. At the time, Ralfie was working as a bookkeeper at the Copra factory. One day the foreman called Clara, looking for him. He explained that lately Ralfie had been returning extremely late from his lunch break. Clara said nothing about this to her husband but went immediately to Pella.

The winds began to pick up as Clara made her way to Pella's lonely cottage on the steep cliffs high above the sea. For a while the two women sat sipping tea on the veranda, quietly watching the whitecaps. Gazing into Pella's clear, fathomless eyes whose cataracts had once been burned away by a special lotion, Clara talked about the white-baby dreams. Without a word, Pella read the leaves at the bottom of Clara's teacup. She then took broken pieces of crystal and arranged

them on the chipped black plate where she had put out the pieces of
gizzarda they had eaten, so that now the shards mixed with sweet
crumbs of cake. She studied the patterns of light distilled through the
slivers of glass. She shook her head and turned her gaze back to the
sea. "Ralfie have malaria," she finally told Clara. "De kind dat sleep
and wake, de kind whose fever drive people insane."

Clara leaned toward Pella, whose eyes remained locked upon a
distant point. She remembered that when Pella was a little girl, both
her parents were drowned in a boating accident somewhere out on that
sea, which was why, people claimed, she could divine past and future.
"You sure what you saying?" Clara asked.

Pella turned back to Clara with brooding eyes. "Listen me, woman,
you must be careful of Ralfie. Him could turn against you. If you go
to find him now, you must first stop at de cane field down de road and
cut yaself a joint to lash him."

But Clara believed in her own power to control her son. And when
she left Pella's house, she fled as soon as she got to the cane rows.

"Him disappear again," the foreman told her when she reached the
Copra factory. He shrugged. "Somebody see him out near Freemont
Street."

Clara sensed why Ralfie had gone to Freemont Street; something
told her it had all led up to this next hour of her life: Dora Cambridge
lived out there.

The trade winds kept blowing all afternoon and they were saying
a hurricane was brewing down by the Antilles. The air was chilling
fast as Clara rushed through the streets. She saw ravaged red trumpets
of hibiscus in the gutters. A merchant's milk cart had been upset and
gallons of clotted cream had whitewashed the cobblestones. Shadows
were stretching between the stucco walls of houses and shops as Clara
kept hurrying toward Freemont Street. The wind howled through the
cane fields and she saw the sea ruffling into whitecaps and the heads
of palm trees bend and frazzle.

As Clara passed the spire of the Methodist church, she quietly
prayed that what she felt in her heart was wrong. And yet, at that
moment she foresaw her arrival at Dora's house and knew she would
hear those strange noises of a fallen world coming from inside. She

heard those sounds even before she got to the front door and began pounding with the knocker. There were scuffling footsteps, and then Ralfie darted into the side alleyway.

Clara ran after him. She smelled garbage bins and suddenly felt dirty and foul. He was peering at her with his proud, imperious face that so resembled his father's, looking at her as though she were a stranger. His face was marked by Dora's scratches, and blood was running from his eyes.

"Ya filthy wretch!" Clara cried out above the wail of the winds. "Ya not mine again, ya devil child, ya disgrace . . . me whole life!" And then suddenly, the gusts tore off a guango limb, which crashed down upon the roof of Dora's house.

By now Clara's voice was shaking pitifully and she stood up from the kitchen table. The pot of rice and peas was bubbling on the stove. She balled her hands into fists and stared confusedly at the green kitchen wall, her face pulsing with terror. "Suddenly him grabbed me arm," she went on. "Me try to twist away. But I smell dose fever sweats and him was rank. Him lash his fingers to me throat and me couldn't breathe. Me managed to bust me knees against his chest. But den was like we both were into a boat pitching dis way, dat way . . . and I saw up de sky rolling over me eyes. Me heart cry out, 'Stop from now, Ralfie, what you doing me? Stop it child. Stop it!'

"Den I fall forward and strike me head on some sort of pipe protruding from de ground. And den him was grabbing hold to me hips and by den me couldn't speak at all. Was just froze as me watch de devil's violence break 'pon his face. Him force . . ."—her voice was rasping—"his way wid me. Seemed me was lying there in de dust forever. At first telling meself, 'Girl, you only dreaming, it's na true, you'll wake like you wake from de white-baby dream.' "

Clara's face suddenly shriveled up with a bewildering thought. "Yes, was like . . . for a while me did fall asleep . . . or something." She paused. "Don't quite know. I thought I was at de beach looking 'pon de combers breaking lovely and seeing de porpoise winging through de water. You know how dem porpoise mouth always smile? Den it grow dark around me and I realize de weight was off. Open me eyes and dere was Ralfie, looming over, staring down with a look like him know me again, trying to say to me de simplest of all words. 'Ma,' him said. 'Mama?'

" 'Ralfie, don't you know?' me managed to whisper. 'Don't you realize . . . is me?' "

These last words echoed like gunshot in the kitchen. David stood up to fight off his confusion. His mouth had gone dry and there was an incredible pressure behind his eyes. Through the living-room window, he could see a train hurtling along a distant trestle toward Coney Island. He looked back into Clara's daunted face. "And that's when he went to that yellow villa—the one on the cliffs?"

Clara's head nodded ever so slightly.

"How could you?" David suddenly cried. "How could you let him do that to you?"

Clara looked amazed for a moment and then she blinked as though the question made no sense. "What do you mean—how could I?"

"You said yourself, when you get angry . . . I mean, don't you remember that night we drove into Rye? You know you have the power to fight back, to protect yourself. I just don't understand." He was feeling breathless and crazy.

"You don't understand?" Clara echoed him. "But him did leave his head. Him have de strength of ten men." A single beat of hatred passed through her face; it was the first time she had ever looked at David this way. "And don't you remember what I tell you?" she cried out. "What I said happen when me love up somebody?"

She had told him love crippled her power to do violence, love tormented her until she grew frail. But this situation was different; it had involved her own self-preservation. David was suddenly remembering the afternoon the spacemen touched the moon, when he had put his hands up Clara's legs—what then must have gone through her mind? He felt so confused. How could she have carried around such a secret for all this time?

She spoke again. "Why you think me couldn't say a damn thing, couldn't even protest my hurt when you call me a nigger?"

David looked mystified. "What do you mean by 'protest'? You left me!" he exclaimed.

Clara shook her head. "You know why I leave, so don't give me no bullshit!" She turned to the kitchen window. Some ladies with shopping carts were gossiping loudly by the corner. David could make out the distant fluency of patois. "Me get three o' dem fe same price. . . . It go up since last week—dem na have it again."

Still looking down to the street, Clara murmured, "You and I, we saw de end in sight."

"What end?"

Clara now looked at him again. "Dat me couldn't be ya muddar and you couldn't be me son," she said softly in a shudder. For a moment her weary eyes searched his. "When me did tell you dat night before I gone dat morning I forget what race you were, I also found myself forgetting you had a muddar, thinking you could be mine always. Too much longing for a son again. Was always frightened you'd find out Ralfie dead and what him do me." She sighed. "Seems dat night we both knew it have to break. I told you go to ya muddar; and you told me something I could never forgive."

David was having difficulty looking directly at Clara; he was afraid she would know he felt ashamed of what had happened to her. "You were so determined to find out everything, till no more mystery to Clara," she told him, as though lack of mystery would kill his feelings

David reached for her hand, and as he did so a wave of nausea went through him. He wanted to say how sorry he was about what she had gone through, knowing it was something she had relived many times since then. He wanted to tell her how it didn't make a difference in the amount he cared for her. But what he wanted most of all was to get away and think.

Clara bent her head on David's shoulder and they held one another for a while. She was bracing herself for the next moment, upon which she had wagered for several hours. She picked up her head and looked at him. "So should I get us something to eat now?" she asked softly

He was silent as Clara rose from the table to get some plates.

"Clara . . . I can't stay," David said suddenly. "We're supposed to be leaving soon. They'll wonder where I am."

"Don't you think dem know you gone already? Stay and eat something wid me," she urged softly.

David shook his head and looked away. "I can't."

Clara turned the stove off with a flick of her wrist and stared, injured, at the pot of food.

David stood up. "Come walk me to the door," he told her gently. But she refused to follow him.

"Please?"

She sat there and watched him moving down her hallway, battling her tears for a few moments. But finally she had to go unlatch the locks and open the door for him.

As David passed into the outer corridor, he grabbed her by the shoulders and forced her to look at him. But she was lifeless in his arms. "I understand why you had to lie to me," he told her. "And you were right to. When I was younger, I never would have understood."

"Eh-heh" was all Clara said before she retreated back inside the exile of her apartment and relocked the three locks on her door.

While waiting for the elevator to come, David heard a single outburst of sobbing and then silence.

Soon he was out in the streets, the sun dipping behind the tombs, the distant buildings of Brooklyn tinted like antique photographs. A mother was strolling her child, and two men were waxing an old car. Reggae music drifted toward David from their transistor radio. The men stopped to stare at him and he thought of how people must have stared at Clara in Port Antonio fifteen years ago. It was a long time to be sentenced to shame.

He reached the entrance to the subway and was about to go underground when suddenly he felt dizzy and had to grab on to the banister. He saw a vision: Clara's son on a promontory high above the sea, several hundred feet from the combers. He wondered if in that last moment of his life, Ralfie had been sane enough to be pressed with the dilemma of whether to live or die. Perhaps, as he stood there, the wind shifted, bringing the scent of orange blossoms, which tempted him to live, but then he had looked out over the jade-colored water —a whole other dreamworld of sandbar plateaus, coral valleys, black spines of sea urchins—and been lured to take that fatal step.

Suddenly, David surged with regret. He knew that he alone had the power to forgive Clara. Tears of his own shame running down his cheeks, he hurried back through the streets toward her building. "I'm sorry," he kept saying. "You're forgiven, you're forgiven." People turned to look at him, frolicking children giving wide berth, as though they'd known all along he'd have a change of heart.